*The Single Market Review*

AGGREGATE AND REGIONAL IMPACT

# THE CASES OF GREECE, SPAIN, IRELAND AND PORTUGAL

# *The Single Market Review* series

EUROPEAN COMMISSION

*The Single Market Review*

AGGREGATE AND REGIONAL IMPACT

# THE CASES OF GREECE, SPAIN, IRELAND AND PORTUGAL

*The Single Market Review*

SUBSERIES VI: VOLUME 2

OFFICE FOR OFFICIAL PUBLICATIONS
OF THE EUROPEAN COMMUNITIES

KOGAN PAGE . EARTHSCAN

This report is part of a series of 39 studies commissioned from independent consultants in the context of a major review of the Single Market. The 1996 Single Market Review responds to a 1992 Council of Ministers Resolution calling on the European Commission to present an overall analysis of the effectiveness of measures taken in creating the Single Market. This review, which assesses the progress made in implementing the Single Market Programme, was coordinated by the Directorate-General 'Internal Market and Financial Services' (DG XV) and the Directorate-General 'Economic and Financial Affairs' (DG II) of the European Commission.

This document was prepared for the European Commission

by

# ESRI

It does not, however, express the Commission's official views. Whilst every reasonable effort has been made to provide accurate information in regard to the subject matter covered, the Consultants are not responsible for any remaining errors. All recommendations are made by the Consultants for the purpose of discussion. Neither the Commission nor the Consultants accept liability for the consequences of actions taken on the basis of the information contained herein.

The European Commission would like to express thanks to the external experts and representatives of firms and industry bodies for their contribution to the 1996 Single Market Review, and to this report in particular.

Office for Official Publications of the European Communities
2 rue Mercier, L-2985 Luxembourg
ISBN 92-827-8807-5                    Catalogue number: C1-72-96-002-EN-C

Kogan Page . Earthscan
120 Pentonville Road, London N1 9JN
ISBN 0 7494 2339 0

# Table of contents

# List of tables

# List of figures

# List of abbreviations

| | |
|---|---|
| CEC | Commission of the European Communities |
| CGE | Computable General Equilibrium |
| CSF | Community Support Framework |
| EC | European Community |
| EEC | European Economic Community |
| EMS | European Monetary System |
| EMU | European and Monetary Union |
| ESRI | Economic and Social Research Institute |
| EU | European Union |
| Eurostat | Statistical Office of the European Communities |
| FDI | Foreign Direct Investment |
| GDP | Gross Domestic Product |
| GNP | Gross National Product |
| IDA | Industrial Development Authority |
| IMF | International Monetary Fund |
| IO | Input-output |
| IRS | Increasing Returns to Scale |
| ISIC | International Standard Industrial Classification |
| IV | Instrumental Variables |
| MNC | Multinational Corporation |
| MPC | marginal propensity to consume |
| n.a. | not available |
| NACE | general industrial classification of economic activities in the European Communities |
| NESC | National Economic and Social Council |
| OECD | Organization for Economic Co-Operation and Development |
| OLS | Ordinary Least Squares |
| p.a. | per annum |
| PIH | Permanent Income Hypothesis |
| PSBR | Public Sector Borrowing Requirement |
| R&D | Research and Development |
| SEM | Single European Market |
| SMEs | Small- and Medium-sized Enterprises |
| VAT | Value Added Tax |

# Acknowledgements

The Economic and Social Research Institute project team was co-ordinated by John Bradley. The members were drawn from the following institutions. Economic and Social Research Institute: John Bradley and Joanne McCartan; University College Dublin: Frank Barry and Aoife Hannan; Fundación de Estudios de Economía Aplicada: Simón Sosvilla-Rivero; Universidade Catolica Portuguesa: Leonor Modesto. The following acted as consultants to the project. Karl Whelan: MIT; Peter McGregor and Kim Swales: University of Strathclyde; Demetrius Yannelis: University of Piraeus.

# 1. Summary

As part of the *Single Market Review*, this report analyses the likely effects of the single market and the Community Support Framework (CSF) on the countries of the EU periphery: Greece, Spain, Portugal and Ireland. To this end, macroeconometric models of these economies were constructed which were then subjected to 'shocks' designed to capture the essential elements of the single market and CSF programmes. This procedure allows us to distinguish between developments which would have occurred in these economies in the absence of these programmes, and developments that are instead *due to* the programmes.

The original Cecchini study was based on economic models of four of the large EU economies plus Belgium and the Netherlands, and the EU-wide results were then derived by grossing up the results for these six economies. This presents an inaccurate picture of likely developments in the periphery, however, since developmental processes in the periphery are quite different from those pertaining to the core; for example, the periphery economies are price-takers in the markets for their exports to a much greater extent than are the large core economies. Also, one of the major factors determining periphery development is the inflow of foreign direct investment (FDI) from the core. Although many of the 'shocks' that we apply to our economic models are taken from the Cecchini Report, therefore, we would not expect our results to simply replicate the Cecchini results since the developmental processes modelled are quite different.

The structure of our macroeconomic models is described in Chapter 5 of this report (see in particular Figure 5.1). Manufacturing output, which consists of both tradable and non-(internationally-)tradable components, is determined by a combination of cost-competitiveness and aggregate-demand factors. The greater the tradable component, the larger the impact on output of world demand relative to domestic demand. Ireland is the most open of the four economies in this regard, and Spain the least open. Given the level of output determined in this way, manufacturing-sector employment and investment are determined in a cost-minimization process by relative factor prices. Since output of the services sector is typically far less internationally tradable than is manufacturing output, the services sector in each economy is driven largely by conventional Keynesian aggregate-demand processes.

To allow for unemployment we present a wage-bargaining model of the labour market. Wage demands are influenced by inflation, productivity growth, unemployment, and the tax wedge. These various influences differ in strength across the different countries. Not surprisingly, given its very high current level of unemployment, the impact of unemployment on wage bargaining is found to be lowest in Spain.

Having given this brief description of the economic models, we now describe the 'shocks' entailed in our analysis of the effects of the single market programme. We make no effort to determine the extent to which the programme has actually been put into effect; rather we assume that the programme as set out in the Cecchini Report is phased in over a 10-year period, 1987–97. To the extent that elements of the programme remain to be introduced after that date, the effects we identify will take place later than at the dates shown in our tables of results.

For the small-open-economies under discussion, the effects of the single market can be classified at a theoretical level as static, dynamic, locational and growth-dependent. In our analysis, however, the dynamic effects can be subsumed under the static and locational categories. The static effects are those that arise as various sectors expand and others contract in each country in the wake of EU market integration. To determine which sectors expand and which contract, we make use of a detailed study of the competitiveness of industrial sectors in each EU country carried out by the European Commission (European Commission, 1990b). The successful sectors expand through capturing increased foreign market share and the unsuccessful sectors decline through losing home market share. Our analysis suggests that this static shock is positive for Ireland, marginally negative for Portugal, moderately negative for Spain and strongly negative for Greece. The reason for this is that Ireland and Portugal are found to have the largest shares of employment and output in the sectors in which these individual countries are expected to benefit from the single market, relative to those in the country-specific sectors that are expected to be adversely affected.

For both Spain and Portugal, however, these adverse static shocks are more than compensated for by beneficial locational effects; by this is meant the increased FDI inflows that these economies have experienced in recent years. These increased inflows can be ascribed either to EU entry or to the single market programme; to the extent that the latter is responsible, the net static plus locational effects for Ireland, Spain and Portugal are all positive. The 'growth-dependent' effects arise since, with further trade liberalization increasing the proportion of internationally tradable goods relative to non-tradable goods, the peripheral economies will be more strongly affected by growth in the EU core than is the case at present.

The overall effects of the single market, then, are sensitive to whether we ascribe the increased FDI inflows into Spain and Portugal to the SEM or not. If we deem that they are *not* due to the SEM, then the single market has almost insignificant effects on Greek and Spanish GDP by the year 2010; Irish GDP is over 9% higher than it would otherwise have been, however, while Portuguese GDP is 7.5% higher. This strong showing for Portugal, in the face of a negative static shock, is due primarily to the growth-dependent effects; as Portugal becomes much more open, its response to increases in core-country GDP is correspondingly stronger.

If the increased FDI flows are instead ascribed to the SEM, then the positive effects on Spain and Portugal are very much stronger. In this case the SEM raises Portuguese GDP by almost 11.5% by the year 2010; Spanish and Irish GDP are raised by 9%, though the effect on Greek GDP remains insignificant. Note that for the first three countries these effects are roughly twice the size of the average GDP effects estimated by Cecchini. Greece remains an outlier for two reasons: first, because so many of its indigenous industries are deemed uncompetitive by the European Commission study referred to earlier (which makes the static shock strongly negative), and second, because inflows of FDI remain low. Our feeling, however, is that the low FDI inflows are a consequence of the current unsettled nature of Greek macroeconomic policy and so, if these problems could be overcome, the Greek position in our analysis would appear much more favourable.

Of course, one of the main reasons for the introduction of the Community Support Framework, consisting of the Delors I (1989–93) and Delors II (1994–99) packages, was the fear that gains to core countries from the single market would dominate the gains to the periphery. Our study presents a separate analysis of the impacts of the CSF on the EU periphery countries. These programmes have effects on both the demand side of the economy (in the sense of increasing aggregate spending) and on the supply side (in the sense of increasing the productive capacity of the economy). The mechanisms underlying the first set of effects, being Keynesian in nature, are far less complex than those underlying the supply-side effects.

There are three main channels through which the supply-side effects operate: the CSF improves the physical infrastructure of the economy, raises the level of human capital (through enhancing the skills and education of the labour force), and directly assists the private sector by subsidizing investment. The latter channel is relatively straightforward; modelling the impact of the first two channels on private sector costs, however, brings us into relatively uncharted territory. We attempt to capture the first two effects through incorporating externality mechanisms into the models. Thus, public investment in infrastructure and human capital bring spillover benefits to private industry. There is little consensus, however, on the size of these spillover benefits, so we report results for high, medium and zero estimates of the size of the spillover effects. Clearly, the long-term effects of the CSF also depend critically on whether the programmes end in 1999 or whether they can be assumed to continue indefinitely. Again, we report results for both scenarios.

Appropriately enough, since Greece is found to benefit least substantially from the single market, we find that it, along with Portugal, benefits most substantially from the CSF. The benefits to Ireland and Spain are very much less. The relative size of these effects is due primarily to the relative size of the CSF funds allocated to each economy. For example, although Ireland does well in per capita terms from the CSF allocations, its relatively large GDP per head means that the CSF allocations as a ratio of GDP are smaller than the equivalent ratios for Greece and Portugal (see Table 9.1).

The general flavour of our results on the CSF (in isolation from any single market shocks) may be gleaned from the following. For the case where there are no beneficial spillover effects for the private sector, but where CSF funding continues indefinitely, Greek GDP in the year 2010 is almost 6% above what it would otherwise be; Portuguese GDP is 7% higher, while the figures for Ireland and Spain are only 1% higher. For the case where financing is withdrawn after 1999 on the other hand, but where there are relatively strong spillover effects, Portuguese GDP is over 2% higher, but Irish, Greek and Spanish GDP are all less than 1% above what they would otherwise be. This suggests that the long-run supply-side effects, to the extent to which we have captured them correctly through the externality mechanisms, are very much weaker than the Keynesian demand-side effects.

To arrive at a definitive answer to the question of the combined effects of the single market and the CSF programmes requires choosing amongst a range of scenarios: for example, are the increased FDI flows into Spain and Portugal to be attributed to the SEM? Is the CSF funding temporary or permanent? Are the economic mechanisms that generate long-run supply responses to CSF programmes strong or weak? In the light of the most recent research, we do not yet have definitive answers to these difficult questions.

To take the worst case scenario, suppose that the FDI effects are unrelated to the SEM, the CSF funding ends after the year 1999 and the CSF investments contribute nothing to long-term growth (i.e. the so-called externality effects are zero). Here, the SEM effects come from Table 8.1(a); the CSF effects come from Table 9.6. Under this worst case scenario, these are actually zero. Thus, the combined effects on GDP of the SEM and the CSF are effectively zero for Greece and Spain by the year 2010, and are 7.5% and 9% for Portugal and Ireland, respectively. The interpretation is as follows. Greece experiences strong adverse effects on its manufacturing sector, but these are offset by the benefits derived from an increased openness to EU growth. Spain suffers smaller adverse restructuring in its manufacturing sector, but remains relatively less open. Portugal suffers only a small adverse restructuring effect, and this is dominated by the benefits of increased openness. Ireland, on the other hand, benefits directly both from manufacturing restructuring and from greater openness.

The most positive effect on the cohesion objective arises when FDI effects are assumed to derive from the SEM, the CSF funding is maintained unchanged after the year 1999, and the CSF investments are assumed to contribute to long-term growth. Here, the SEM effects come from Table 8.1(b); the CSF effects come from Table 9.4. Greece experiences an increase of 7.5% to its GDP by the year 2010, the lowest of the four countries. Almost all of this effect is associated with the permanent CSF expenditure, i.e. it is Keynesian in origin. Both Ireland and Spain experience similar impacts in the range 11% to 12.6%, where almost three quarters comes from the SEM and only one quarter from the CSF. Finally, Portugal experiences the strongest impact, amounting to 23%, split equally between the contributions of the SEM and the CSF. The effect of the CSF is so strong in this case: first, since the CSF funds represent a high proportion of GDP, and second, because the Portuguese investment multiplier is so large (see Chapter 4).

# 2. Introduction

The purpose of this report is to present the results of a study of the macroeconomic effects of the single market on the four 'cohesion' countries (Greece, Ireland, Portugal and Spain) using adaptations of the HERMIN econometric models for each of these countries as previously described in Bradley, Herce and Modesto (1995b). The study was originally structured as a four-stage programme of research as follows:

(a)     exploration of likely single market impacts on the cohesion countries by means of adaptation and application of the original Catinat-Italianer 'parametric' methodology for use with the HERMIN model;[1]

(b)     definition of an appropriate counterfactual simulation to describe the likely evolution of the four cohesion economies in the absence of the single market initiatives and in the absence of the accompanying investment oriented EU initiatives such as the Community Support Frameworks (CSFs) and the cohesion funds;

(c)     use of the four HERMIN models for Greece, Ireland, Portugal and Spain, suitably adapted, to carry out simulations of the single market initiatives and the CSFs, where impacts would be measured in terms of deviations from the counterfactual derived in (b) above;

(d)     investigation of 'developmental' issues that go beyond the Catinat-Italianer methodology to explore how the single market initiatives are likely to induce structural change as the cohesion countries are obliged to open up and adapt to greater exposure to the external EU and wider world economies.

In this report the results of the project to date are described and the present work is set in a context that permits these results to be compared with existing published single market research on the cohesion countries and wider research on the core countries.[2]

Chapter 3 provides some brief background information on macroeconomic structures in the EU periphery, with a particular focus both on intra-periphery comparisons and on comparisons between the core and the periphery. This material has relevance in order both to arrive at qualitative views on the manner in which the periphery is likely to react to the single market developments and to set the context for the HERMIN modelling framework that has been used to carry out numerical simulations.

Chapter 4 reviews the research that is already available on the impacts of the single market and the CSF on the four 'cohesion' countries. In addition, since the wider impacts of the single market on the rest of the EU are certain to have important consequences for the periphery, in a situation where the periphery is likely to function in a post-recursive way relative to the much larger and more developed core, the likely top-down macroeconomic impacts of the single market on the core are briefly reviewed.

---

[1]     The Catinat-Italianer methodology was based largely on exogenous shocks to the HERMES and INTERLINK models that lowered prices and costs and boosted external demand in the context of a given relatively stable model structure. For details of the 'parametric' methodology, see Catinat and Italianer, 1988.

[2]     In what follows we will sometimes use the term 'periphery' to refer to the four economies being analysed: Greece, Ireland, Portugal and Spain. The more exact term 'cohesion' countries will also be used.

It must be kept in mind that this project was carried out in a context where the peripheral Member States were not analysed separately as part of the original research project on the economics of 1992 (Cecchini, 1988; Emerson *et al.*, 1988). In that project, a simple 'grossing up' process was used to extend the detailed macroeconometric results from seven core economies to the total of the 12 Member States.[3] Since the GDP of the remaining six economies represented only 11.7% of the total in the year 1985, the overall effect on the EU, as estimated in the 1988 studies, is unlikely to be very sensitive to the method used to 'gross up' the results for the periphery. However, the strong assumption that the impacts on the individual peripheral economies (and the cohesion subset in particular) are likely to be the same as for the more developed core economies needs to be examined more closely than was the case in the Cecchini/Emerson 1988 study. The bulk of the report is devoted to this task.

Prior to developing the methodology for analysis of the SEM and the CSF, in Chapter 5 we describe the key features of the HERMIN macroeconometric modelling framework being used in this project to define a no-single-market and no-CSF counterfactual (or *antimonde*) as well as to carry out the simulations of the impacts of the single market and CSF initiatives. Since the HERMIN models have been extensively modified for use in this project, the earlier model descriptions presented in Bradley, Herce and Modesto (1995b) need to be updated. Some of the technical details on the model are outlined in Chapter 5.

In Chapter 6, we develop our empirical methodology for studying the impact of the single market on the periphery. In addition to applying variations of the Catinat-Italianer methodology used in the 1988 studies for the 'core' Member States, we develop approaches that attempt to take into account the reality that the periphery is less developed than the core and that the onset of the single market is likely to induce major structural changes to the economies of the periphery.

Since the arrival of the single market has been accompanied by major increases in structural funds for the periphery, through the Community Support Framework (CSF) and the cohesion funds, Chapter 7 briefly describes the methodology used to address how the HERMIN models can be used to explore the way in which these Community structural initiatives are likely to influence the peripheral economies.

Chapter 8 presents simulation results for the single market shocks for each of the four HERMIN country models. Since many of the effects depend on parameters whose magnitudes are difficult to specify econometrically, and on mechanisms whose association with the single market might be disputed (e.g. the influence on foreign direct investment inflows into the periphery), we also report some sensitivity analysis to search for effects that are crucially important to the simulation results.

Chapter 9 presents simulation results for the CSF shocks for each of the four HERMIN country models. As in the previous case of the SEM shocks, many of the effects depend on parameters whose magnitudes are difficult to specify econometrically (e.g. the magnitude of externality elasticities), so we also report some sensitivity analysis to search for effects that are crucially important to the simulation results.

---

[3]     The seven countries included in the 1988 studies were Belgium, Germany, France, Italy, Luxembourg, the Netherlands and the United Kingdom. Although the remaining five 'peripheral' countries were excluded from the macroeconometric analysis, some were included in the microeconomic survey-type studies.

Chapter 10 provides a detailed evaluation and discussion of the simulation results of the SEM and CSF shocks from different points of view. First, the single market and CSF impacts are examined for each of the four models separately. Second, the four cohesion country results are compared and contrasted with a view to examining how their different levels of openness and their different internal structure are likely to influence their response to single market and CSF initiatives. Finally, the impacts on the cohesion countries are compared with the likely impact of the single market on the core countries, as quantified in the original Emerson 1988 study and updates, in order to judge whether or not the cohesion objective can be attained over a reasonable time horizon.

# 3. The cohesion countries: background economic issues[4]

The purpose of this chapter is to describe the similarities in economic structure that characterize the peripheral EU countries – Greece, Ireland, Portugal and Spain – and to analyse the structural changes that have taken place in these countries since they joined the EU.

We begin by looking at the convergence experience of the periphery (i.e. the extent to which these regions have caught up to the core in terms of GDP per capita). Although some convergence has occurred, these countries remain the poorest in the Union and it is not surprising therefore that they share many characteristics. Some of these are more apparent than others; the relative importance of agriculture and the underdevelopment of physical infrastructure in the periphery, for example. Less obvious, however, are features such as the extent of unemployment and underemployment, the relative share of producer and consumer services, and the relative lack of increasing-returns-to-scale segments of manufacturing industry.

## 3.1. The convergence experience of the EU periphery

The term 'EU periphery' is used to denote those countries all or most regions of which have 'Objective 1' status. These regions, with 75% or less of the EU average GDP per capita, comprise the western and southern seaboards of the Union.

Have the relatively poor regions been converging on the richer regions, in terms of GDP per capita, or not? The conventional wisdom in economic growth theory is that regions should converge over time. The world data (depicted in Barro and Sala-i-Martin (1995) for example), however, shows divergence rather than convergence. These authors and many others argue, however, that when the stock of human capital is controlled for, conditional convergence appears.

Walsh (1993) and O'Grada and O'Rourke (1994) control for this, though, and still find Ireland to be a slow-growth outlier in terms of European convergence. Prados *et al.* (1993) report similar findings for the whole European periphery. Many of these findings, however, depend strongly on the time period of the sample. Table 3.1 takes a broad look at the convergence experience and indicates fairly rapid convergence in recent years.

Using Barro and Sala-i-Martin's average convergence speed (2% p.a.), each country except Greece is found to have performed somewhat better than expected (in terms of GDP per head) since its accession to the EU.[5] This may be partly attributable to the CSF programmes, though there is some empirical evidence that trade integration promotes convergence (Ben-David, 1993).

If living standards are more accurately measured by private consumption per capita, however, as shown in Table 3.2, relative living standards are found to have fallen in all four peripheral

---

[4]   This chapter draws on material contained in Barry, Bradley and Duggan (1996).

[5]   Note that there is controversy in Ireland over the accuracy of recent GDP figures, many economists holding that they are overestimated due to the transfer pricing behaviour of multinational companies.

Member States between 1973 and 1991.[6] (Ireland, on this measure, lies much closer to the lower levels of Portugal and Greece than to the relatively high level of Spain.) The convergence experience is not therefore unambiguous. It becomes of great interest to look at the structural differences between core and periphery, and to ask whether the two groups of regions have been becoming more similar in these respects or not.

**Table 3.1.     Relative GDP (GNP) per capita in purchasing power parity terms (EUR12=100)**

|          | 1960    | 1973    | 1980    | 1985    | 1990    | 1993    |
|----------|---------|---------|---------|---------|---------|---------|
| Ireland  | 61 (62) | 59 (59) | 64 (62) | 65 (58) | 71 (62) | 77 (69) |
| Spain    | 60      | 79      | 74      | 71      | 75      | 76      |
| Greece   | 39      | 57      | 58      | 51      | 47      | 49      |
| Portugal | 39      | 56      | 55      | 51      | 56      | 61      |

*Source*: European Commission Annual Report (1994).

*[handwritten: increase in GDP    61 – 77 in 33 yrs.]*

**Table 3.2.     Economic indicators in the periphery**

|                          | Greece | Ireland | Portugal | Spain | EU  |
|--------------------------|--------|---------|----------|-------|-----|
| Unemployment rate (%)    |        |         |          |       |     |
| 1960                     | n.a.   | 4.7     | 1.9      | 2.4   | 2.5 |
| 1973                     | 2.0    | 6.2     | 2.6      | 2.6   | 2.6 |
| 1993                     | 7.8    | 18.4    | 5.2      | 21.2  | 10.4 |
| Private consumption/capita |      |         |          |       |     |
| 1973                     | 57     | 67      | 65       | 80    | 100 |
| 1991                     | 54     | 62      | 58       | 76    | 100 |

*Source: European Economy* No. 55 and Eurostat National Accounts (1970–91).

## 3.2.   Structural similarities between peripheral regions

The European Commission's (1990) 'One Market, One Money' report points out that the EU periphery is characterized by higher unemployment than prevails in the EU core. This is a statistical artefact, however, since Spain, the country with the highest unemployment rate, is also by far the largest peripheral economy. However, all the peripheral countries can be seen to suffer from either unemployment or underemployment (which does not show up in the standard data). In what follows, we focus on a number of shared characteristics that are likely to increase the burdens of adjustment on peripheral labour markets, factors such as the relative importance of agriculture, the difficulties of adjusting to free trade, and the relative underdevelopment of financial markets and of physical infrastructure in the periphery. We then move on to analyse other structural similarities between peripheral countries: relative proportions of producer and consumer services, and the share of increasing returns sectors within manufacturing.

### 3.2.1.   Unemployment and underemployment

Table 3.2 illustrates that two of the peripheral countries, Ireland and Spain, have very high unemployment rates, while Greece and Portugal have rates below the EU average. The less

---

[6]    Consumption is measured according to its own specific purchasing power parity (from Eurostat National Accounts 1970–91).

well developed nature of the social welfare systems in Greece and Portugal, however, and the large proportion of the labour force engaged in agriculture in these countries suggest a substantial degree of underemployment.

This is further borne out by the fact that Portugal and Spain have exceptionally low productivity levels in agriculture – only about one third of the already low national level in each case. The professional status of employment also points to agricultural underemployment in Greece and Spain, where 38% and 19%, respectively, of total agricultural employment is classified as unpaid family workers. While the proportion of unpaid family workers in Portugal and Ireland is much lower (less than 10% in each case), in both these countries there are still many small holders with no prospect of long-term viability. Furthermore, in Greece the exceptionally high proportion of non-agricultural employment classified as employer/self-employed (27%) or unpaid family workers (5%, with 11% of females so classified) also suggests underemployment.

Ireland, Spain and Greece also have exceptionally high dependency rates. In Ireland in 1991, there were 21 dependants for every 10 workers, in Spain 20 and in Greece 17, as compared with an EU average of 14. This is due not only to unemployment, but also to the very low labour force participation rates in these countries. This in turn points to a relatively high incidence of discouraged workers.

### 3.2.2. Agricultural orientation

As the *One Market, One Money* report (European Commission, 1990) notes, Objective 1 regions have a relatively high share of employment in the declining agricultural sector. Of the four countries, Greece has the largest proportion of employees in agriculture (22.2% of total employment in 1991). This compares with 17.4% in Portugal, 14.0% in Ireland and 10.9% in Spain (Eurostat, 1993).

This factor adds to the number of workers who must be absorbed into the urban labour force, or else, as in Portugal and Greece, provides a refuge in the form of underemployment for those who, in a more developed welfare system, would add to the unemployment rolls.

### 3.2.3. Underdevelopment of infrastructure and capital markets

Two further characteristics of peripheral regions appear likely to hinder the development of employment opportunities. One is the underdeveloped state of financial markets. Larre and Torres (1991), in a study of Spain, Portugal and Greece, make the following points, many of which apply to Ireland as well:

> In the mid-1980s financial markets were still in their infancy, with ... little or no competition between banks and financial institutions; narrow capital markets; a limited range of savings instruments and a preponderance of public debt securities; credit controls (Greece and Portugal) and administratively fixed interest rates; compulsory portfolio requirements for banks, and a high proportion of subsidized credit.

This theme is echoed in *One Market, One Money* (1990), which reports that the high cost of credit and poor availability of risk capital are among the major factors that firms in peripheral regions identify as growth inhibiting.

The same report also notes that firms identify infrastructural deficiencies in the areas of education and training, transport and communications, and the supply and cost of energy, as more important impediments than geographic factors such as the proximity of suppliers and of customers. The available data on the stock of infrastructure in peripheral regions provides supporting evidence. Table 3.3 below, adapted from Biehl (1986), reports relative infrastructural levels for an aggregate of transportation, telecommunications, energy and education. It reveals that Ireland, Spain and Portugal fell further behind the EU average between 1979 and 1985, while Italy and Greece converged slightly.

**Table 3.3.    Relative infrastructural levels in EU countries**

|          | 1979–80 | 1985–86 |
|----------|---------|---------|
| Italy    | 81.7    | 85.4    |
| Spain    | 77.7    | 74.3    |
| Ireland  | 71.1    | 67.1    |
| Greece   | 54.5    | 56.0    |
| Portugal | n.a.    | 38.7    |
| EU       | 100.0   | 100.0   |

*Source:* Biehl (1986).

### 3.2.4.  Difficulties of adjustment to free trade

Progressive trade liberalization within Europe is likely to entail substantial industrial disruption in the periphery, while sectoral restructuring within core EU countries, which have fairly similar factor endowments, is more likely to take place through the development of market niches rather than through the wholesale disappearance of existing industries. Evidence in this regard is provided by Neven (1990) who shows that Greece and Portugal have less intra-industry trade than the other EU countries; Ireland, Spain and Italy have intermediate levels, while Germany, France, the Netherlands, the UK and Belgium are characterized by intense intra-industry trade. Adjustment problems are therefore likely to be greater in the periphery.

As Krugman (1987) notes with respect to the southern periphery's accession to the EU:

> The trade expansion produced by EC enlargement is simply not likely to be as painless as the trade expansion produced by the formation of the Community and earlier enlargement. There will certainly be income distribution problems created by the changes, and also quite possibly some real costs in terms of unemployment.

A massive shake-out of jobs in Irish and Spanish 'traditional' industry occurred as trade liberalization progressed. The low productivity sectors in Greece and Portugal are also likely to face intense pressures in the next decade.

Further confirmation of the structural changes likely to be in store for Greece and Portugal is provided by the size structure of enterprises in peripheral regions, shown in Table 3.4. The National Economic and Social Council (1989) documents how the average size of establishments in Ireland declined in the wake of free trade as indigenous firms in increasing-returns sectors were wiped out. Something similar may have happened in Spain.[7] Portugal may therefore be thought to resemble the pre-free-trade Irish position, while the fact that nearly three fifths of Greek non-agricultural employment is concentrated in micro-enterprises with less than 10 employees probably does not augur well for their ability to compete internationally.

**Table 3.4.    Non-agriculture employment shares by enterprise size, 1988**

|  | Greece | Ireland | Portugal | Spain | EU |
|---|---|---|---|---|---|
| Micro (0-9) | 59 | 34 | 36 | 36 | 30 |
| Small (10-99) | 21 | 30 | 27 | 30 | 25 |
| Medium (100-499) | 11 | 18 | 17 | 17 | 16 |
| Large (500+) | 9 | 17 | 20 | 17 | 30 |

*Source:* First Annual Report of the European Observatory for SMEs (1993).

### 3.2.5.   The structure of the services sector

The economic geographers Keeble, Offord and Walker (1988) noted that the structure of the services sector differed significantly between core and periphery, with the core being relatively more specialized in producer services.[8]

Table 3.5 below shows the ratio of employment in producer relative to consumer services. It shows, as Keeble *et al.* suggested, that there is a substantial difference between the relative proportions accounted for by producer and consumer services in the core *vis-à-vis* the periphery.

It is clear that the core-periphery distinction is significant and long-lasting. Ireland, however, seems to have extricated itself from its peripheral position, particularly between 1978 and 1983, while Greece appears as the periphery outlier, with a ratio of producer to consumer services more like that of the core. The latter is easily explained, however, by the fact that Greece, containing as it does a large number of islands, possesses an unusually large transport, communications and storage sector which is part of producer services. Keeble *et al.* (1988) suggest that Ireland's core-like characteristics appear to be evidence of successful industrial policies.

Why does the core appear to be relatively specialized in producer services? Hansen (1990) argues that:

> in an increasingly information-oriented economy, producer services play a pivotal role in the ... expanding division of labour, which in turn creates productivity increases throughout the economy. Regions that have a high density of producer services are thus likely to have higher per capita incomes than other regions.

---

[7]    On the basis of Ireland's adjustment, we would regard small initial firm size in increasing-returns sectors as a competitive disadvantage, rather than as representing an opportunity for the exploitation of further scale economies in an integrated market, as in Neven (1990).

[8]    Producer services are defined in the NACE and ISIC classifications as categories 7 (Transport and Communications) and 8 (Banking and Financial Services), while consumer services are categories 6 (Distribution, Hotels and Catering) and 9 (Community, Social and Personal Services).

**Table 3.5.     Ratio of employment in producer versus consumer services**

|             | 1968  | 1978  | 1983  | 1987  |
|-------------|-------|-------|-------|-------|
| Belgium     | .299  | .33   | .327  | .332  |
| Germany     | .342  | .316  | .318  | .314  |
| France      | .343  | .351  | .344  | .343  |
| Netherlands | .522  | .308  | .359  | .362  |
| Ireland     | .241  | .251  | .354  | .332  |
| Italy       | .40   | .267  | .262  | .267  |
| Portugal    | n.a.  | .259  | .24   | .225  |
| Spain       | n.a.  | .294  | .289  | .269  |
| Greece      | n.a.  | .457  | .378  | .345  |

*Source:* Duggan (1995).

Causation can equally plausibly run in the opposite direction. The fact that 'core regions almost always contain above-average concentrations of highly qualified workers' can be related to studies by Beyers *et al.* (1986) and Wier (1992) which showed that the producer services sector is dominated by professional and technical employees, while consumer services are typically labour-intensive low-productivity low-wage jobs. Whichever direction of causation is more important, it is clear that a high ratio of producer to consumer services jobs is beneficial.

### 3.2.6.   Increasing returns to scale in manufacturing sectors

Equivalently, it is beneficial for a region to have a high share of the manufacturing sectors that exhibit increasing returns to scale (IRS). As Heffernan and Sinclair (1990) note, average productivity in the regions that capture these sectors rises relative to that prevailing elsewhere.

One of the potential difficulties that the periphery faced in adjusting to EU membership was the possibility that as trade barriers fell these industries would be attracted more to the core because of economies of agglomeration. Indeed, as Barry (1994) showed, this process *did* result in the decline of Irish indigenous industry in IRS sectors.[9] However, the influx of multinational companies in precisely these sectors more than dominated this decline, so the share of Irish employment in IRS sectors has increased substantially.

**Table 3.6.     Developments in IRS industries**

|                              | 1973   | 1980   | 1993   |
|------------------------------|--------|--------|--------|
| Indigenous employment        | 25,209 | 27,440 | 22,565 |
| Share of total manufacturing | 12.46% | 11.86% | 11.64% |
| Multinational employment     | 32,735 | 50,114 | 59,055 |
| Share of total manufacturing | 16.18% | 21.67% | 30.46% |

*Source:* IDA Employment Survey.

Summing multinational and indigenous employment, we find the share of IRS sectors in total manufacturing employment has risen from 29% in 1973 to 42% by 1993. While this is still small relative to the equivalent share in the core EU countries (see Table 3.7 below), it has been increasing over time rather than decreasing.

---

[9]   The IRS sectors are identified by O'Malley (1992) on the basis of Pratten's (1988) study of engineering economies of scale.

**Table 3.7.      Employment in IRS sectors as a % of total manufacturing employment**

|            | 1968 | 1979 | 1983 | 1989 |
|------------|------|------|------|------|
| Germany    | 55   | 60   | 65   | 63   |
| France     | 42   | 55   | 55   | 51   |
| Netherlands| 50   | 62   | 54   | 54   |
| Belgium    | 42   | 57   | 55   | 53   |
| Italy      | 49   | 54   | 56   | 55   |
| Ireland    | 21   | 35   | 40   | 45   |
| Spain      | n.a. | 38   | 39   | 37   |
| Portugal   | n.a. | n.a. | 28   | 25   |
| Greece     | n.a. | n.a. | 36   | 35   |

*Source:* Eurostat: *Structure and Activity of Industry*, various years.

Once again, we see a very clear core-periphery pattern emerging, with the periphery less specialized in IRS sectors. Unfortunately, the paucity of data precludes an analysis of how this situation has changed over the course of the 1980s.

If the Irish experience is anything to go by, however, we can say that the periphery is likely to be capturing an increasing share of IRS industries. The data on foreign direct investment in manufacturing (from the *OECD*, 1993) reveal that while the Irish share of foreign direct investment (as a proportion of GNP) was twice as large as Spain's and three times as large as Portugal's in the early 1980s, the Portuguese and Irish shares had been equalized by the early 1990s, and the Spanish share was now twice as large as these. Only the Greek share remained low, and stagnant.

# 4. Macroeconomic impact of the SEM and the CSF: a review of research

This chapter reviews the quantitative studies that have assessed both the impact of the SEM and the CSF on the peripheral countries of the EU. The analysis of the Irish case is probably the most comprehensively documented and it is presented in greater detail than the other country studies. Having reviewed the Irish case, available Spanish, Portuguese and Greek studies are then described, beginning with a review of the SEM literature followed by a review of the CSF literature.

## 4.1. Quantifying the impact of the SEM

The studies that quantify the impact of 1992 through empirical research have been extremely useful and have greatly enhanced the analysis. For example, the special issue of *European Economy/Social Europe* (European Commission, 1990), devoted to a study of the impact of the single market by industrial sector, is used extensively in the methodology to quantify the magnitude of the switch in manufacturing sectors from non-tradable to tradable goods due to the SEM (see Chapter 6). The review of SEM studies treats the four countries individually, wherever possible dividing the analysis into aggregate and sectoral studies.

### 4.1.1. Ireland: aggregate studies

*O'Sullivan (1989)*

In one of the first empirical studies that applied the Cecchini-type analysis to Ireland, O'Sullivan suggested that Ireland stands to gain overall in the long run but that there would be considerable costs to bear in the short run (i.e. 1990–94). His analysis, carried out in 1989 using an early four-sector version of the Irish HERMES model (Bradley *et al.*, 1989), examined impacts to the year 1994. He suggested that the improved external environment, falling interest rates and the speeding up of technical progress would be the main influences of the SEM on Ireland. His results are less optimistic than those of the Cecchini Report, 1988, and he predicted that the benefits for Ireland would accrue mainly to the industrial sector. Overall, O'Sullivan predicted that GNP would increase by 1.7% by the year 1994, industrial output by 2.8%, investment by 6.2% (due to increasing capacity and falling interest rates), employment by 6,000, with price and wage levels falling by approximately 1%.

*Bradley, Fitz Gerald and Kearney (1992)[10]*

This study was the first comprehensive quantitative analysis of the impact of the SEM on Ireland using the ESRI HERMES model of the Irish economy.[11] The impact was analysed under two general headings: the changes in the *trading environment* and the changes that occur *within* Ireland as a result of 1992. The average effects of 1992 as analysed by the 1988 Cecchini Report (i.e. a 4.5% increase in GDP by 1998, a 6.1% reduction in price levels, a 1%

---

[10]    This study also quantifies the impact of the CSF on Ireland.

[11]    Full documentation of the HERMES-Ireland model is given in *HERMES-Ireland: A Model of the Irish Economy: Structure and Performance*, J. Bradley *et al.*, 1989, The Economic and Social Research Institute, and further details of a later version are given in Bradley and Fitz Gerald (1991).

improvement in the external balance and a 2.2% improvement in the budgetary balance) are taken as given exogenous shocks to Ireland's trading environment. The ESRI study imposed both these shocks and the changes occurring within Ireland as exogenous shocks to the HERMES model, and compared their results to those in the Cecchini Report under the following headings:

(a)    the relaxation of border controls;
(b)    the opening up of public procurement;
(c)    the liberalization of financial services;
(d)    the 'supply effects' (such as lower production costs and higher productivity gains).

These forecasts are summarized in Table 4.1.

**Table 4.1.    Macroeconomic consequences for Ireland, effects of 1992 to the year 1998**

| Changes (as %) relative to benchmark[1] | GNP | Consumer prices | Employment ('000s) | Budgetary balance | External balance |
|---|---|---|---|---|---|
| Border controls | 0.2 | -0.9 | 340 | 0.04 | -0.01 |
| Public procurement | 1.1 | +0.3 | 7,780 | 0.29 | 0.13 |
| Financial services | 1.1 | -1.0 | 8,480 | 0.24 | -0.10 |
| 'Supply effects' | 2.0 | -1.6 | 15,870 | 0.42 | -0.08 |
| Overall effect | 4.5 | -3.1 | 33,660 | 1.00 | -0.01 |
| Cecchini average[2] | 4.5 | -6.1 | 1,840,000 | 2.2 | 1.0 |

[1] The benchmark represents a probable evolution of the Irish economy in the absence of 1992.
[2] Cecchini Report for EUR-12, medium term (six years).
*Source:* Tables 3.1–3.5, pp. 32–42. Bradley *et al.* (1992).

A stylized projection for the Irish economy to the year 2000 was used as a baseline for the analysis. Counterfactual experiments were then carried out, considering, in turn, the contribution to the growth of the economy from each of the four headings outlined above. The results were compared to the baseline to determine the separate impact of the SEM.

Bradley *et al.* imposed a cut in public sector employment by 300 in 1993 and a reduction in costs by 1% over 6 years (same as the Cecchini analysis) to assess the impact of the abolition of border controls. In the medium term the simulated effects on Ireland are not as pronounced as those predicted by Cecchini, 1988, for all of the EC: prices fall by 0.9% compared to a 1% fall in the latter. This is because the increase in labour supply prevents the growth in the economy from tightening the labour market. There is no crowding-out of the growth stimulus arising from higher wage rates. The wage equation in the HERMES Ireland model displays both hysteresis and the downward inflexibility of Irish nominal wages. This explains why the price reduction is not as large as that predicted by Cecchini.

Due to the openness of the Irish economy before 1992, the report suggested that the opening up of public procurement has little impact on prices, but may lead to Irish firms reaping the benefits of an increase in external demand. Their model predicted that employment will rise by nearly 8,000 in the medium term as a result of the opening up of public procurement.

In the Cecchini analysis, the liberalization of financial services is predicted to equalize interest rates as capital is free to locate wherever the rate of return is highest; the Cecchini model forecasts a 0.5% reduction in the interest rates. The report predicted that the large size of the Irish national debt would restrict the scope for a fall in interest. However, the increased efficiency of the financial sector would lead to a reduction of 1,000 jobs over a five-year period and a price reduction of 0.5%. The results from the HERMES Ireland model due to liberalization of financial markets were not as strong as those in the Cecchini Report. In the medium term, Irish prices were predicted to fall by 1.0% (-1.4% according to Cecchini) and GNP to rise by 1.05% (1.5% according to Cecchini).

As in the Cecchini Report, the impact of the 'supply-side effects' (i.e. firms facing lower production costs and higher labour productivity) on the overall forecast dominated all other policy categories in the ESRI study. This shock was implemented by simulating a reduction in *ex ante* domestic unit costs of production over a six-year period. The simulation resulted in a 2.0% increase in GNP (similar to the 2.1% increase in the Cecchini Report), but a smaller price reduction of 1.4% than the EC-wide reduction of 2.3% found by Cecchini.

The ESRI forecast of the total effect of 1992 on the Irish macroeconomy compares favourably to the Cecchini predictions except in the context of prices. Cecchini found a 6.1% reduction in consumer prices by the year 1998 while the ESRI study suggested that prices would fall by only 3.1%. The ESRI prediction of the impact on GNP is almost identical to that of Cecchini, as is also the prediction of a sustained increase in the total numbers employed.[12]

### 4.1.2. Ireland: sectoral studies

Most of the sectoral studies review historical trends and do not quantify the impact of 1992 on the sectors in question. This criticism is true of all the papers in the publication *The Single European Market and the Irish Economy* (Foley and Mulreany, 1990), some of which are reviewed below.

*Foley (1990)*

Foley was pessimistic about the impact of the SEM on Irish indigenous industry. He predicted that benefits from the reduction in transport costs would be outweighed by the removal of barriers, which increases competition from foreigners on the domestic market. Foley claimed that unless firms who concentrate on the domestic market became exporters, they would not gain from the SEM. Foley's assertions about the demise of indigenous industry were not based on empirical analysis, nor did he quantify the impact of 1992 on indigenous industry at a disaggregated level.

*Jacobson and Andreosso (1990)*

A similar pessimistic view was held by Jacobson and Andreosso (1990) who reviewed Ireland's ability to attract foreign direct investment once barriers were abolished. They foresaw adverse economic consequences for Ireland in this regard due both to increased competition from EC partners and to the erosion of artificial country-specific advantages (such as low corporate taxes and government assistance). Future flows of FDI into Ireland would be uncertain, according to the authors.

---

[12] The simulation results reported in Chapter 7 are based on a smaller HERMIN model, but can be compared to the earlier ESRI HERMES-based analysis. The fact that the HERMIN models are available for all four cohesion countries serves to offset the loss of sectoral detail due to HERMIN's four sectors.

The two aforementioned papers and those by Keegan and Hennessy (1990) reviewing the building and construction sector and Ferris (1990) analysing transport costs, all concluded that the benefits to Ireland would be outweighed by the loss incurred due to the SEM. However, the lack of formal empirical analysis in any of these studies weakens the strength of their conclusions.

### Durkan and Reynolds-Feighan (1992)

In a micro-study of transport costs, Durkan and Reynolds-Feighan (1992) found transport costs faced by Irish firms to be high compared to other EC countries. There were also regional differences in cost within Ireland, where regions suffer competitive disadvantages within Ireland as well as externally. The study predicted that this would have serious implications not only for export trade but also for domestic markets. The authors found that transport costs accounted for a little over 4% of the value of sales of manufactured goods. They predicted that internal Irish transport costs would be reduced in the medium term once the EC proposal for VAT harmonization was implemented, since this was one factor highlighted by firms as keeping transport costs high. Although the investment in better Irish infrastructure was a major component in the effort to reduce transport costs, the study suggested a need for proportionally higher investment in road infrastructure in Ireland than elsewhere in Europe, if any significant reduction in Irish transport costs was to be realized.

### NESC (1989)

The National Economic and Social Council (1989) survey included a very comprehensive historical analysis of the Irish economy, but no empirical analysis. The NESC concluded that Irish industry would benefit from price reductions and increased competitiveness but that the indirect effects of the SEM, such as economies of scale, would have an ambiguous effect. Their general conclusion was that 'the long run benefits of the SEM are likely to be unevenly distributed – with the greatest benefit accruing to regions in which industries with economies of scale and highly innovative sectors are most prevalent. Ireland is not such a region' (p. 526). They predicted that the convergence of income disparities would not necessarily follow from the SEM. This overall conclusion differs from the more optimistic conclusions of O'Malley (1990 and 1992).

### O'Malley (1990, 1992)

O'Malley quantified those disaggregated manufacturing sectors most likely to be affected by 1992, based on the approach by Buigues *et al.* (1990) in a *European Economy/Social Europe* special edition assessing the impact of the single market by industrial sector. O'Malley concluded that Ireland was in a relatively favourable position to face the SEM and benefit overall from freer trade. The findings from the O'Malley (1990) study are used extensively in our subsequent methodology, allowing us to take into account the structural changes to the economy that trade liberalization might bring, by quantifying the magnitude of the switch from non-tradable to tradable (see Chapter 6).

O'Malley (1990) picked out 39 'sensitive' sectors (three-digit NACE code sectors) accounting for 46.7% of total manufacturing employment. The 'sensitive' sectors were those manufacturing sectors most likely to be affected either positively ('strong sectors') or adversely ('weak sectors') by the abolition of non-tariff barriers within the EC. O'Malley assessed their competitiveness using a range of indicators such as the intra- and extra-EC import/export ratio (1985-87) and the percentage change in that ratio over the 1980–87 period. About 28% of manufacturing employment was in the relatively strong sensitive sectors (16 sectors) as compared to 19% in potentially vulnerable sectors (24 sectors). He drew attention to the dualistic structure that existed within these 39 sectors. Firstly, high-technology, mostly foreign owned, companies (accounting for 56% of the sensitive sector employment, higher than the 42.8% share in total manufacturing employment) accounted for almost 70% of the strong sectors. The fact that foreign firms produced mainly for the export market strengthened their concentration in the strong sectors. Secondly, the traditional manufacturing indigenous firms were less export-oriented and had a poorer record in international competition. The suggestion that the foreign-owned companies might not expand in Ireland due to the new opportunities of the single market was rejected by O'Malley. As the multinational firms produce mainly for the export market, the removal of non-tariff barriers would seldom create a new motivation to close Irish plants. The net benefits to Irish industry were positive according to O'Malley, but he pointed out that companies would need to inform themselves about international developments in order to gain any real advantages from these opportunities.

O'Malley (1992) also reviewed the relative importance of economies of scale for the individual sensitive sectors and considered the implications for foreign and Irish owned firms separately. He found that Irish indigenous industry was relatively highly concentrated in sectors where economies of scale were less important, and were unlikely to gain much from attaining greater benefits from economies of scale. The bulk of foreign owned industry (accounting for 23% of total manufacturing employment) was in sectors with substantial economies of scale and was likely to be significantly affected by the removal of non-tariff barriers. O'Malley predicted that these firms would benefit from both the single market and the ability to take greater advantage of economies of scale. On balance, O'Malley suggested that industry in Ireland would benefit proportionally less from economies of scale than the EC average, but argued that the overall benefits, though limited, would still be positive.

### 4.1.3. Spain: aggregate studies

The two main aggregate studies of the Spanish economy outlined below quantify the impact of the SEM on the Spanish economy.

*Collado et al. (1992)*

The first study by Collado *et al.* (1992) is similar to that by Bradley *et al.* (1992) reviewed above, and followed a methodology close to that of the Cecchini Report, comparing their results for the Spanish economy to those reported by Catinat and Italianer (1988). The authors used the MIDE model[13] in their analysis. This is a dynamic macro-sectoral econometric model, based on the 1980 input-output table, which considers 43 separate activity branches, complemented with information from Eurostat *National Accounts* data.

The model consists of three blocks: production, income prices and accounting identities. The first block determines the final demand, the intermediate consumption, and the production, productivity and employment in each of the 43 activity branches at constant prices, being the

---

[13] MIDE are the Spanish initials for a Macroeconomic Intersectoral Model of Spain built at the Fundación Tomillo, a private organization that offers economic research [see Collado (1992, Appendix 1) for a detailed account of the model structure].

sum of final demands equal to GDP. The income-prices block determines sectoral value added at current prices (i.e. wages, profits, taxes and price index for each branch); the sum of sectoral value added gives nominal GDP. The final block, through macroeconomic identities and behavioural equations, converts the nominal GDP into disposable income, and distributes it among households, firms and the government. The model is closed by the production block and the income-prices block.

Collado *et al.* (1992) considered the macroeconomic effects of the SEM under four headings, similar to that of the Cecchini Report (1988):

(a)     the abolition of border controls;
(b)     the opening up of public procurement;
(c)     the liberalization of financial services;
(d)     'supply effects' due to increased competition.

In addition, they consider the effects of the fiscal harmonization of indirect taxes.

Regarding the removal of customs barriers within the EEC, they simulated a reduction of 8,000 jobs and a cut in the export and import prices according to the average cost reduction by product categories provided in Catinat and Italianer (1988). Given that the competitiveness of the bulk of industries where public purchases are concentrated is relatively poor, the authors evaluated the impact of the opening up of public procurement using the higher values of those reported in Catinat and Italianer (1988). Regarding the effect of financial liberalization, they examined the effects of a reduction in the price of financial services due to greater competition by a gradual reduction to 21% (the mean of the Cecchini Report estimates for Spain) in the 1993–2000 period. They evaluated the effects of a reduction in the cost of production due to increased competition and economies of scale similar to that in Catinat and Italianer (1988) and Pratten (1988). Finally, the effects of the harmonization of indirect taxes were evaluated, leading to VAT rates of 14% and 20% in 1996, and a harmonization of the excise taxes (10% increase of excise rates on alcoholic beverages between 1994 and 1995, and 20% increase in tobacco).

They predicted that the aggregate potential consequences of the completion of the single market for Spain in the medium term (by 1998) would be as follows: a 1.1% increase in GDP over the baseline (mainly due to a 1.3% increase in exports and a 1.17% increase in consumption); a reduction of approximately 2% in prices; a 0.87% deterioration in the trade balance; a 1.17% improvement in the public deficit; and an increase in employment by 217,400 jobs (reducing the unemployment rate by 1.36%). These Spanish forecasts are not as optimistic as those predicted by the Cecchini Report for the EC core Member States or those suggested for Ireland in the Bradley *et al.* (1992) ESRI study.

### Polo and Sancho (1993)

The authors used a computable general equilibrium (CGE) model to forecast the consequences of the SEM for Spain. Their static, single-country CGE model included four types of agents: producers (12), consumers (8), the public sector and two foreign sectors (the EEC and the rest of the world), as well as 36 goods and three production factors (two types of labour and capital).

The authors considered the macroeconomic effects of the elimination of barriers to trade, the financial liberalization and the fiscal harmonization of indirect taxes. Regarding the first effect, they simulated both the elimination of tariffs and quantitative restrictions (through a total elimination of tariffs on EEC imports and a 25% increase in the elasticities of substitution between domestic products and imports – the latter to capture the greater openness of the Spanish economy), and the removal of administrative barriers and standards (proxied by a 2% cut of import prices and a 1.7% reduction in production costs as estimated in the 1988 Cecchini Report). Regarding the effects of financial liberalization, they examined the effects of a reduction in the price of financial services due to greater competition (simulating a 21% cut, as in Collado, 1992). For the evaluation of the harmonization of indirect taxes, they studied both the effects of harmonization of VAT rates leading to 6%, 14% and 20% rates and the effects of harmonization of the excise taxes (20% increase of excise rates on alcoholic beverages, tobacco and mineral oil).

Their estimations suggested that the global effect of these shocks would lead to substantial gains in production (6.35%), employment (a reduction of 2.79% in the unemployment rate), government revenues (leading to an improvement of 0.61% in the public deficit/GDP ratio), and consumers' welfare (4.51% in the short run and 5.41% in the long run). The deterioration of the trade deficit with the EEC (30% fall in the export/import ratio) was found to be the most negative effect of integration.

This study suggested greater benefits for the Spanish economy due to the SEM than Collado *et al.* (1992). CGE models are a very useful tool in modelling the effects of policy changes such as tax harmonization across a disaggregated level of sectors, by considering the changes in the relative prices throughout the economy rather than through aggregate mechanisms. In the context of modelling economic growth and structural adjustment, static CGE models are exposed to criticism. A static equilibrium solution, as in the case above, is put forward as a long run equilibrium towards which the economy moves, but how rapidly the economy adjusts is left rather vague.

### 4.1.4.  Spain: sectoral studies

Most of the sectoral studies of the Spanish economy forecast positive returns from the SEM. However, the magnitude of the effect differs across the studies.

*Gonzalez-Romero (1989)*

The analysis contained in this paper is based on a study of business perceptions of the prospects opened up by the completion of the SEM. It concludes that manufacturing production will increase by 8.7% (greater than the 5% expected for the EEC as a whole), due to a 4.9% increase in productivity and a 3.8% increase in employment. However, the effects vary within the manufacturing sector. Those with strong, medium and weak demand will experience an increase in production of 10%, 7.8% and 8.9% respectively, while employment in those same sectors will increase by 5.2%, 3.1% and 4.7% respectively. This prediction is quite optimistic and suggests that the SEM would significantly boost the Spanish manufacturing sector.

*De la Oliva and Orgaz (1989)*

De la Oliva and Orgaz (1989) also predicted a positive effect on Spanish manufacturing as a consequence of the completion of the single market, but a relatively smaller impact on Spain than on the EEC as a whole. They reached this conclusion since the 40 industrial sectors that are likely to be positively affected represent 34.3% of total industrial value added in Spain (versus 48.9% in the EEC), and are more sensitive to import penetration.

*Martin (1990)*

Martin studied the 40 sensitive manufacturing sectors in Spain that were identified by the European Commission to be substantially affected by the creation of the SEM. This paper was part of the *European Economy/Social Europe* special issue (1990) and follows the same structure as O'Malley's (1990) study of Irish manufacturing. The paper concluded that these 40 sensitive sectors are more exposed to external competition than the remaining sectors of Spanish manufacturing, due to their lower export/import ratio and smaller share of domestic production in apparent consumption. Moreover, it also found that Spanish firms seemed to perform relatively more strongly in products which were characterized by weak demand, relatively low capital/labour ratios, low R&D content and less scope for scale economies. As with the O'Malley study, we use Martin's classification in our own simulations, to be reported in Chapter 8 below, in order to quantify the magnitude of the switch from non-tradables to tradables for the Spanish manufacturing sectors.

*Viñals et al. (1990)*

The authors analysed the economic performance inside the EEC to evaluate the likely evolution of trade flows, output and employment following the completion of the SEM, concentrating on the transitional period.[14] This study analysed Spain's integration with the EC in a historical context, but it does not quantify the effects of the SEM on the Spanish economy. It characterized the Spanish economy before integration as having a relatively less open current account and more open capital account, a rigid labour market, and a solvent financial system, leading them to conclude that the adjustment costs from the 'EEC cum 1992' shock may be larger in goods and labour markets than in financial markets.

Their study of the Spain-EEC inter- and intra-industry trade suggests that a significant effect on Spain's industrial structure is expected to exploit both its comparative advantage and scale and scope economies. Viñals *et al.* use a CGE model similar to that used by Smith and Venables (1988) to assess empirically the distributional and efficiency adjustment costs to the new structure, finding that this relocation of production was likely to be across sectors rather than within sectors, involving a fair amount of inter-sectoral capital and labour flows. Moreover, given the rigidities in the labour and capital markets, such costs were expected to be quite important if no appropriate economic measures are implemented.

---

[14]   Viñals (1992) offers a more detailed discussion of these topics, as well as the sectoral studies carried out to evaluate the likely impact of the growing openness of the Spanish economy.

*Collado (1995)*

In a later paper, Collado (1995) studied the convergence between the occupational structures of Spain and the EC, concluding that although convergence has occurred at the aggregate level, the gap has widened in several sectors of the Spanish economy. Sectoral convergence is associated with reductions in comparative advantage and relatively lower levels of foreign investment. However, he does not quantify the effects of convergence in this paper.

## 4.1.5. Portugal: aggregate studies

Unlike the Bradley *et al.* (1992) and the Collado *et al.* (1992) quantitative studies, no such similar aggregate study, to our knowledge, has been carried out for the Portuguese economy assessing the impact of the SEM, based on formal empirical macroeconometric or CGE models.

*De Macedo (1990)*

De Macedo assessed the impact of the SEM on Portugal but does not quantify his conclusions using formal empirical models. He predicted that the size, inefficiency and uncompetitive nature of the Portuguese public sector was an obstacle to integration within the EC. The public sector has been described as 'frozen' until 1989, due to political policies of central planning, and has only recently been reformed (de Macedo, 1990: 336–42). De Macedo found that the manufacturing sector was concentrated in weak-demand sectors such as textiles and leather goods, with growth in employment and investment occurring in these sectors. He concluded that in order to remain competitive, the manufacturing sector would have to undergo restructuring and invest in differentiated products to benefit from export growth.

## 4.1.6. Portugal: sectoral studies

*Goncalves (1990)*

This paper, in the *European Economy* special issue, identified 47 Portuguese sensitive manufacturing sectors likely to be affected by the SEM. These sectors are used later in Chapter 7 in the HERMIN-based methodology in a similar manner to those of Martin (1990) and O'Malley (1990), outlined above. The sensitive sectors account for 60% of value added and 70% of employment in industry, where the majority (37 sectors) are in weak demand sectors. Goncalves' overall assessment was negative, predicting that these weak demand sectors would be likely to suffer competitiveness loss due to the SEM unless technological co-operation agreements can be concluded or efficient foreign companies were to set up in Portugal.

## 4.1.7. Greece: aggregate studies

*Capros, Karadeloglou and Mentzas (1990)*

This study used the GEM-NTUA four-sector model developed by the National Technical University of Athens to examine the effects of *1992* on the Greek economy, using a methodology similar to the Cecchini Report (1988). The GEM-NTUA model represents the behaviour of four economic agents: households, firms, the government and foreigners. It also has four sectors of production: agriculture, manufacturing (including mining), energy utilities and services (public and private).

Of particular interest are the multiplier properties of the model. For example, the impact public investment multiplier (defined as $\Delta GDP/\Delta IG$, where IG refers to public investment), is 1.18, and declines to a value of 0.7 in the long run. Similarly, the model is very sensitive to changes in the external growth rate. The main use of the model has been in the study of energy-environment interactions, in association with the MIDAS model of energy supply and demand.

The findings of this study were quite pessimistic. For example, the positive effects of 1992 were found to be significantly lower than for the core EU members or, indeed, for Ireland. GDP was shown to increase by 2.4% as a result of all of the 1992 measures, compared with the core economies' increase of 4.5%. In addition, the fall in prices is less (1.5% compared to 6.4%). Hence, the study suggested that the SEM measures would exacerbate the disparity between Greece and the core economies. The poor showing for 1992 seemed to be concentrated in the negative effects of public procurement liberalization (due to the existence of a significant protectionist environment for some Greek firms producing exclusively for the public sector), and the rather modest supply-side effects. On balance, the study is difficult to evaluate, since very little detail is presented.

### 4.1.8.  Greece: sectoral studies

*Mardas and Varsakelis (1990)*

The authors identified 45 sensitive sectors as being likely to be affected by the SEM, in a paper contained in the *European Economy/Social Europe* (1990) special issue. As with Ireland, Spain and Portugal, this analysis is used in our own later quantification of the structural shift from non-traded to traded behaviour due to the impact of the SEM. The 45 sensitive sectors accounted for 57% of value added and 62% of employment in Greek industry. As with Portugal, the authors found that the majority of the sectors (37) were vulnerable to the SEM process and likely to be negatively affected. They pointed out that highly labour intensive sectors, such as textiles, clothing and footwear, were relatively more protected in Greece than was the case for the EC average. The eight sectors that experienced strong trade performance belonged mainly to the clothing/footwear industries. Being weak demand sectors, the authors questioned whether these sectors would respond well to the challenge of increased competition. In general, this paper suggested that Greece would suffer adversely from the SEM.

*Katseli (1990)*

Katseli claimed that trade liberalization had reduced the existing intra-industry specialization in manufacturing in Greece. She predicted that inter-industry specialization would arise out of the removal of barriers to entry in Greece, and that employment would fall in the short run. In the long run, Katseli suggested that trade liberalization would lead to competitive gains, increased efficiency and eventually a restructuring of industry. However, neither the short run nor the long run results are quantified in the paper using formal empirical models. The author suggested policy changes necessary for adjustment to freer trade: the active promotion of entrepeneurship; that government policy should integrate structural adjustment policies (increased efficiency in industry) with macroeconomic policies (controlling the external balance) in order to add credibility to the government's commitment to the single market.

*Sarris (1990)*

Sarris developed a two-sector model of the Greek economy, one sector exhibiting fixed prices, the other flexible prices. He made this distinction as opposed to the general traded (large-scale) sector, non-traded (small-scale) sector since a sizeable proportion of Greek exports are composed of agricultural products, textiles and garments, and hence subject to fixed prices. The model shows that 'the maintenance of high public spending and deficits imply a healthy level of GDP but at the expense of an appreciating currency in real terms'. Yet, if the structure of the economy does not change in line with freer trade, GDP will not necessarily rise in the short term. This is due to the low Phillips curve effect, where unemployment in some sectors induced by increased competition does not lead to reduced wages and increased employment in others. The author predicted that the opposite effects will occur with financial liberalization.

### 4.1.9. Southern peripheral countries of the EU: aggregate studies

*Larre and Torres (1991)*

This paper analysed the convergence of the southern peripheral countries in Europe to the OECD and European average. It suggested that Portugal and Spain have converged due to increased foreign investment and the structural changes that have occurred in their economy, which in turn has lead to increased investment and the deregulation of the labour market as well as the removal of barriers to trade. Greece has not experienced such convergence, due to a slower removal of the impediments to freer trade. This paper does not specifically deal with the impact of the single market on the above-mentioned countries, but the focus of the analysis, on such issues as structural adjustment and FDI, gives an insight into the mechanisms of convergence as were experienced by the southern peripheral countries.

*Neven (1990)*

This paper was optimistic about the likely southern peripheral country gains from the SEM. It predicted that Greece and Portugal (and, to a lesser extent, Spain) would benefit greatly due to their strong comparative advantage in the (labour intensive) clothing and footwear sectors, with half the labour costs of their northern neighbours. He uses firm size as an indication of the extent to which scale economies are exploited. From our point of view, Neven appears overly optimistic in that he suggests that the relative smallness of firms in the southern periphery industrial sectors, characterized by economies of scale, will allow them to expand under liberalized trade. As the NESC (1989) report on the Irish experience indicates, however, the small indigenous firms in these sectors in Ireland were wiped out because they were too small to compete.

## 4.2. Quantifying the impact of the CSF 1989–93

The first reformed programme of structural intervention, the CSF or Delors I package, covered the five years from 1989 to 1993. The analysis of the Irish CSF 1989–93 is probably the most comprehensively documented of the four cohesion countries. The Greek CSF 1989–93 has been the subject of three studies, but the level of detailed documentation of results and methodology is quite limited. Although the Portuguese CSF 1989–93 has not been analysed using a conventional macroeconometric model, it has been studied using an experimental optimal growth model which could potentially yield some new insights over and above the more conventional analysis based on macroeconometric models. No formal macro-model-based quantifications for the Spanish CSF 1989–93 were available to the authors of this report.[15]

## 4.2.1.  Ireland: CSF 1989–93

The Irish CSF 1989–93 was structured as a series of operational programmes, set in the context of a comprehensive framework for tackling the structural problems of the Irish economy. Each programme concentrated on a priority – a particular sector or structural problem – and specified objectives to tackle the problem or the challenges faced by the sector. For the purposes of more logical economic analysis, they were re-classified under six more economically relevant headings:

(a)  *Human resources*

   The single biggest category, accounting for 42% of expenditure. Spent on different training schemes and on the improvement of the educational system.

(b)  *Physical infrastructure*

   Accounting for 27% of expenditure, the bulk spent on upgrading port facilities and road infrastructure.

(c)  *Farm income support*

   Accounting for 10% of expenditure, designed to boost agricultural incomes, such as compensatory (headage) payments.

(d)  *Grants to industry*

   To reduce the cost of setting up new installations or expanding existing plants.

(e)  *Agricultural investment*

   Accounting for 8% of expenditure, to increase productive potential in forestry and farm improvement schemes.

(f)  *Aid to marketing and research and development*

   To promote the marketing potential of existing firms and increase the level of expenditure on R&D.[16]

The ESRI[17] carried out the analysis in terms of the six-way classification described above, and then analysed all the programmes together and assessed the impact of the CSF when taken as a whole. Because of the arbitrariness and uncertainty about the pure supply-side effects of the CSF, they were separated out so that the sensitivity of the conclusions to alternative assumptions concerning the long-term response of the economy to the CSF could be examined.

---

[15]   A study of the short run demand effects of the CSF 1989-93 has been carried out by Beutel, 1993, using input-output models for the four Objective 1 countries, for the Mezzogiorno region of Italy and for Northern Ireland.

[16]   *Source:* Bradley, Fitz Gerald and Kearney (1992).

[17]   The study was carried out by Bradley, Fitz Gerald and Kearney (1992). They also assessed the impact of the SEM on Ireland, which is discussed in greater detail above in our review of the impact of the SEM on Ireland.

Because of the particular interest in the long-term impact on potential growth, the analysis was not ended in 1993 but was continued out to the year 2000. While the first CSF only ran until 1993, the simplifying assumption was made that it remained unchanged in real terms in all its details after 1993.[18]

This review focuses on the total impact of the CSF, and the reader is referred to Bradley, Fitz Gerald and Kearney (1992) for more detail. The study suggested that the medium-term contribution to growth was likely to be about 2.7% of GNP. The effects on GNP per capita were somewhat smaller, due to the impact of increased inward migration flows into the Irish labour market. The creation of around 30,000 additional jobs by the year 2000 substantially reduces net emigration and increases the population. As a result, by the year 2000, GNP per capita was projected to be only 0.8% above the benchmark no-CSF scenario.

The CSF policies were found to be very 'supply-side friendly', in that the international and public sector finance balances improved unambiguously, wage rates eventually returned to their no-CSF levels after a period of demand-led inflation during the implementation phases, unemployment was down, in particular the long-term component, emigration was reduced, and the debt/GNP ratio was improved by about 6 percentage points.

The single most important area of expenditure under the CSF is the range of programmes under the broad human resources heading. These programmes are designed to improve the human capital of the Irish labour force and to increase labour market participation by marginal groups. The ESRI study showed that, if successful, these policies could raise GNP significantly in the short to medium term, with even greater long-term effects. However, considerable uncertainty remained about the precise quantification of the supply-side effects of these measures.

A particularly important aspect of the CSF programme was the extent to which it induces a long-run positive supply-side stimulus to the economy, since these effects represent the permanent value of the CSF as distinct from the transitory demand shock which accompanies implementation. As in the Emerson-Cecchini report, the exploration of these supply-side effects could, at best, be tentative since the techniques involved are at the frontier of economics. The ESRI study posited long-run supply effects under all the headings with the exception of the agricultural income transfers. They were found to be particularly important under two headings: human resources and infrastructure. The supply-side effects grew steadily over time. On these assumptions, by the end of the first CSF plan in 1993, they would add about 0.75% to the volume of GNP. However, by the end of the decade, the supply-side stimulus would have more than doubled and the level of GNP would have increased by almost 2%.

## 4.2.2.  Spain: CSF 1989–93

There does not appear to have been any analysis of the impact of the Spanish CSF 1989–93 based on formal models of any sort. The one Spanish model in the public domain (MOISEES) is a single sector model based on neo-Keynesian disequilibrium switching regimes. Hence, the

---

[18]    It should be noted that the Greek work to be reported on below does not extend the period of analysis much beyond the terminal date of CSF 1989–93. Since one does not know much about the long-term properties of the Greek models involved, perhaps it is just as well to keep the time horizon short, and stay in the 'Keynesian' demand regime.

size of its multipliers is extremely sensitive to the initial state of the economy. Consequently, it is not possible to use the multipliers tabulated for MOISEES as guidelines for CSF analysis (Molinas *et al.*, 1990).

### 4.2.3.  Portugal: CSF 1989–93

There has been no published or accessible unpublished analysis of the Portuguese CSF based on a conventional macroeconometric model. However, a study by Gaspar and Pereira (1991) was based on an innovative small-scale one-sector model of endogenous growth that was parameterized and calibrated using Portuguese data for 1986. The object of that study was twofold: to analyse the effects of financial integration of the Portuguese economy with the rest of the EC, and to analyse the impact of unilateral public capital transfers, such as the CSF.[19]

Since CSF transfers are subject to the complementarity principle (which requires that national governments contribute funds proportional to EU funding), and the additionality principle (which attempts to prevent the recipient countries from decreasing their own financial allocations in other areas), the net impact of the EU CSF funding on the domestic budget is ambiguous. The model developed by Gaspar and Pereira builds on the work of Barro (1990) and Barro and Sala-i-Martin (1990). Basically, public capital is assumed to play the role of an externality, i.e. a source of increasing returns.

The growth model was used to analyse the effects of the EC CSF funding in the usual way. A baseline scenario was constructed from 1989 to beyond the year 2010, with no increase in the CSF funding above the 1988 baseline. For the period 1989–93, the actual increases in the EC CSF funding were inserted. Beyond 1993, they were assumed to grow at a rate of 3% per annum. The difference in the two simulations was taken as a measure of the impact of the CSF funding, since in both simulations the composition and magnitude of the domestic funding were kept unchanged.

In addition, the model was used to analyse the effects of Portuguese financial integration with the rest of the EC, mainly in terms of a gradually narrowing domestic-foreign interest rate differential as a result of increasingly free capital mobility. This is, in part, the impact of a combination of the financial deregulation of 1992, combined with Portugal's membership of the EMS/EMU process.

The impact of the CSF on the growth of GDP was found to be stable and permanent, at around 0.4%, reaching 0.6% in the long run. Hence, with the particular evolution of the CSF funding in the simulation experiment, the long-run level of Portuguese GDP is increased by over 7% relative to a non-CSF baseline.

The impact of the CSF funding on the optimal public sector deficit was relatively small. Public deficits show a slight deterioration in the short run. Public investment increased by 1.5% of GDP, while public consumption decreased by 1.2%. The relatively high cost of international funds, in the complete absence of financial integration, together with the additionality and complementarity provisions, caused public investment under CSF policies to crowd out public consumption essentially on a one-to-one basis.

---

[19]    Essentially the same model framework was extended to include Greece and Ireland in Pereira, 1992.

The most surprising result is that the inflow of CSF public transfers causes an increase in the optimal amount of foreign financing, less outflow in the absence of financial integration. The authors suggested that the traditional Keynesian result may not generalize to the context of an optimal intertemporal growth model of a capital importing economy. Also, in the absence of financial integration, no substantial optimal re-allocation of structural funds for consumption activities occurred, due to the relatively high cost of funds.

Finally, a comprehensive series of sensitivity analyses were carried out, where all the assumed parameters of the model were varied. The authors suggested that the model could be generalized to include human capital (which was ignored in the first version), to consider international flows of labour as well as of capital within the EC, and to disaggregate the one-sector formulation into a traded/non-traded two-sector formulation. The Portuguese model provides an intriguing and novel application of optimal growth theory in the presence of externalities that generate increasing returns. However, the work remains very experimental in nature and sheds only limited empirical light on the impact of CSF 1989–93 on the Portuguese economy.

### 4.2.4. Greece: CSF 1989–93

The Greek CSF 1989–93 has been the subject of three unpublished studies that make explicit use of macroeconometric models. The first, by Capros and Karadeloglou (1989), used the GEM-NTUA four-sector model, described in Capros et al. (1988). The second, carried out by researchers at the Bank of Greece, used a small one-sector model (Lolos and Zonzilos, 1992). The third, by Bourguignon et al. (1992), uses a modified CGE approach. We review briefly these three studies and comment on their reliability and the robustness of their conclusions.

*Capros and Karadeloglou (1989)*

The model developed by the National Technical University of Athens (GEM-NTUA) is documented in Capros et al. (1988). This model has already been referred to above in the review of Greek SEM studies.

In the analysis of the Greek CSF 1989–93, a baseline scenario was constructed for the period 1989–95, using forecast exogenous variables, where the EC funding injections for the CSF followed pre-1989 trends. The CSF policy scenario was based on the same exogenous assumptions, except that the EC funding of the CSF reflected the actual transfers to Greece. These funds were introduced in constant drachmas, and endogenously inflated inside the model, where the ECU-drachma exchange rate was assumed to be unaffected by the CSF. The actual timing of the expenditures over the period 1989–93 were taken from the Greek CSF documentation (European Commission, 1990a), and it was assumed that the funding was to be continued in real terms beyond the terminal year 1993.

The broad pattern of results was very like those in the Irish case (ignoring the specifically Irish open labour market and endogenous migration mechanism). In the medium term, by the year 1995, GDP increased by 1.85% over the benchmark case, with the main expenditure increase coming in investment (public and private). However, employment only increased by 0.51%. Prices were relatively unchanged, public sector borrowing as a percentage of GDP improved, as also did the balance of payments.

It is significant that the increase due to the CSF (at 1.85%) was less than the gap between the effects of 1992 on the Greek economy and the developed core economies (at 2.08%). Hence, according to this study, the relative position of the Greek economy would deteriorate under the combined 1992 and CSF effects. Also, the study showed that exports never increased above the non-CSF baseline. Indeed, they remained systematically below the baseline, reaching almost 1% less by the year 1995. Correspondingly, imports were up, so the balance of trade (not separately identified in the Greek documentation) must have deteriorated. Hence, the improvement in the balance of payments must be due entirely to the capital inflows from the EU CSF aid.

On balance, this study is somewhat difficult to evaluate, since very little detail of methodology or simulations is presented. The effects look like purely Keynesian ones, although the deterioration in the balance of trade would either point to a suboptimal use of the CSF funds by Greek policy-makers, or simply to an inadequate incorporation of the CSF policies into the model instruments and equations.

### Lolos and Zonzilos (1992)

The study by Lolos and Zonzilos (1992) specified and estimated an aggregate dynamic econometric model of the Keynesian type. A special characteristic of the model is that it uses advanced error correction mechanisms and co-integration techniques for estimation. No documented testing of the model is given, however, nor are any multipliers extracted for examination. However, its Keynesian specification seems to be fairly standard.

The study used the same temporal distribution as the previous study by Capros and Karadeloglou (1989) described above. Three main channels of CSF influence are identified as:

(a)   public investment in infrastructure (about 50% of the total);
(b)   investment in training and skill formation (about 25% of the total);
(c)   restructuring of productive capacity and improvement in competitiveness, through various forms of financial assistance.

The manner in which the impact of the CSF was examined is as follows. First, an initial simulation was carried out, which included all CSF funding, both domestic and EC. This was called the base run, or the CSF scenario. Then a modified run was made, reducing the magnitude of the exogenous variables related to the CSF implementation to the extent that they were funded by EC transfers. The impact of the CSF was defined as the difference between the base run and the modified run.

The study found that Greek GDP was boosted by slightly over 2% by 1993, equivalent to an increase in the growth rate of about 0.5% per annum. This is quite a significant result, given that the average annual growth rate in Greece over the previous decade was only 1%. Private non-residential investment was raised by 2.5%, but there was some crowding out by the public sector. The unemployment rate was lowered by 1%.

These results are broadly in line with the previous study, where it must be remembered that Lolos and Zonzilos are analysing the impact of the total EC CSF transfers (i.e. relative to a zero base line), while Capros and Karadeloglou used a 3% growth of CSF funding as their baseline. Given that the CSF funding was roughly doubled, compared to the level in 1988, one would expect the Lolos and Zonzilos impact on GDP (at 2.06% by 1993) to be approximately twice the impact as defined by Capros and Karadeloglou (at 1.55%).

It must be said that, as with the previous study, the Lolos and Zonzilos analysis is very limited, since it used a model that focused only on the demand-side impact of the CSF. In such a model-based framework, a cessation of the CSF funding would reverse almost all the previous beneficial impact unless hysteresis effects were present, which would serve to prevent the economy from returning to its initial position, once the CSF funding ended. There appears to have been no Greek study of CSF 1989–93 that examined possible long-term supply-side effects.

*Bourguignon et al. (1992)*

Probably the most interesting study of the Greek CSF 1989–93 is that prepared by Bourguignon *et al.* (1992), using a hybrid Keynesian-CGE modelling approach. The study adapted a modelling framework originally built for the OECD Development Centre and the World Bank to evaluate the likely impact of structural adjustment policies in developing countries (Bourguignon, Branson and de Melo, 1993).

The version of the model used for the assessment of the Greek CSF combined a standard CGE model with a wide variety of macroeconomic closures. The Greek economy was disaggregated into nine sectors and five socio-economic groups. Agents were assumed to operate in four markets (goods and services, labour, money and foreign exchange). In the goods market, adjustment was either Keynesian (a non-competitive mark-up pricing rule with quantity adjustments or changes in capacity utilization), or classical (competitive Walrasian price adjustment).

The macroeconomic closure chosen for Greece was at the frontier between Keynesian and classical: some sectors (agriculture, commerce) were held to be close to full employment, while there was held to be underemployment of capacity in others (energy). In the former, any expansion would be met by price increases, resource reallocation and imports; in the latter, any contraction would be met by a fall in capacity utilization and employment.

The analysis was performed using three simulations. The first, a base run, included all the policy initiatives in CSF 1989–93. The second eliminated all the supply-side phenomena assumed to be associated with the CSF programme, i.e. all the effects which were assumed to modify exogenously the production potential of the economy. This was called the CSF-demand simulation, since only demand effects are left. The third simulation eliminated all expenditures explicitly linked to the CSF programme, in infrastructure, training, etc., as well as the current transfers from abroad and the corresponding entries into the government accounts. This was called the no-CSF scenario.

The analysis was carried out for two different regimes or macro closure rules. The first (case 1 in Table 4.2) was the normal Keynesian or underemployment rule. The second (case 2 in Table 4.2) was a classical rule, and assumed the Greek economy was at full employment.

In the Keynesian rule, the simulations suggested that the CSF could raise Greek GDP by 1.3% in 1992 and 1993, and by a little less in the previous years. However, more than half the effect was essentially coming from the demand side of the programme and would cease as soon as the programme comes to an end, ignoring possible hysteresis effects. Supply-side effects, which last even after the end of the CSF, were more moderate in case 1, contributing only approximately 0.5% of the GDP increase in 1992 and 1993.

Case 2 explored the other extreme, the full employment case. This simulation showed the sensitivity of the results with respect to the macroeconomic closure rules used. In this case, the demand-side effects were zero. Any additional demand simply crowded out existing demand, leaving total output unchanged, except for some reallocation across sectors.

**Table 4.2.    CSF 1989–93 (Greece): Keynesian and classical regimes**

| Case 1: Keynesian framework | | | | | | | |
|---|---|---|---|---|---|---|---|
| **Real GDP** | **1989** | **1990** | **1991** | **1992** | **1993** | **1994** | **1995** |
| Supply | 0.19 | 0.29 | 0.47 | 0.47 | 0.46 | 0.55 | 0.54 |
| Demand | 0.48 | 0.68 | 0.76 | 0.84 | 0.84 | -0.46 | -0.46 |
| Total | 0.68 | 0.97 | 1.23 | 1.3 | 1.3 | 0.09 | 0.09 |
| Case 2: Classical (or full employment) framework | | | | | | | |
| **Real GDP** | **1989** | **1990** | **1991** | **1992** | **1993** | **1994** | **1995** |
| Supply | 0.16 | 0.46 | 0.9 | 1.43 | 1.97 | 2.6 | 3.2 |
| Demand | 0.03 | -0.04 | -0.1 | -0.11 | -0.12 | -0.04 | -0.03 |
| Total | 0.19 | 0.42 | 0.8 | 1.32 | 1.86 | 2.56 | 3.17 |

*Source:* Bourguignon *et al.* (1992).

The comparison between the two cases also gives an order of magnitude of the loss in the efficiency of the CSF due to the macro environment in which it takes place. If the CSF were implemented in a full employment economy, it would raise growth by 3% more than it would probably do in reality.

# 5. Macroeconometric modelling of the cohesion countries: HERMIN

This chapter provides a summary overview of the structure and properties of the four HERMIN models of Greece, Ireland, Portugal and Spain, focusing on similarities and differences between the structures of the various peripheral countries. The summary is brief, since more detailed descriptions of earlier versions of three of the models are available elsewhere (Bradley, Herce and Modesto, 1995b).[20]

Each national HERMIN model consists of three broad subcomponents: a supply side, an absorption side and an income distribution side. Obviously, the models function as integrated systems of equations, with interrelationships between all their subcomponents. However, for expositional purposes, the HERMIN modelling framework is described in terms of the above three subcomponents, which are schematically illustrated in Figure 5.1 below.

Conventional Keynesian mechanisms are at the core of the HERMIN model. Thus, the absorption and income distribution subcomponents (shown in Figure 5.1) generate the standard income-expenditure mechanisms of the model. However, the model also has neoclassical features, mainly associated with the supply subcomponent (illustrated in Figure 5.1). Thus, output in manufacturing is not simply driven by demand. It is also influenced by price and cost competitiveness, where firms seek out minimum cost locations for production (Bradley and Fitz Gerald, 1988). In addition, factor demands in manufacturing and market services are derived using a CES production function, where the capital/labour ratio is sensitive to relative factor prices. The incorporation of a structural Phillips curve mechanism in the wage bargaining mechanism introduces further relative price effects. Finally, in the Irish model, labour migration is sensitive to relative labour market conditions in Ireland and the UK.

The HERMIN models are econometric in that the key behavioural equations are estimated using annual time series. However, a very simple approach to econometric estimation has been taken with all four models. The behavioural equations are estimated by ordinary least squares (OLS), with correction for first order auto-correlation where needed. Some experimentation with instrumental variables techniques (IV) has been carried out. However, since we use annual time series data, covering only the period 1977–90 in the Portuguese case, more sophisticated techniques may be of limited value.

In most cases, we have taken little account of the non-stationarity that one would expect to find in most economic variables. However, it is well known that if our behavioural equations were in fact co-integrating relationships, then the simultaneity bias in OLS would disappear asymptotically. With improved and extended data series, it may be possible to address issues of non-stationarity and the dynamic specification of the equations using co-integration analysis and its associated error-correction model, combining the latter flexibility in dynamic specification with desirable long-run properties.

---

[20] The HERMIN model for Greece was newly constructed by the project co-ordinator in conjunction with the Greek consultant and is described for the first time in this section.

**Figure 5.1.    The HERMIN model schematic**

**Supply aspects**

*Manufacturing sector*

Output = $f_1$( World Demand, Domestic Demand, Competitiveness, t)

Employment = $f_2$( Output, Relative Factor Prices, t)

Investment = $f_3$( Output, Relative Factor Prices, t)

Capital Stock = Investment + (1-$\delta$) Capital Stock$_{t-1}$

Output Price = $f_4$(World Price * Exchange Rate, Unit Labour Costs)

Wage Rate = $f_5$( Output Price, Tax Wedge, Unemployment, Productivity )

Competitiveness = National/World Relative Production Cost and Prices

*Service sector*

Output = $f_7$( Weighted Domestic Demand, World Demand)

Employment = $f_8$( Output, Relative Factor Prices, t)

Investment = $f_9$( Output, Relative Factor Prices, t)

Capital Stock = Investment + (1-$\delta$)Capital Stock$_{t-1}$

Output Price = Mark-Up on Labour Costs

Wage Inflation = Manufacturing Sector Wage Inflation

*Demographics and labour supply*

Population Growth = $f_{11}$( Natural Growth, Migration ) – (Ireland)

Migration = $f_{12}$( National/EU Labour Market Conditions ) – (Ireland)

Labour Supply = $f_{13}$( Population, Replacement Ratio, Unemployment )

Unemployment = Labour Supply - Labour Demand

**Absorption aspects**

Consumption = $f_{14}$( Personal Disposable Income )

Net Trade Surplus = Output - Domestic Demand

**Income distribution**

Income = Output

Personal Disposable Income = Income + Transfers - Direct Taxes

Balance of Payments = Net Trade Surplus + Net Factor Income from Abroad

Public Sector Borrowing = Public Expenditure - Tax Rate * Tax Base

Public Sector Debt = ( 1 + Interest Rate ) Debt$_{t-1}$ + Borrowing

**Key exogenous variables**

*External:* World output and prices; EU core labour market conditions; exchange rates; interest rates.

*Domestic:* Public expenditure; tax rates.

The national HERMIN models were estimated using the TSP 4.3 econometric software. The models were simulated using the SIMPC software developed by Henk Don (Don, 1993). SIMPC uses a TSP-like model equation language and TSP-compatible data inputs. In addition, it is very user friendly, permits conventional and model-consistent expectations, has excellent graphic output, and is very fast. All four models have been developed with a common structure and notation.[21]

## 5.1. The supply block of HERMIN

Basically this block concerns the determination of output, factor inputs, output prices and factor prices for the four-way sectoral disaggregation of GDP into manufacturing (T), market services (N), agriculture (A) and government (G).

### 5.1.1. Manufacturing sector

*Manufacturing output (OT)*

A standard form of manufacturing output equation (OT) is specified for each of the four models. This takes the form

$$\log(OT) = a_1 + a_2 \log(OW) + a_3 \log(ULCT / POT)$$

$$+ a_4 \log(FDOT) + a_5 \log(POT / PWORLD) + a_6 t$$

where $OW$ is 'world' manufacturing output, $ULCT$ is unit labour costs, $POT$ is the output price, $FDOT$ is a measure of domestic demand weighted by manufacturing output content (derived from the I-O table), and $PWORLD$ is the world manufacturing price.

In estimation the Irish and Spanish models appear as polar opposites. The small size and extreme openness of the Irish economy, and the dominant position occupied by branch plants of foreign-owned multinational firms, dictate a particular approach to manufacturing output determination, with consequences for the behaviour of manufactured exports. Domestic demand is found to play a relatively small part in the long-run decisions of Irish manufacturing firms, and output prices are almost completely determined abroad. Irish manufacturing output is driven primarily by world demand and cost competitiveness.

In the Spanish HERMIN model, on the other hand, manufactured output responds strongly to changes in both domestic demand and world demand conditions. Spanish prices are also more strongly affected by domestic costs, in contrast to the strong degree of externally determined pricing behaviour found for Irish manufacturing.

---

[21] Annotated listings of all four HERMIN models are available in a separate document (Bradley and McCartan, 1996).

Table 5.1 shows the estimated and imposed coefficients in the manufactured output equation for all four models. For reasons explained later in Chapter 6, we impose certain restrictions on the relative size of the coefficients $a_2$ and $a_4$ (i.e. on the relative strengths of the world and domestic demand variables).

**Table 5.1.    Coefficients on the OT equation**

|        | Greece | Ireland | Portugal | Spain |
|--------|--------|---------|----------|-------|
| $a_2$  | 0.25*  | 0.51    | 0.37     | 0.18  |
| $a_3$  | -0.25* | -0.31   | -0.25*   | -0.20*|
| $a_4$  | 0.50*  | 0.26    | 0.74     | 0.54  |
| $a_5$  | -0.25* | -0.34   | -0.25*   | -0.20*|
| $a_6$  | 0.0096 | 0.036   | -0.001   | 0.0095|

*Denotes imposed coefficient.
*Source*: Own estimations.

*Factor demands in manufacturing (LT, IT)*

Since the Cobb-Douglas production function is too restrictive, we use the CES form of the added value production function and impose it on both the manufacturing (T) and market service (N) sectors:

$$Q = A \left[ \delta \left\{ \exp(\lambda_L t) L \right\}^\rho + (1-\delta) \left\{ \exp(\lambda_L t) K \right\}^\rho \right]^{\frac{1}{\rho}}$$

In this equation, $Q$, $L$ and $K$ are added value, employment and capital stock, respectively, $A$ is a scale parameter, $\rho$ is related to the constant elasticity of substitution, $\delta$ is a factor intensity parameter, and $\lambda_L$, $\lambda_k$ are the rates of technical progress embodied in labour and capital respectively.

In both the manufacturing and market service sectors, factor demands are derived on the basis of cost minimization subject to given output, yielding a joint factor demand equation system of the form:[22]

$$K = g_1 \left( \left( Q, \frac{c}{w} \right) \right)$$

$$L = g_2 \left( \left( Q, \frac{c}{w} \right) \right)$$

Here, $w$ and $c$ are the cost of labour and capital, respectively. Simple autoregressive expectational lags can be imposed by making actual factor demands a function of lagged values of the driving variables.

The above simple scheme, using a putty-putty model of the capital stock (i.e. malleable *ex ante* and *ex post*), proved difficult to estimate in practice. This is not surprising in light of the

[22]    A profit maximization approach, used in an earlier version of the Portuguese model, leads to essentially the same empirical formulation of factor demands, although it has different implications for output determination. In all models we have standardized on the cost minimization approach.

derived nature of the capital stock data. Hence, a switch was made to a marginal, or putty-clay, system where investment, the new vintage of capital stock, is driven by output and relative factor prices, and the capital stock is assumed to be malleable *ex ante* but not *ex post*. In the absence of data on vintage output and labour inputs, the corresponding marginal output and employment are crudely proxied by the total levels of these variables. Alternatively, we can focus an the long-term formulation of the equation, when the ratio of capital to output is proportional to the ratio of investment to output:

$$\frac{I}{Q} = \frac{(\delta + g)}{(1+g)} \frac{K}{Q}$$

where $g$ is the growth in output and $\delta$ is the depreciation rate. Hence, the modified joint factor demand system can be written in the form:

$$I = h_1\left(Q, \frac{c}{w}\right)$$

$$L = h_2\left(Q, \frac{c}{w}\right)$$

where the capital stock is now generated by a perpetual inventory formula,

$$K_t = I_t - (1-\delta)K_{t-1}$$

Although the central factor demand systems in the manufacturing and market service sectors are functionally identical, together with their ancillary identities, they will have different estimated parameter values and other crucial differences. For example, in the Irish case a fraction of manufacturing sector profits is repatriated through the balance of payments, mirroring the known behaviour of multinational firms that dominate the Irish manufacturing sector. This profit repatriation mechanism is not yet included in the Greek, Portuguese and Spanish models, where the role of multinationals as a share of total manufacturing activity is considerably smaller. No such mechanism is included in the market service sector, where distributed profits simply go directly into private income.

Focusing first on production functions, we summarize below the elasticities of substitution between capital and labour in the manufacturing sector. The main finding (shown in Table 5.2) that comes through is the fact that the Irish elasticity is much smaller than those for Portugal and Spain.[23]

The smaller elasticity for Ireland can be understood as follows. In a traditional and/or relatively closed economy, the substitution of capital for labour as a result of shifting relative factor prices normally takes place within the economy. However, in an economy dominated by multinationals, this substitution will often involve a shift in production capacity to other countries (i.e. capital will not replace labour in the Irish factory but will instead seek out lower costs elsewhere). Due to difficulties with the Greek estimation, we have imposed the

---

[23] The volume of output is held constant in determining the values of these elasticities.

Portuguese elasticity of substitution, but estimated the other CES parameters freely from the data.

**Table 5.2.    Elasticities of substitution in manufacturing sector production functions**

| Ireland | Portugal (and Greece) | Spain |
|---------|----------------------|-------|
| 034 | 0.88 | 0.77 |

*Source:* Own estimations.

A note on the role that the production function plays in the model is necessary. Macroeconometric models can feature production functions of the form:

$$Q = f(K, L)$$

without output being determined by this relationship. We have seen above that manufacturing output is determined in HERMIN by a mixture of world and domestic demand, together with price and cost competitiveness terms. Having determined output in this way, the role of the CES production function is to constrain the determination of factor demands in the process of cost minimization that is assumed. Hence, given $Q$ (determined however), and given (exogenous) relative factor prices, the factor inputs, $L$ and $K$, are determined by the CES constraint. Hence, the production function operates in the model as a technology constraint and is only indirectly involved in the determination of output. In later chapters, we will see that it is partially through these interrelated factor demands that the longer run efficiency enhancing effects of the SEM and the CSF are held to operate.

*The price of manufacturing output (POT)*

Output prices in the manufacturing sector are determined as a mixture of price taking (PWORLD) and a mark-up on unit labour costs (ULCT).

$$\log(POT) = a_1 + a_2 \log(PWORLD) + (1 - a_2)\log(ULCT)$$

Ireland stands out as a more extreme case of price-taking, with an elasticity of 0.80 on PWORLD. Greece has a value of 0.70 and Portugal 0.62. Spain is lowest, with a value of 0.41. In every case, price homogeneity was imposed, ensuring that the mark-up elasticity was 1 minus the price-taking elasticity.

*Average annual earnings in manufacturing (WT)*

The behaviour of the industrial sector tends to be dominant in the area of wage determination. Wage rates are modelled as the outcome of a bargaining process that takes place between well-organized trade unions and employers, with the frequent intervention of the government. Formalized theory of wage bargaining points to four paramount explanatory variables (Layard, Nickell and Jackman, 1990):

(a)    Output prices: the price that the producer can obtain for output clearly influences the price at which factor inputs, particularly labour, can be purchased profitably.

(b)    The tax wedge: this wedge is driven by total taxation between the wage denominated in output prices and the take home consumption wage actually enjoyed by workers. The wedge effect arises because workers try to bargain in terms of a take home wage denominated in consumer prices and not in terms of gross pre-tax wages denominated in producer prices.

(c)   The rate of unemployment: the unemployment or Phillips curve effect basically states that the more people are unemployed in an economy, the lower will be the subsequent wage demands from those still employed or who seek jobs. In this formulation, for trade unions unemployment is inversely related to bargaining power. The converse applies to employers.

(d)   Labour productivity: the productivity effect comes from workers' efforts to maintain their share of added value, i.e. they want at least to enjoy some of the gains from higher output per worker.

The form of manufacturing wage equation estimated for the Irish and Spanish models is as follows:

$$\log(WT) = a_1 + a_2 \log(POT) + a_3 \log(WEDGE) + a_4 \log(LPRT) + a_5 UR$$

where $WT$ and $POT$ are the wage rate and output price, $WEDGE$ is the tax wedge, combining all direct and indirect tax effects, $LPRT$ is labour productivity and $UR$ is the unemployment rate. This equation could also be written in rate-of-change form, and the issue of hysteresis explored through using the level and change in UR in the Phillips curve term. Wages in the Greek and Portuguese models are determined in a slightly simpler way and use the consumption deflator (incorporating only an indirect tax wedge), as follows:

$$\log(WT) = a_1 + a_2 \log(PC) + a_3 \log(LPRT) + a_4 UR$$

In all cases, we imposed full price indexation, which was not rejected by the data in the case of Ireland and Portugal. In the case of Spain, we believed that anything less than full price indexation would complicate the interpretation of the long-run simulation analysis that is required for SEM and CSF investigations. While international studies show dramatic differences in the pass-through of productivity, they tend to show full indexation to prices in the long run (Drèze and Bean, 1990). We failed to estimate sensible equations for wage setting in Greek manufacturing and were forced to impose the following properties: full indexation to consumer prices; full pass-through of labour productivity; and a Phillips curve effect that is the same as in the case of Portugal.

It is in the impact of unemployment on wage demands (the 'Phillips curve' effect) that the four wage equations differ most. The effects on the wage rate of a 1% rise in the rate of unemployment are shown in Table 5.3.

It is clear that wage bargaining in the manufacturing sector is least influenced by the level of unemployment in the Spanish case. The Phillips curve parameters are very similar in the cases of Greece, Ireland and Portugal. However, the labour supply is exogenous in the cases of Greece and Portugal. Hence, deviations of unemployment from a baseline can only be removed through changes in the demand for labour. For Ireland, on the other hand, the labour supply is highly elastic, due to the presence of an unemployment-sensitive migration mechanism in the Irish model. This will serve to drive any deviations of the Irish unemployment rate to zero in the medium term, as the British-Irish equilibrium is re-established. Hence, the long-run effective role of the Phillips curve mechanism is very diminished in the Irish model.

**Table 5.3.    Phillips curve effects[1]**

|  | Manufacturing |
|---|---|
| Ireland | -0.021[1] |
| Portugal | -0.022 |
| Greece | -0.025 |
| Spain | -0.0054 |

[1] Percentage change in wages resulting from 1 percentage point rise in unemployment.
*Source:* Own estimations.

### 5.1.2.  Market services

*Output in market services (ON)*

Once again, a standard form of the service sector output equation (ON) is specified for all four models. Initially this was in double log form:

$$\log(ON) = a_1 + a_2 \log(IH + IBC) + a_3 \log(FDON) + a_4 \log(OW) + a_5 t$$

where *IH* is housing investment, *IBC* is other building and construction investment, *FDON* is a measure of domestic demand weighted of services output content and *OW* is world manufacturing. We separate out the building and construction investment from the other components of domestic demand since this element has a large weight in determining output in the service sector (remember, building and construction activity is included in the market services sector (N)).

Given the heterogeneous nature of output in market services, the above equation and its linear form proved difficult to estimate. However, this equation plays a crucial role in generating Keynesian multiplier effects. In particular, the impact of changes in investment in building and construction is central to the analysis of the effects of CSF infrastructural investments, since building and construction activities are part of the market services sector. Since it is known that activities such as road building have a high market service output content, it is necessary to have reasonable values for the coefficient $a_2$. It is easier to constrain this coefficient in a linear form of the ON equation, and this is the form incorporated into the model, i.e.:

$$ON = a_1 + a_2(IH + IBC) + a_3 FDON + a_4 OW + a_5 t$$

Estimation yielded the following results:

**Table 5.4.    Coefficients on the ON equation**

|  | Greece | Ireland | Portugal | Spain |
|---|---|---|---|---|
| $a_2$ | 0.786 | 0.709 | 0.80* | 0.80* |
| $a_3$ | 0.837 | 0.591 | 0.80* | 0.917 |
| $a_4$ | 0.458 | 9.726 | 432.6 | 0.491 |
| $a_5$ | 2.62 | 123.1 | 884.1 | 0.00 |

* Denotes imposed coefficient.
*Source:* Own estimations.

*Factor demands in market services (LN, IN)*

A CES production function is also used in the market service (or N-sector) for each model. We summarize below the elasticities of substitution between capital and labour in the market service sector. The main finding that comes through is the fact that the Irish elasticity is much smaller than those for Portugal and Spain.[24]

**Table 5.5.   Elasticities of substitution in market services production functions**

| Ireland | Greece and Portugal | Spain |
|---------|---------------------|-------|
| 0.20 | 0.70 | 0.51 |

*Source:* Own estimations.

*Market services output price (PON)*

Market services output prices (PON) are determined as a mark-up on unit labour costs (ULCN) is all four models. However, in Portugal, there is a small world price-taking element, with an elasticity less than 0.20.

*Average annual earnings in market services (WN)*

Visual inspection indicated that the sectoral wage inflation rates in manufacturing and market services were almost identical. So we invoke labour market homogeneity, as in the Scandinavian model of Lindbeck, 1979, and pass on the manufacturing-sector wage inflation to the market service and government sectors. This assumption seems to fit all countries reasonably well, even if it is a gross simplification of the real world situation.

## 5.1.3.   Agriculture

The agricultural sector is treated exogenously in all four models. Basically, output (OA), employment (LA), and capital stock (KA) are modelled as time trends. Output prices are exogenously determined within the Common Agricultural Policy (CAP).

## 5.1.4.   Government sector: output and employment

Public sector employment and investment are exogenous instruments. GDP arising in the public sector is set equal to the real and nominal wage bill, plus a real and nominal non-wage residual. Further details of taxation and expenditure are given below in the income distribution block, in Section 5.3.

## 5.1.5.   Labour supply

*Labour supply and migration*

In the case of Ireland, the supply of labour by households is modelled carefully in order to take into account the known open properties of the Irish labour market. Population of working age is driven by an exogenous 'natural' growth rate, modified by migration outflows and inflows. The participation rate is influenced by unemployment (the discouraged worker effect) and the replacement ratio (i.e. the fraction of average earnings replaced by social welfare transfers)

---

[24]   The volume of output is held constant in determining the values of these elasticities.

(Newell and Symons, 1990). International migration is driven by relative expected earnings and employment probabilities between Ireland and Britain (Walsh, 1974).

Unfortunately, estimation of the crucial migration relationship is not very robust, due to the poor quality of the inter-censal estimated data on new migration flows. However, the migration mechanism in the Irish model is quite unique among macroeconometric models in the EU, and, for example, no other European macromodel treats migration endogenously. The performance of the Irish labour market is crucially dependent on the migration outlet as a means of providing employment for excess Irish population in world (mainly British) labour markets. Later, when we analyse the economic benefits of training and other EC regional and social CSF policies that boost the demand for labour, we will see that the resulting net inflows of migrants can often bring about a radical change in outcome compared to the case of a closed labour market.

With respect to labour supply, the Irish and Greek/Portuguese models are also polar extremes, with the labour supply exogenous in the Portuguese and Greek models and both endogenous and highly elastic (because of the migration links between Ireland and the UK) in the Irish case. The Spanish model permits some endogeneity to enter via discouraged worker effects in the male and female labour force participation decisions. Consequently, in the Portuguese and Greek models there is a one-to-one relationship between employment and unemployment: at the margin, a job created means one less unemployed person. Once again however, we argue that the Portuguese model may become more similar to the Irish case as the Portuguese labour market integrates with labour markets in the European core economies. Alternatively, the labour supply may be quite elastic due to internal migration (e.g. of the classic Harris-Todaro rural-urban kind). This obviously is an area where further research is needed, given the importance of the Phillips curve effects in all the model simulations.

## 5.2.   The absorption block of HERMIN

### 5.2.1.   Private consumption

In the standard version of HERMIN, the determination of household consumption is quite simple and orthodox. Private consumption is related to real personal disposable income. In practice, consumers in the periphery are found to be mainly liquidity constrained, a fact that is not surprising in light of the less sophisticated financial sectors in these countries.[25]

The estimation results for the simple liquidity constrained consumption functions were as follows:

**Table 5.6.    Long-run marginal propensity to consume (MPC)**

|  | Greece | Ireland | Portugal | Spain |
|---|---|---|---|---|
| MPC | 0.790 | 0.800 | 0.826 | 0.882 |

*Source*: Own estimations.

---

[25]   At the suggestion of the academic panel, we experimented with hybrid liquidity constrained and permanent income models of consumption, using the Irish model as a test case. We found that the properties of the model were relatively invariant to the choice between a hybrid and a pure liquidity constrained function. Of course, if a forward looking model of wage income were used, the properties of the model would change radically (Bradley and Whelan, 1996).

## 5.2.2. Net trade surplus

Drawing on the theory on regional and small open economy macromodels (reviewed in Appendix A), exports and imports are not modelled separately in the HERMIN models. Rather, the net trade surplus, in current and constant prices, is determined as a residual by subtracting domestic demand from output. Thus, in current prices,

NTSV = GDPMV - (CONSV + GV + IV + DSV)

and in constant prices,

NTS = GDPM - (CONS + G + I + DS)

where *GDPM(V)* denotes *GDP* at constant (current) market prices; *CONS(V)* is private consumption, *G(V)* is public consumption, *I(V)* is investment, and *DS(V)* are inventory changes.

Hence, the HERMIN models can say nothing about the separate behaviour of exports and imports. Only the impact on the net trade surplus can be examined.

## 5.3.  The income distribution block of HERMIN

With a view to subsequent policy analysis, HERMIN includes a moderate degree of institutional detail in the public sector along conventional lines. Within total public expenditure we distinguish public consumption (mainly wages of public sector employees), transfers (social welfare, subsidies, debt interest payments), and capital expenditure (public housing, infrastructure, investment grants to industry). Within public sector debt interest, in the Irish and Spanish cases, we distinguish interest payments to domestic residents from interest payments to foreigners, the latter representing a leakage out of GDP through the balance of payments.

If we leave tax rates unchanged in simulated public expenditure increases, the stock of outstanding government bonds could rise without bound relative to GNP, as increased interest payments on new debt compound with previous debt. Hence, it would become difficult to evaluate the wider effects of different expenditure shocks if the final debt positions were very different.

Obviously, one needs a method of altering public policy within the model in reaction to the economic consequences of given policy shock. If all the policy instruments are exogenous, this is not possible, although instruments can be changed on the basis of off-model calculations.

The issues here have been clearly stated by Bryant and Zhang, 1994:

> Plausible models capable of analysing fiscal policy issues must be specified so that the government's budget constraint is satisfied, in any given year and across the whole sequence of years. That condition in turn means that the models must incorporate some form of 'intertemporal fiscal closure rule'. [This] is a reaction function for the behaviour of a key instrument variable under the control of the fiscal authority.

We include a closure or policy feedback rule into HERMIN, the task of which is to ensure that the direct tax rate is manipulated in such a way as to keep the debt/GNP ratio close to an exogenous notional target debt/GNP ratio. The policy feedback rule presently used in the Irish

HERMIN model is based on the IMF world model, MULTIMOD (Masson *et al.*, 1989), and takes the following form:

$$\Delta GTYPR = \alpha \left\{ \frac{(GNDT - GNDT^*)}{GNPV} \right\} - \beta \left\{ \frac{(GNDT - GNDT^*) - (GNDT_{-1} - GNDT_{-1}^*)}{GNPV} \right\}$$

Here, *GTYPR* is the (fractional) direct tax rate, *GNDT* is the total national debt, *GNDT\** is the target value of *GNDT*, *GNPV* is nominal *GNP*, and the values of the parameters $\alpha$ and $\beta$ are selected in the light of model simulations. The performance of the rule can be quite sensitive to the choice of the numerical values of $\alpha$, $\beta$.

There is effectively no monetary sector in HERMIN, so both the exchange rate and domestic interest rates are treated as exogenous. Thus, the nominal 'anchor' in each model is the world price in foreign currency. Furthermore, the financing of public sector borrowing is handled in a rudimentary fashion and public debt is simply the accumulated stock of the net flow of annual borrowing.[26] For the Irish case, these assumptions are not as serious as they would be in a model of a larger, more closed, economy such as France, Germany, Italy or the United Kingdom. In fact, they accord very well with Ireland's pre-EMS and post-EMS history of financial integration (Bradley and Whelan, 1992). However, these assumptions are very questionable in the cases of Greece, Portugal and Spain and will require much further research.

In effect, by treating exchange rates and interest rates as exogenous in Greece, Portugal and Spain we are positing a future process of EMU-type financial integration rather than modelling their actual past behaviour. While the projections of the Irish model are broadly consistent with this exogeneity assumption, it will be important to check the consistency in the case of the other three countries. In stylized base-line projections to the year 2010, over which the behaviour of the model shocks are explored, we assume a world inflation rate of 2.5% per annum and a world growth rate of 4% per annum, fixed exchange rates and low nominal interest rates. However, any permanent deviation of cost competitiveness from the baseline is not accommodated by an exchange rate depreciation.[27] Rather, the full costs of adjustment fall on the labour market.

### 5.4. How the models react to exogenous shocks

In all four models, an attempt has been made to carry out comparable shocks to observe how each model reacts. We briefly review the responses of each model to a range of shocks that serve to illustrate certain mechanisms that are central to the subsequent analysis of the SEM and the CSF. These shocks originate from the year 1990, and are carried out against the background of a baseline *antimonde* projection that runs from 1987 to 2010. The baseline is not intended to be a formal forecast of the likely evolution of these four economies. Rather, it is a conjectural projection that has reasonably stable properties (i.e. stable public debt/GDP

---

[26]   In the Irish and Spanish cases, the domestic (local currency) debt is maintained as a given fraction of GNP. Residual financing is by means of foreign currency borrowing, all at exogenous interest rates and exchange rates. Debt financing in the cases of Greece and Portugal is assumed to be of domestic origin, also with exogenous interest rates.

[27]   A simple link between the exchange rate and cost competitiveness could have been posited in the Portuguese and Spanish models but would have complicated the interpretation of the shocks.

ratio, stable or declining rate of unemployment, etc.). In effect, the models are reasonably linear in behaviour, so the magnitudes of partial derivatives with respect to exogenous variables are relatively invariant to the actual level of the baseline.

Our choice of five test shocks is carefully designed to illustrate properties of the HERMIN model that will prove to be important in the SEM and CSF simulation exercises that follow. For example, the response of each model to a stimulus in world activity (specifically, to world manufacturing output, OW) is important when analysing the impact on the periphery of growth in the rest of the EU. The shock to public sector employment (LG) permits the evaluation of standard fiscal multipliers both in the case of debt financing and in the case of tax financing. The shock to public sector investment (IGV) permits the evaluation of Keynesian-type expenditure multipliers, where the specific response of the private sector to better quality infrastructure is ignored for the moment.[28] The shock to social welfare income transfers explores the standard Keynesian impacts associated with Social Fund-type expenditures.[29] Finally, the shock to the rate of personal income tax illustrates the way in which the policy feedback rule, described above, works in attempting to remove imbalances in the public sector borrowing requirement relative to a baseline.

## 5.4.1. The impact of world manufacturing activity (OW)

The results are shown in Table 5.7. The Irish results stand out in this table in that the manufacturing sector responds strongly to the world demand boost. This arises from the form of the manufacturing output equation, where there is a higher elasticity with respect to OW than is the case in the other three models. The least responsive models are the Greek and Spanish, where once again this merely reflects the characteristics of the country coefficients of the manufacturing output equation. Since domestic demand plays a greater role in the southern periphery models, the service sector responds relatively more strongly than in the Irish case to secondary effects of a rise in manufacturing output. In addition, the direct impact of changes in OW is greatest in the case of Greece (i.e. the elasticity of ON with respect to OW is largest), and smallest in the case of Ireland.

Besides boosting GDP, the world demand shock improves the public finance situation: borrowing falls, as does the public debt level. In Table 5.7 we also show for the Irish and Spanish models the case where the policy rule is switched on in an effort to leave the debt unchanged at the end of the period. In the case of Ireland and Spain, we see that this produces a further boost to domestic output since direct tax rates can be cut.[30]

---

[28]  Chapter 7 shows how the Keynesian multipliers effects can be enhanced through the incorporation of externality mechanisms that attempt to capture the complex reponse of the private sector to improved infrastructure.

[29]  Once again, Chapter 7 explores how mechanisms can be used to enhance the Keynesian effects through externalities associated with transfers spent on education and training.

[30]  A similar policy of fiscal relaxation was used in the Cecchini Report (Cecchini, 1988, pp. 99–102).

**Table 5.7.    World demand shock: 1% of 1989 figure[1]**

| Year | 1990 | 1991 | 1995 | 2000 | 2010 |
|---|---|---|---|---|---|
| **Greece** | | | | | |
| **% dif. in OT** | 0.26 | 0.23 | 0.25 | 0.24 | 0.24 |
| **% dif. in ON** | 0.34 | 0.40 | 0.48 | 0.52 | 0.59 |
| **% dif. in GDPFC** | 0.21 | 0.24 | 0.29 | 0.31 | 0.37 |
| **dif. in RDEBT** | -0.23 | -0.50 | -0.85 | -0.99 | -1.20 |
| **Ireland** | | | | | |
| **% dif. in OT** | 0.49 | 0.46 | 0.49 | 0.52 | 0.55 |
|  | (0.50) | (0.47) | (0.52) | (0.58) | (0.63) |
| **% dif. in ON** | 0.23 | 0.28 | 0.28 | 0.31 | 0.37 |
|  | (0.23) | (0.28) | (0.31) | (0.35) | (0.43) |
| **% dif. in GDPFC** | 0.26 | 0.27 | 0.30 | 0.33 | 0.39 |
|  | (0.26) | (0.28) | (0.32) | (0.37) | (0.44) |
| **dif. in RDEBT** | -0.45 | -0.67 | -0.76 | -0.96 | -1.44 |
|  | (-0.44) | (-0.66) | (-0.64) | (-0.56) | (-0.33) |
| **Portugal** | | | | | |
| **% dif. in OT** | 0.37 | 0.36 | 0.42 | 0.44 | 0.48 |
| **% dif. in ON** | 0.19 | 0.25 | 0.33 | 0.40 | 0.52 |
| **% dif. in GDPFC** | 0.18 | 0.20 | 0.25 | 0.28 | 0.34 |
| **dif. in RDEBT** | -0.16 | -0.26 | -0.36 | -0.39 | -0.32 |
| **Spain** | | | | | |
| **% dif. in OT** | 0.22 | 0.25 | 0.24 | 0.25 | 0.26 |
|  | (0.23) | (0.27) | (0.34) | (0.43) | (0.50) |
| **% dif. in ON** | 0.17 | 0.22 | 0.22 | 0.25 | 0.32 |
|  | (0.18) | (0.23) | (0.29) | (0.38) | (0.48) |
| **% dif. in GDPFC** | 0.15 | 0.19 | 0.19 | 0.20 | 0.25 |
|  | (0.16) | (0.20) | (0.25) | (0.32) | (0.40) |
| **dif. in RDEBT** | -0.11 | -0.19 | -0.47 | -0.84 | -1.68 |
|  | (-0.11) | (-0.18) | (-0.29) | (-0.28) | (-0.13) |

[1] All differences are from national baseline scenario.

*Legend*
OT          Output in the traded sector (constant prices)
ON          Output in the non-traded sector (constant prices)
GDPFC    Gross domestic product at factor cost (constant prices)
RDEBT    National debt as a percentage of GDP
*Note:*      Numbers in brackets indicate simulations where the fiscal policy rule (to target RDEBT) was switched on
               (refer to Section 5.3).

## 5.4.2.  The impact of an increase in government employment (LG)

The results are shown in Table 5.8. In each case, public employment numbers have been permanently raised by 5% of their 1989 baseline value. Table 5.8 shows both the case where no attempt is made to finance the increased public expenditure by raising taxes and the case where the policy feedback rule is used to attempt to prevent deviations in the national debt to GDP ratio from its baseline values.

We calculate a multiplier by taking the ratio of the rise in real GDP (relative to the baseline) to the increase in public consumption (in real terms, relative to the baseline). For all four models, the long-run fiscal multipliers are quite high in the policy unconstrained case, ranging from about 1.5 for Ireland to about 2 for Greece. In this case, for Greece, Ireland and Portugal it is seen that there is a serious deterioration in the fiscal position (i.e. a rise of about 10% in the debt/GDP ratio).

**Table 5.8.     Public sector employment shock: 5% of 1989 figure[1]**

| Year | 1990 | 1991 | 1995 | 2000 | 2010 |
|---|---|---|---|---|---|
| **Greece** | | | | | |
| **Multiplier** | 1.12 | 1.32 | 1.72 | 1.79 | 1.96 |
| | (1.51) | (1.88) | (1.78) | (0.48) | (-1.14) |
| **dif. in RDEBT** | -0.65 | -1.35 | -0.10 | 3.34 | 10.43 |
| | (-0.37) | (-0.97) | (1.06) | (3.75) | (0.55) |
| **Ireland** | | | | | |
| **Multiplier** | 1.18 | 1.41 | 1.40 | 1.43 | 1.50 |
| | (1.10) | (1.24) | (0.86) | (0.46) | (0.08) |
| **dif. in RDEBT** | -1.19 | -1.40 | 1.56 | 4.72 | 9.90 |
| | (-1.27) | (-1.65) | (0.06) | (0.57) | (-0.58) |
| **Portugal** | | | | | |
| **Multiplier** | 1.02 | 1.22 | 1.55 | 1.64 | 1.91 |
| | (0.96) | (1.05) | (0.94) | (0.68) | (0.75) |
| **dif. in RDEBT** | -0.06 | 0.14 | 2.72 | 5.97 | 11.44 |
| | (-0.31) | (-0.21) | (2.11) | (2.61) | (2.76) |
| **Spain** | | | | | |
| **Multiplier** | 1.27 | 1.66 | 1.51 | 1.52 | 1.53 |
| | (1.14) | (1.39) | (0.85) | (0.50) | (0.42) |
| **dif. in RDEBT** | -0.13 | -0.08 | 0.67 | 1.73 | 4.15 |
| | (-0.20) | (-0.32) | (-0.53) | (-1.17) | (-2.26) |

[1] All differences are from national baseline scenario.

*Legend*
The multiplier is calculated as dif(GDPE)/dif(G) where differences are taken relative to the no-shock baseline. GDPE is gross domestic expenditure (at constant prices) and G is public consumption (at constant prices).

*Note:*     Numbers in brackets indicate simulations where the fiscal policy rule (to target RDEBT) was switched on (refer to Section 5.3).

In the policy constrained case, shown in brackets in Table 5.8, the policy rule is endogenized to attempt to moderate the rise in the debt/GDP ratio over its baseline. The rule is not perfect, but it is reasonably successful in controlling deviations in the debt/GDP ratio. The fiscal multipliers are drastically reduced in the policy constrained (semi-balanced budget) case. The reduction is greatest in the case of Greece, where they become negative towards the end of the simulation period. In the case of Ireland, the multiplier falls eventually to zero, indicating that the balanced budget multiplier is zero in the medium to long term.

### 5.4.3.   The impact of an increase in public sector investment (IGV)

The results are shown in Table 5.9. In this shock, we raise nominal public investment (an exogenous variable in all four models) by 1% of nominal GDP in the base year 1989, i.e. the year immediately preceding the shock. In the policy unconstrained case, the long-run multipliers are seen to be in the range 1.0 to 1.8, with Ireland at the lower end and Portugal at the higher end. For all four models, there is a serious deterioration in the long-run debt/GDP ratio, ranging from 9% in the case of Spain to about 14% in the case of Portugal.

The results in brackets in Table 5.9 show the case where the policy feedback rule is switched on in an effort to prevent the rise in the debt/GDP ratio from its baseline. The results for Ireland indicate an approximately zero balanced budget multiplier. For Portugal and Spain, the multiplier is drastically reduced. In the case of Greece, the policy feedback rule does not appear to be working very well.

## Table 5.9.    Public investment shock[1]

| Year | 1990 | 1991 | 1995 | 2000 | 2010 |
|---|---|---|---|---|---|
| **Greece** | | | | | |
| **Multiplier** | 0.98 | 1.17 | 1.45 | 1.44 | 1.46 |
| | (1.29) | (1.67) | (1.44) | (-0.01) | (-2.08) |
| **dif. in RDEBT** | 0.14 | 0.28 | 2.81 | 6.45 | 12.32 |
| | (0.40) | (0.64) | (3.84) | (6.59) | (2.53) |
| **Ireland** | | | | | |
| **Multiplier** | 0.85 | 0.98 | 0.95 | 0.96 | 0.98 |
| | (0.76) | (0.79) | (0.35) | (-0.12) | (-0.42) |
| **dif. in RDEBT** | -0.58 | -0.31 | 3.47 | 6.84 | 10.78 |
| | (-0.73) | (-0.71) | (1.29) | (1.25) | (-1.09) |
| **Portugal** | | | | | |
| **Multiplier** | 0.91 | 1.12 | 1.41 | 1.50 | 1.76 |
| | (0.85) | (0.95) | (0.78) | (0.44) | (0.41) |
| **dif. in RDEBT** | -0.03 | 0.40 | 4.01 | 8.23 | 13.58 |
| | (-0.16) | (0.05) | (1.58) | (1.49) | (-0.10) |
| **Spain** | | | | | |
| **Multiplier** | 1.23 | 1.52 | 1.37 | 1.37 | 1.37 |
| | (1.09) | (1.24) | (0.55) | (-0.06) | (-0.16) |
| **dif. in RDEBT** | 0.03 | 0.34 | 2.20 | 4.54 | 8.89 |
| | (-0.14) | (-0.19) | (-0.37) | (-1.46) | (-3.07) |

[1] All differences are from national baseline scenario.

*Legend*
The multiplier is calculated as dif(GDPE)/dif(IG) where differences are taken relative to the no-shock baseline. GDPE is gross domestic expenditure (at constant prices) and IG is public investment (at constant prices).
*Note*:     Numbers in brackets indicate simulations where the fiscal policy rule (to target RDEBT) was switched on (refer to Section 5.3).

## 5.4.4.   The impact of an increase in income transfers (GTRSW)

The results are shown in Table 5.10. In this shock we have increased social welfare income transfers by an amount equivalent to 1% of nominal GDP in the base year 1989. In the policy unconstrained case, we see a pattern of multipliers ranging from 0.7 (in the case of Greece) to 0.9 (in the case of Portugal and Spain), with a deterioration in the debt/GDP ratio in every case of about 12%. Switching in the policy feedback rule partially eliminates the build up of debt and drastically reduces the size of these multipliers.

## Table 5.10.  Income transfer shock[1]

| Year | 1990 | 1991 | 1995 | 2000 | 2010 |
|---|---|---|---|---|---|
| **Greece** | | | | | |
| **Multiplier** | 0.35 | 0.58 | 0.67 | 0.68 | 0.69 |
| | (0.57) | (0.88) | (0.73) | (0.04) | (-0.83) |
| **dif. in RDEBT** | 0.42 | 0.68 | 2.86 | 6.42 | 13.82 |
| | (0.69) | (1.07) | (4.13) | (7.08) | (3.36) |
| **Ireland** | | | | | |
| **Multiplier** | 0.55 | 0.62 | 0.63 | 0.66 | 0.73 |
| | (0.48) | (0.47) | (0.18) | (-0.11) | (-0.25) |
| **dif. in RDEBT** | -0.02 | 0.47 | 3.61 | 7.32 | 13.98 |
| | (-0.14) | (0.15) | (1.66) | (1.83) | (-0.16) |
| **Portugal** | | | | | |
| **Multiplier** | 0.28 | 0.52 | 0.64 | 0.71 | 0.92 |
| | (0.22) | (0.37) | (0.14) | (-0.21) | (-0.38) |
| **dif. in RDEBT** | 0.64 | 1.12 | 4.25 | 7.74 | 12.23 |
| | (0.51) | (0.78) | (1.92) | (1.35) | (-0.89) |
| **Spain** | | | | | |
| **Multiplier** | 0.81 | 0.98 | 0.90 | 0.91 | 0.93 |
| | (0.68) | (0.72) | (0.13) | (-0.37) | (-0.43) |
| **dif. in RDEBT** | 0.20 | 0.61 | 2.72 | 5.59 | 11.93 |
| | (0.05) | (0.13) | (0.08) | (-1.17) | (-3.86) |

[1] All differences are from national baseline scenario.

*Legend*
The multiplier is calculated as dif(GDPE)/dif(GTR) where differences are taken relative to the no-shock baseline. GDPE is gross domestic expenditure (at constant prices) and GTR are income transfers (at constant prices).

*Note:*    Numbers in brackets indicate simulations where the fiscal policy rule (to target RDEBT) was switched on (refer to Section 5.3).

### 5.4.5.   The impact of an increase in the personal income tax rate (GTYPR)

The results are shown in Table 5.11. This simulation is designed to illustrate the effects of raising the rate of direct income tax, the policy instrument that is used in the feedback rule to influence deviations of the public debt/GDP ratio from its baseline path. In these simulations, the personal income tax rate is first exogenized and then raised by an amount required to increase direct tax revenue by 1% of nominal GDP in the base year 1989.

In all cases, the effect of the increased tax revenue is to cut the borrowing requirement and reduce the debt/GDP ratio by some 15% in the long run. The negative effects in the Greek, Irish and Portuguese models are rather similar causing a reduction of between 0.7% and 0.85% in GDP in the long run. The Spanish case is slightly different, in that the negative effects on GDP are larger. It appears that the very small Phillips curve coefficient is producing this result since the rise in Spanish unemployment is exerting too weak a downward pressure on wage bargaining.

**Table 5.11.    Direct tax rate shock: 1% of GDP in 1989[1]**

| Year | 1990 | 1991 | 1995 | 2000 | 2010 |
|------|------|------|------|------|------|
| **Greece** | | | | | |
| **% dif. in GDPE** | -0.40 | -0.67 | -0.76 | -0.77 | -0.76 |
| **dif. in RDEBT** | -0.48 | -0.79 | -3.35 | -7.47 | -16.04 |
| **Ireland** | | | | | |
| **% dif. in GDPE** | -0.55 | -0.56 | -0.59 | -0.61 | -0.66 |
| **dif. in RDEBT** | -0.92 | -1.66 | -4.46 | -7.87 | -14.19 |
| **Portugal** | | | | | |
| **% dif. in GDPE** | -0.31 | -0.59 | -0.70 | -0.74 | -0.85 |
| **dif. in RDEBT** | -0.68 | -1.21 | -4.53 | -8.69 | -16.36 |
| **Spain** | | | | | |
| **% dif. in GDPE** | -0.95 | -1.01 | -1.18 | -1.15 | -1.13 |
| **dif. in RDEBT** | -0.98 | -2.16 | -5.26 | -9.09 | -16.88 |

[1] All differences are from national baseline scenario.

*Legend*
GDPE        Gross domestic expenditure
RDEBT      National debt as a percentage of GDP

## 5.5.    Overall perspective on the HERMIN models

In the Irish case, the HERMIN model reflects an economy whose manufacturing sector reacts rather rapidly to movements in world demand, indicating the close supply-side links with foreign multinational activity. The somewhat limited role for domestic fiscal expansion is reflected in the fiscal multipliers, which are effectively zero in the balanced budget case when the national debt is capped.

In the Greek and Portuguese cases, the HERMIN model reflects economies that are only partially exposed to international competition. Increases in world demand bring only limited increases in domestic production, reflecting the more traditional nature of their exports and the predominance of imports of finished goods. The fiscal multipliers also appear to be relatively large, though they probably characterize an era that has now passed, when Portugal and Greece were relatively insulated from world economic forces. We suspect that both these economies may become much more like the Irish case in future years.

The Spanish results are interesting. Our prior assumption was that Spain would behave as a semi-closed economy, given its large size relative to Greece, Ireland and Portugal. This is partially borne out in the world output shock. However, the fiscal multipliers were found to be rather smaller than expected. The institutional rigidities of the labour market, captured in a stylized way by the very small Phillips curve parameter in the wage bargaining equation, appear to be responsible for this, but the matter clearly merits further research and investigation.

# 6. The single market impacts on the cohesion countries: methodology

The terms of reference of this study require us to examine the impact of the SEM on the cohesion countries, conditional on the role of the CSF. Hence, two quite separate methodologies are required. The first must be designed to address the SEM impacts directly, and needs to focus mainly on the effects of trade liberalization. The second must be designed to address the CSF impacts, both short-run Keynesian and long-run supply-side effects. In this chapter, we describe our SEM methodology, which is essentially new to the study. In Chapter 7, we describe our CSF methodology, drawing on and extending previous work by Bradley *et al.* (1995a, 1995b). Simulations carried out using the HERMIN models for the SEM are presented in Chapter 8 and those for the CSF are presented in Chapter 9. The results are reviewed and interpreted in the concluding Chapter 10.

## 6.1. Trade liberalization

The employment effects of trade liberalization are ambiguous in the context of distorted labour markets, as are the effects on inflation and growth. In this chapter, we use the HERMIN macroeconometric modelling framework of the countries of the EU periphery (Greece, Ireland, Portugal and Spain) to try to quantify the various ways in which the SEM will influence these economies. For some aspects of the impact of the SEM, we use results derived from the Cecchini Report and from background studies to that report. However, in addition, we develop a methodology that allows us to take into account the structural changes to the economy that trade liberalization brings, changes that were not always included as part of the Cecchini analysis of the developed 'core' EU Member States.

Just as it is well known that the impact of protectionism on employment is ambiguous when the labour market is distorted (Buffie, 1987; Grinols, 1991), so the effects of trade liberalization on employment can go in either direction when the labour market does not adjust flexibly. In the same way, it has been argued that since closed economies are more insulated from world shocks, trade liberalization may be growth reducing in periods of deficient world demand (see, for example, Diaz Alejandro, 1984). Thus, the demand-pull effects on growth of increased openness may be positive or negative depending on the ratio of world growth to domestic-demand growth. The price-level effects of increased openness will also be ambiguous, depending on the strength of world inflation relative to domestic cost developments.

Recently, a further argument has been advanced by Krugman and Venables (1990) as to why the impact of trade liberalization on welfare might be ambiguous. Focusing on the interaction between trading costs and economies of scale in determining the impact of trade liberalization on the periphery, their work suggests two contrasting scenarios:

(a)   In the first scenario, as trade is liberalized, production shifts from the periphery to the core because of the importance of scale economies and the necessity of locating close to the larger market.

(b)   In the second scenario, the opposite occurs, as the competitiveness premium of the periphery (due to lower labour costs) attracts production from the core.

The pessimistic scenario is more likely when trading costs begin to decline from a high level, while the optimistic one is more likely when trading costs decline from an already relatively low level. Barry (1996) suggests that this model provides a rationale for Williamson's (1965) well-known hypothesis that the process of trade and market integration generates divergence in its initial stages and later leads to convergence. In this chapter, we develop a methodology that takes us some way towards a quantification of these various ambiguous effects.

In our description of the HERMIN macro-econometric models in Chapter 5, we model the peripheral countries as small open economies producing both traded and non-(internationally-) traded goods. The defining characteristics of the tradable components of manufacturing and services are that prices are determined exogenously by the law of one price, mediated through the exchange rate, and that all output produced can be sold abroad at these exogenous world prices. The Irish manufacturing sector can be used to illustrate some of the issues involved. In the case of the Irish economy, where foreign direct investment plays a crucial role in manufacturing, output levels are determined by the proportion of multinational direct investment that Ireland can capture or retain (Bradley and Fitz Gerald, 1988). This, in turn, is influenced by the Irish manufacturing sector's level of cost competitiveness. Hence, an increase in world demand raises Irish production of tradables for a given level of competitiveness by causing internationally trading companies to expand production at all their production sites, including the Irish site. Therefore, the responsiveness of Irish manufacturing output to world demand, for a given level of competitiveness, is central to defining the extent of tradables in Irish manufacturing. For non-tradables, on the other hand, prices are a mark-up on unit labour costs, and output is driven by domestic demand.

The structural change that we focus upon is the fact that, as trade liberalization proceeds, major subcomponents of the manufacturing and services sectors switch from being essentially non-tradable to being internationally tradable. In the case of the SEM and the CSF programmes, this change would result from the dismantling of non-tariff barriers such as restrictive public procurement policies, or from, for example, a decline in transport costs.

As these changes occur, the elasticities with respect to world influences in both the output and pricing equations will rise and those with respect to domestic factors will fall. The effects of incorporating these structural changes are that the country will now expand more rapidly when world demand increases, and will be less directly dependent on domestic demand growth. Inflation will also become even more linked to world inflation and will be less influenced by domestic cost conditions. The negative aspects of these developments are that world recessions will now impact more strongly on the periphery, and the power of domestic demand management tools in the periphery to counteract these effects will be diminished. These trade-offs are implicit in Krugman, 1987. *A priori*, then, in line with theory, the effects on employment, inflation and growth are ambiguous.

Our methodology contrasts with previous studies that took the economic structure as given and analysed the implications for individual countries of the world output and competitiveness changes that emerged from the Cecchini Report (Emerson *et al.*, 1988, and for the case of Ireland and Spain, Bradley, Fitz Gerald and Kearney, 1992, and Collado *et al.*, 1992). Such work entailed shocking the exogenous price and world activity variables within models that were largely structurally invariant with respect to the SEM policy initiatives.

In computing the proportions of manufacturing that make the transition from being non-tradable to being tradable, we recognize that some sectors will be successful in this transition (in the sense that they will be competitive internationally, and so will expand) while other sectors will be unsuccessful, and will therefore contract. In categorizing such sectors, we draw on the special edition of the *European Economy/Social Europe* (European Commission, 1990) which classifies individual sectors in each country into those that are likely to be positively affected by the SEM and those that are likely to be adversely affected. This, in turn, helps us to compute the static (positive and negative) output shocks that the SEM entails for each of the countries under discussion.

## 6.2.  Classification of the effects of trade liberalization

The effects of the SEM can be classified into four broad categories: static, locational, growth-dependent and dynamic, and in this chapter we describe the main features and processes of each. However, in their practical implementation in the HERMIN econometric models, these four categories are not entirely separate, but become inter-related. Thus, for example, we will see that locational processes, mainly associated with foreign direct investment (FDI) flows, will serve to modify static gains to trade liberalization. Also, growth dependent effects will be seen to magnify the static gains from a structural shift towards greater openness.

### 6.2.1.  Static effects

Traditional trade theory teaches that as trade liberalization proceeds, the economy restructures in line with its comparative advantage. Thus, at unchanged levels of world and domestic demand, some sectors expand and others contract as input costs and output prices change in response to liberalization. These standard static effects for a two-good economy are depicted in Figure 6.1. The two goods are denoted by D (to indicate that these sectors are to go into decline) and S (indicating that these are the successful sectors). The bow-shaped curve is the economy's production possibility frontier, depicting the various combinations of both goods that can be produced with full and efficient use of the economy's stocks of capital and labour. As the economy adjusts from the pre-trade (autarky) equilibrium at point 1 to the free-trade equilibrium at point 2, production of good D declines and production of good S increases. The welfare gain is illustrated by the fact that the trading economy can consume on the indifference curve $IC_2$ which lies further from the origin than $IC_1$.

With undistorted markets the static gains represented by the expansion of the S sector (valued at world prices) outweigh the static losses associated with the contraction of the declining sector. However, with distorted markets (particularly, for present purposes, distorted labour markets) the net effect becomes ambiguous as not all the economy's resources can be shifted easily between sectors. The analysis is further complicated by the possibility of international capital mobility, since it is then less clear-cut whether all the economy's initial capital stock shifts from the D to the S sector.

We are now faced with the difficulty of estimating the extent of the expansion of the S sector in response to trade liberalization. In the textbook case depicted in Figure 6.1, one could simply measure the stocks of capital and labour released by the projected decline of the D sector and, taking likely productivity gains into account, compute the expansion of the rest of the economy entailed by their reallocation to S.

**Figure 6.1.    Static effects of trade liberalization**

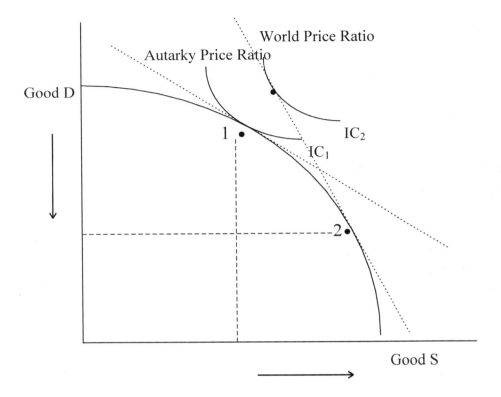

The estimates of the productivity gains entailed in the SEM are taken from the Cecchini Report (Emerson, 1988, pp. 251–264). The question remains as to how to compute the projected decline in the D sectors and the projected expansion in the S sectors in Figure 6.1 above. The answer is implicit in the assumptions we make about the increased export-orientation of the economy that arises as the SEM proceeds. For the S sectors, the export-output ratio rises through an increase in exports with no change in home-market sales, for a given level of domestic demand.[31] For the D sectors, the increased export orientation occurs through a decline in home market sales as import penetration proceeds. This procedure allows us to compute the net static gain (or loss) to manufacturing that is operationalized as an exogenous shock to the macroeconometric models.[32] The manner in which this shock is implemented is described in detail below.

## 6.2.2.  Locational effects

Trade liberalization generally affects the location decisions of multinational companies. If foreign direct investment inflows were previously oriented towards sales on the domestic market, then trade liberalization could result in reduced inflows. Given the almost complete export orientation of those multinational companies (MNCs) currently located in Ireland, however, we would not expect an outward flight in response to the SEM. Similarly, the FDI/GDP ratio has

---

[31]    This ignores the possibility of intra-industry trade. This might not, however, affect the output results, since increased trade of this type would entail a reduction in home market sales alongside an even greater expansion in exports.

[32]    In the diagram above depicting the static output effects, the net exogenous shock must clearly be positive; however, if the Krugman-Venables (1990) analysis is correct, the net static effect can be negative. We allow for the latter possibility.

increased dramatically for Portugal in recent years (Cabral, 1995), and most of this inflow is aimed at the external market (Simoes, 1992). There has also been a substantial increase in the FDI inflow into Spain (Bajo-Rubio and Sosvilla-Rivero, 1994). Only the Greek share remained low, and relatively stagnant, at least until 1992.[33]

A major issue arises concerning the relationship between observed FDI inflows and the SEM. At one extreme, we could assume that all increases in FDI inflows after 1987 resulted directly from the SEM and anticipation of the SEM. At the other extreme, we could assume that the FDI inflows arose as a result of EU entry (in the cases of Portugal and Spain), and of EU membership (in the case of Ireland and Greece), and that any connection with the SEM was tenuous. We will discuss these choices later in the chapter when we implement them in detail.

## 6.2.3. Growth-dependent effects

With an increased proportion of tradables in the manufacturing sector and a diminished proportion of non-tradables, the peripheral economies would clearly become more directly dependent on world-demand growth and less directly influenced by domestic-demand growth. Thus, the increase in world demand in the EU as a whole, predicted by and quantified in the Cecchini Report, will have even stronger effects on the periphery than an equivalent world demand shock before the structural changes brought about by the SEM. Our methodology allows us calculate the increased responsiveness of both output and prices to changes in world activity. Indeed, this is one of the central methodological contributions of the present study.

## 6.2.4. Dynamic effects

There are a range of effects that are commonly called 'dynamic'. These include the intensification of competition that trade liberalization entails, and the rationalization of sectors in which economies of scale are important. The first of these factors we have attempted to capture through our quantification of the productivity gains and cost reductions associated with the SEM, drawing on the original Cecchini research. We handle the second in our estimates of which sectors are likely to respond successfully and which are likely to be unsuccessful, derived from the *European Economy/Social Europe* special issue (European Commission, 1990).

Other dynamic effects possible in the case of the SEM are studied by Baldwin (1989) in the context of the Solow and endogenous-growth models. In the Solow model, savings drive investment. However, we do not feel that this is appropriate for the peripheral economies, given their access to, and insignificant impacts on, international capital markets. Again, while it is likely that the SEM will stimulate technological development, which is the linchpin of the endogenous-growth effects Baldwin discusses, we feel that these will impact on the periphery primarily through inflows of foreign direct investment, which we do take into account (including their contributions to increased productivity). Clearly, this is an area that will have to be the subject of further and deeper research.

---

[33]    *OECD International Direct Investment Statistics Yearbook 1994.* Unpublished data from the Bank of Greece confirm that FDI inflows remained low until 1992.

## 6.3.    Quantification of the exogenous shocks

Macroeconomic analysis of the SEM impacts carried out by Emerson (1988) was structured in terms of four categories that were closely identified with the policy initiatives. These were the removal of frontier controls; the opening up of public procurement; the liberalization of financial services; and supply effects, or the strategic reactions of firms in the new competitive environment.

Although the above four categories are useful when relating the SEM legislative initiatives to the macroeconomic consequences, all four categories contain a common core of economic impacts that differ in magnitude rather than in kind. For example, all four categories have an impact on import prices and other external prices and costs; all four have an impact on manufacturing output. For our purposes, it is more useful to work directly with the main economic impact mechanisms.

Hence, in our empirical analysis, the impact of the SEM consists of a sequence of seven separate, but inter-related, shocks that are illustrated schematically in Figure 6.2. Three of the shocks are derived directly from the results of the earlier Cecchini analysis. These are the reduction in world prices and costs (shock (ii)); the modest reduction in public sector employment as a result of abolition of customs barriers (shock (iii)); and the reduction in the subsector of market services associated with rationalization of distribution and financial services (shock (vi)). These require little explanation beyond that provided in Emerson (1988), and are described very briefly.

Two further shocks have their origins in the Cecchini analysis, but are modified in their implementation by the special features of the peripheral Member States. These are the gains in manufacturing productivity associated with increased competitiveness (shock (i)); and the static gains to manufacturing output that follow directly from trade liberalization (shock (v)). The two remaining shocks require a new methodology and take into account factors that were excluded from the Cecchini analysis. These are the structural changes to the models as the economies become more open and exposed to direct world influences – a static effect (shock (iv)); and the increased impact of faster world growth on the structurally changed models – a growth dependent effect (shock (vii)). These latter four shocks require detailed explanations, which are provided in the chapters which follow.

**Figure 6.2.    Taxonomy of SEM shocks**

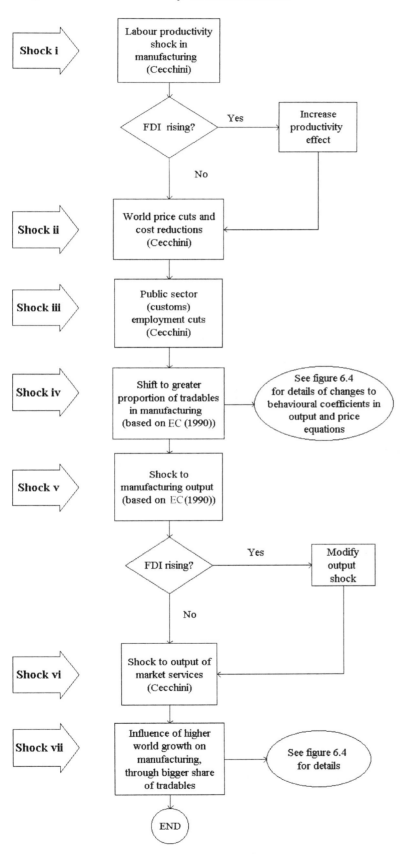

## 6.3.1. Static effects

Ignoring for the moment the three 'Cecchini' shocks (shocks (ii), (iii) and (vi) in Figure 6.2), the other static exogenous shocks we impose to represent the effects of trade liberalization are threefold. The first, rather uncontroversial one, is an increase in manufacturing-sector productivity that represents the effects of the more competitive post-SEM environment (shock (i) in Figure 6.2). Based generally on the Cecchini research, we assume that productivity will grow by a cumulative 5% over the ten-year period 1988 to 1998, but this needs to be modified in the context of increased FDI flows that may be associated with trade liberalization. We return to this point later in the next chapter.

However, the second static shock, involving a shock to manufacturing output, is more difficult to quantify and requires computing the extent to which output in the expanding (S) sectors will grow, and output in the contracting (D) sectors will decline (shock (v) in Figure 6.2). The third static shock requires us to implement modifications to the output and price equations in the manufacturing sectors of the models to reflect the increased openness due to trade liberalization in the context of unchanged output volume (shock (iv) in Figure 6.2).

In our quantification of the above three shocks (numbered (i), (iv) and (v) in Figure 6.2), we make a great deal of use of the special issue of *European Economy/Social Europe* (European Commission, 1990), which analysed the impact of the SEM by individual industrial sector. That study identified 40 out of the 120 NACE 3-digit manufacturing sectors which were likely to be affected by the development of the SEM. These sectors, characterized by high price dispersion across states, are ones in which public procurement policies were deemed to be restrictive or in which differences in national standards were found to hinder trade.

On the basis of the four individual peripheral country studies in the *European Economy/Social Europe* special issue (subsequently *European Economy*, 1990), and on subsequent work by the author of the Irish study, O'Malley (1992), we classify these sectors by three-character codes as follows:

(a)    The first character, S (successful) or D (declining), describes whether the sector is expected to be positively or adversely affected by the transition to the SEM. This classification, which derives from *European Economy* (1990), is based on revealed comparative advantage; it depends largely on the export-import ratios prevailing in each sector, and on movements in these ratios over time.[34] S-sectors are those with high and rising export-import ratios (amongst other characteristics) and are therefore predicted to grow as a result of the SEM, and D-sectors are those predicted to decline.

(b)    The second character can take a value of 1 or 2; these describe whether the EU-wide sectors are likely to be strongly affected by the SEM (as is the case for those for which strongly restrictive public procurement policies applied pre-SEM) or are likely to be only weakly affected (as is the case for those for which only low non-tariff barriers applied).

(c)    The third character describes whether world demand growth for the sector's products is strong (a value of 1), moderate (a value of 2) or weak (a value of 3).

---

[34]    We identify some weaknesses in the *European Economy* (1990) methodology below, and will attempt to correct for them at that time.

Tables showing these classifications for each of the four countries are presented in Appendix B, with that for Ireland reproduced below in Table 6.1, along with the export-market (X/Y) and home-market (H/Y) orientation of each sector, and each sector's share in manufacturing output (Y/YM).

*Static manufacturing output effects (shock (v) in Figure 6.2)*

How are the projected decline in the D sectors and the projected expansion in the S sectors computed? The answer is implicit in the assumptions we make about the increased export orientation of the economy that arises as the SEM proceeds. For the S sectors the export-output ratio (X/Y) rises through an increase in exports with, for a given level of domestic demand, no change in home-market sales. For the D sectors, the increased export orientation occurs through a decline in home market sales as import penetration proceeds.

Since we lack any firm data on the extent of the change in export orientation, we are forced to implement simple stylized rules, as follows. For the less strongly affected S2 and D2 sectors in Greece, Portugal and Ireland, we assume the home-market orientation falls by 25%, with an offsetting rise in the export market orientation. We would expect Spain, as a much larger economy, to remain more closed; thus, for Spain we assume the home-market orientation of the S2 and D2 sectors falls by only 15% rather than 25%. For the first three countries, we do not force the home-market orientation of any individual S2 or D2 sector to fall below 10%, while for Spain the equivalent is 40%.[35] For the more strongly affected S1 and D1 sectors, we raise the export orientation to 90% (for Greece, Portugal and Ireland) and to 60% for Spain, and assume that the expansion or contraction of these sectors (many of which are already close to these limits) is in the same proportion as applies to the S2 and D2 sectors.

Where does our assumption about a 25% reduction in home-market orientation of the S2 and D2 sectors come from? It is in fact the reduction that occurred for indigenous sectors of Irish manufacturing (other than the food, drink and tobacco sectors) as the Irish economy opened up much earlier to free trade between the 1950s and the 1980s.[36] During the mid-1960s, at a time when over 70% of Irish trade was with the United Kingdom, the Anglo-Irish Free Trade Agreement effectively ushered in complete free trade for Ireland. We draw on the resulting behaviour of the Irish indigenous sector to gain some insight into how the other three peripheral Member States might react to a similar shock associated with the SEM. Although we believe our assumptions to be plausible, they will need to be checked against firm data, as they become available.

For the S (or successful) sectors then, we compute dX/Y (where Y, the initial level of output, equals exports, X, plus the unchanging level of home-market sales, H) from the formula:

$$(X+dX)/(Y+dX) = (X/Y)+(1/4)(H/Y)$$

---

[35] The assumptions about the rise in export orientation and the decline in home sales will be explored in the sensitivity analyses to be carried out during the computations reported in Chapter 8.

[36] If we included the highly export-oriented foreign sector of Irish manufacturing, the decline in home-market orientation would, of course, be much more dramatic. We deal with FDI effects later in this chapter. Data for the home-market orientation of indigenous industry in the early 1950s comes from Table 5.5 of O'Malley (1989) and data sources for the present come from O'Malley (1992).

The left-hand side of the equation shows the new export-to-output ratio, which is equal to the initial ratio (X/Y) plus 25% of the initial home-market orientation ratio (H/Y). Simple algebra then reveals that

dX/Y = 1/3

Therefore an increase in output of one-third, accounted for completely through increased exports, will raise the export-output ratio in the required proportion.[37] Since the S sectors in Ireland comprise 56% of manufacturing output, our calculations therefore imply an exogenous (positive) manufacturing-output shock of 19%, i.e. (1/3)*0.56 (see Table 6.1 and Appendix C). With the S sectors comprising 30% of total manufacturing output in Portugal and 14% in Greece, the beneficial output shocks in these countries work out at 10% and 5% respectively (see tables in Appendix B). For Spain, whose home-market orientation is reduced by 15% rather than 25% (see above), dX/Y is 15/(100-15), or 17.6%, rather than 25/(100-25), or 33.3%, so the beneficial output shock is this proportion of the initial 20% of manufacturing output located in these sectors, which is 4% (see table in Appendix B).

The calculations of the adverse output effects for the D sectors are a little more complicated. Here, for the D2 sectors (i.e. declining sectors that are only weakly affected by the SEM), the fall in home-market orientation of 25% occurs through a decline in production of goods for sale on the home market, with no offsetting increase in these sectors' exports (for a given level of world demand). In this case we need to compute dH/Y from the formula:

(H-dH)/(X+H-dH) = .75(H/Y)

The left-hand side of this equation shows the new (post-SEM) home-market orientation ratio, which is set at 75% of the initial home market orientation ratio.

In this case, we find, of course, that the more export-oriented the sector is, the smaller is its decline. We predict that a sector with, for example, an initial home-market orientation of 30% will experience a fall of around 10% in output, so that H/Y falls to 20/90 or 22%. On the other hand, a sector with an initial H/Y ratio of 60% will experience an output decline of 27%, so the new home-market orientation ratio is 33/73 or 45%. For the D sectors, the fall in output (as a proportion of total manufacturing) is listed in the columns marked (-dH/YM) in Table 6.1.

The static gains (dX/YM) and losses (-dH/YM) computed in this way for the peripheral countries other than Ireland are shown in Table 6.2.

On the basis of the methodology just described, Ireland would experience a net static gain of 18%. Why, though, do we treat Ireland differently from the other countries? The answer is that many of the S sectors in Ireland are dominated by multinational companies. (These sectors are listed in Table 6.3 below.) If they are to expand in the way that our methodology predicts, they can only do so through substantially increased inflows of FDI. But this FDI effect is in a different category from the shocks being analysed at present. Wishing to leave until later the shocks emanating from increased FDI inflows, we extract from our current calculations the

---

[37]   For example, we assume that a sector with an export-output ratio of 60% initially will expand through exports until its ratio is 70%. This will occur through a 33% expansion in output, so the new export-output ratio is (60+33)/133, which is 70%.

multinational-dominated sectors (which are marked with an 'M' in Table 6.1). This brings the net static gain to Irish manufacturing output down from the level of 18% that emerges from Table 6.1 to the much lower level of 8% (see Appendix B for the classification of the Irish indigenous sectors).

**Table 6.1.    Classification of the sectors to be affected by the SEM (Ireland)**

| | | NACE | Sector | X/Y | H/Y | Y/YM | dX/YM | d(X/Y)* |
|---|---|---|---|---|---|---|---|---|
| S1 | S11 | 330 | Office & data-processing machinery (M) | 98 | 2 | 13.19 | | 0.00 |
| | | 344 | Telecommunications equipment (M) | 87 | 13 | 2.72 | | 0.09 |
| | | 341 | Insulated wires and cables (M) | 70 | 30 | 0.82 | | 0.18 |
| | S12 | 421 | Cocoa, chocolate (I) | 62 | 38 | 2.49 | | 0.70 |
| | S13 | 372 | Medical & surgical equipment (M) | 99 | 1 | 1.68 | | 0.00 |
| S2 | S21 | 251 | Basic industrial chemicals (I) | 43 | 57 | 2.28 | | 0.36 |
| | | 257 | Pharmaceuticals (M) | 97 | 3 | 5.96 | | 0.00 |
| | | 345 | Radios, TVs, etc. (M) | 38 | 62 | 2.12 | | 0.36 |
| | | 346 | Domestic electrical appliances (M) | 78 | 22 | 1.03 | | 0.06 |
| | | 351 | Motor vehicles (I) | 33 | 67 | 0.19 | | 0.03 |
| | | 428 | Soft drinks (M) | 13 | 87 | 1.64 | | 0.39 |
| | S22 | 325 | Plant for mines, steel (M) | 69 | 31 | 0.39 | | 0.03 |
| | | 364 | Aerospace equipment (I) | 40 | 60 | 0.50 | | 0.08 |
| | | 413 | Dairy products (I) | 29 | 71 | 12.01 | | 2.13 |
| | | 427 | Brewing, malting (I) | 13 | 87 | 5.05 | | 1.10 |
| | S23 | 247 | Glass & glassware (I) | 55 | 45 | 0.89 | | 0.09 |
| | | 322 | Machine tools (M) | 69 | 31 | 0.39 | | 0.03 |
| | | 323 | Textile machinery (M) | 69 | 31 | 0.03 | | 0.00 |
| | | 324 | Food, chemical machinery (M) | 69 | 31 | 0.13 | | 0.01 |
| | | 326 | Transmission equipment (M) | 69 | 31 | 0.07 | | 0.00 |
| | | 327 | Other machinery (M) | 69 | 31 | 0.03 | | 0.00 |
| | | 432 | Cotton industry (M) | 84 | 16 | 0.78 | | 0.03 |
| | | 481 | Rubber products (M) | 85 | 15 | 0.71 | | 0.02 |
| | | 491 | Jewellery (I) | 50 | 50 | 0.16 | | 0.02 |
| | | 494 | Toys & sports goods (I) | 85 | 15 | 0.27 | | 0.01 |
| Total | | | | | | 55.53 | 18.51 | |
| | | | | | | | **-dH/YM** | |
| D1 | D12 | 342 | Electrical machinery (M) | 90 | 10 | 0.61 | -0.00 | 0.00 |
| | | 361 | Shipbuilding (I) | 93 | 7 | 0.14 | -0.00 | 0.00 |
| | | 417 | Spaghetti, macaroni (I) | 50 | 50 | 0.04 | -0.02 | 0.01 |
| D2 | D21 | 256 | Other chemical products (M) | 77 | 23 | 0.78 | -0.05 | 0.05 |
| | | 321 | Agricultural machinery (M) | 69 | 31 | 0.39 | -0.04 | 0.03 |
| | | 493 | Photographic labs (I) | 29 | 71 | 0.12 | -0.05 | 0.02 |
| | D22 | 431 | Wool industry (I) | 70 | 30 | 0.44 | -0.04 | 0.03 |
| | | 453 | Clothing (I) | 54 | 46 | 1.43 | -0.25 | 0.16 |
| | | 455 | Household textiles (I) | 74 | 26 | 0.19 | -0.02 | 0.01 |
| | D23 | 248 | Ceramic goods (I) | 91 | 9 | 0.18 | -0.00 | 0.00 |
| | | 347 | Electric lamps (M) | 90 | 10 | 0.07 | -0.00 | 0.00 |
| | | 438 | Carpets, floor coverings (M) | 65 | 35 | 0.30 | -0.04 | 0.02 |
| | | 451 | Footwear (I) | 42 | 58 | 0.15 | -0.04 | 0.02 |
| Total | | | | | | 4.83 | -0.54 | 6.10 |

*Legend*
X/Y: exports as a percentage of gross output, 1986.
H/Y:(100-X/Y) home market sales as a percentage of gross output, 1986.
Y/YM: sectoral share of manufacturing output, 1987.
dX/YM: gain in exports as a percentage of total manufacturing output.
-dH/YM: loss in home-market sales as a percentage of total manufacturing output (detailed explanation below).
d(X/Y)*: output-weighted percentage point change in export-output ratio, adjusted for demand conditions
*Data sources: European Economy*, Special Edition 1990, part C, Ireland, pp. 247–61; Irish CSO Census of Industrial Production 1987.

**Table 6.2.  Static gains and losses of manufacturing output (without FDI effect)
(% of manufacturing output)**

|          | Gain | Loss | Net gain |
|----------|------|------|----------|
| Ireland  | 8    | 0    | +8       |
| Portugal | 10   | 13   | -3       |
| Spain    | 4    | 11   | -7       |
| Greece   | 5    | 19   | -14      |

*Source:* own calculations.

An examination of the pattern of results shown in Table 6.2 suggests certain questions. For example, what explains the fact that the exogenous output shock of the SEM calculated using Table 6.2 for Ireland is strongly positive (at 8%), while all the others are negative, with Greece's being strongly negative (at -14%)?[38] The major factor driving these results is the proportion of manufacturing located in the S (successful) and D (declining) sectors. Even the non-multinational-dominated S sectors in Ireland, for example, account for 24% of manufacturing output while the equivalent D sectors account for only 5%. On the other hand, in Greece only 14% of total manufacturing is in the S sectors while 29% is located in the D sectors.

One possible weakness in the *European Economy* (1990) methodology is that the state of the overall trade balance was ignored in calculating export-import ratios for individual sectors, and in calculating changes in these ratios over time.[39] For an economy with a positive and rising trade balance deficit over the period when these calculations were made – such as Greece, for example – these calculations would be overly pessimistic. For Ireland, on the other hand, the trade surplus was positive and rising, so the calculations in *European Economy* (1990) would be overly optimistic. The cases of Portugal and Spain are less clear-cut.

The fact that the exogenous shocks for some of the countries turn out positive while those for other countries are negative could nevertheless be a reflection of the Krugman-Venables (1990) argument that when economies of scale are important the effects for peripheral regions can go in either direction.[40]

If the Krugman-Venables effects are not so important, however, then the conventional textbook analysis depicted in Figure 6.1 above comes into play. This requires that the sum of exogenous shocks designed to represent trade liberalization must generate static gains (in the case of flexible factor markets), in which case the results of our analysis shown in Table 6.2 may be overly pessimistic, particularly for Spain and Greece. A further factor involved here is that the large (net) negative shocks computed above for Spain and Greece come about through increased import penetration, heavily outweighing the export expansion effect. Thus, trade liberalization in

---

[38]   We may note in passing that the analysis of de Macedo agrees that Portugal is likely to fare better than Spain (de Macedo, 1990, pp. 326-332.)

[39]   Our criticism here of the *European Economy* 1990 methodology is similar to the Aquino (1978) criticism of the Grubel-Lloyd intra-industry trade indices.

[40]   O'Malley (1992) presents a classification of sectors, based on Pratten (1988), that are characterized by economies of scale. According to this classification, 24 of the 40 sectors identified by the special issue of *European Economy* as likely to be affected by the SEM are sectors in which economies of scale are important.

these cases is associated with increased trade deficits.[41] Trade deficits, however, can be viewed as macroeconomic or intertemporal rather than structural phenomena, in which case we might be wary of imposing exogenous shocks with such strong implications for the trade balance.[42]

It is crucial to note, of course, that we are concerned so far only with calculating the exogenous manufacturing output shocks. The overall impact of the SEM will depend on the endogenous response of each economy to such shocks. A crucial component of this response will operate through the Phillips curve, for example, i.e. through the responsiveness of wage demands to unemployment. Since Greece appears to have a more flexible labour market than Spain, this means that the Greek transition process may possibly turn out to be easier than the Spanish one, even though the Greek manufacturing sector is hit with more adverse shocks. Furthermore, since the Irish labour market is very open, with large potential and actual international labour migration flows, and the Portuguese labour market is closed (at least as handled at present in the HERMIN model), then the country labour market responses could differ greatly, even where the Phillips curve semi-elasticities are identical.

## 6.3.2. Locational effects

Here we take into account the likelihood that FDI flows will play a more important role in the process of structural transformation of the periphery than allowed for in the methodology of the *European Economy* (1990) special issue. Our view emerges from studying structural transformation in the Irish economy as a consequence of the trade liberalization that occurred prior to the SEM proposals, indeed to a considerable extent prior to Ireland's accession to the EEC in 1972. The bilateral dismantling of tariff barriers between Ireland and the United Kingdom in 1965 effectively created the conditions of complete free trade for Ireland, since over 70% of Irish exports were directed to the UK market and imports from the UK were also large. However, the major structural transformation of the Irish economy that took place during the 1960s and 1970s was accompanied by large inflows of FDI, the importance of which was largely ignored in *European Economy* (1990).

We argue that the factors focused upon in *European Economy* (1990) would have served as rather inaccurate predictors of the success or failure of individual industrial sectors in Ireland in the face of trade liberalization over the 1960–95 period, or even over the more recent 1973–95 period. It appears crucial to us to understand the role of FDI flows in the structural transformation of the periphery, given the increasing importance of FDI flows into the other cohesion countries at present.

---

[41]   This is in fact consistent with the assessment of the initial trade effects for Spain and Greece, by Viñals *et al.* (1990) and by Katseli (1990) respectively, who predict strong increases in imports with less favourable effects on exports. Macedo (1990) is more optimistic with respect to the Portuguese position.

[42]   Our wariness in this regard would be alleviated if there were mechanisms within the macroeconometric models which ensured long-run current-account equilibrium. Such mechanisms could include the build-up of pressures towards exchange-rate devaluation when the trade balance got too seriously out of line, though this would not be too effective in the present case of full pass-through of prices into wage demands. The other alternative is to have foreign-debt accumulation impacting adversely on domestic demand; only in the Irish model is this mechanism fully operational, since this is the only one of the four countries at present where the gap between GDP and GNP is substantial and where the modelling of the various components of net factor income flows through the current account of the balance of payments is reasonably comprehensive.

For this analysis, then, one possibility is to identify the subset of industrial sectors that are sensitive to SEM effects and in which FDI flows into the periphery are likely to become more substantial. The sectors in which large foreign direct investment flows appear possible are identified, for the Irish case, in Table 6.3 below. We identify these sectors (marked M) by the fact that in Ireland at present employment in foreign companies in these sectors is substantially larger (generally around three times larger) than employment in indigenous industry.[43] As before, data is available in some cases only for more highly aggregated sectors; we again assume that these numbers apply also to the individual sub-sectors.

Table 6.3 reveals that large FDI flows are possible in many of these sectors.[44] This suggests that the authors of the articles in the *European Economy* (1990) special issue may be overly pessimistic about the ability of the peripheral countries to compete successfully in sectors in which they are initially weak (i.e. identified as D sectors).[45]

Therefore the methodology used as outlined in *European Economy* (1990) underestimates the growth potential in many sectors. If the fact that multinational corporation (MNC) employment in an individual sector is high in Ireland can be taken as an indication that FDI flows are possible into this sector in other countries of the periphery, then many of the weak (D) sectors that appear in the Greek, Portuguese and Spanish *European Economy* (1990) studies may actually prosper through inflows of FDI. In fact, using the analogue of the Irish case, 63% (in employment terms) of Spain's D sectors can be denoted as M (i.e. ones where a high potential exists for FDI inflows), and the equivalent proportions for Portugal and Greece are 62% and 37% respectively.

Rather than continuing the analysis at the disaggregated sectoral level, though, we decided, instead, to focus on the macroeconomic level. Data from the OECD *Foreign Direct Investment Statistics Yearbook* indicates that real FDI inflows into Spain and Portugal have increased dramatically in recent years as indicated in Table 6.4 below.[46] For example, real FDI inflows into Spanish manufacturing averaged $ 2,059 million (in 1990 dollars) between 1982 and 1988 and then rose to an annual average of $ 5,469 million. Real inflows into Portugal rose from an average of $ 160 million between 1982 and 1987 to an average of $ 349 million since then. Flows into Ireland showed no change over this period (remaining at very high levels relative to

---

[43]    Our classification is confirmed by data on sectors in the other peripheral countries into which FDI flows have been substantial; they include most of the sectors identified as 'multinational dominated' in the following table, along with Motor Vehicles, into which FDI flows in some of the other countries have been substantial (European Commission, *Foreign Direct Investment*, 1997, p. 28).

[44]    This appears to be particularly the case for sectors deemed likely to be positively affected. This is misleading, however, since one reason why they are deemed likely to be positively affected is their high export to output ratio, which reflects foreign companies' decisions to use Ireland as an export base.

[45]    Applying the methodology used in *European Economy* 1990 to Irish data from the 1960s, the predictions for the high growth sectors are not entirely accurate. Strong growth is predicted for the Food sector: this materialized in the output share (increasing to 40.8% in 1978), yet the employment share declined from 23% in the mid-1960s to 20.9% in 1978. The methodology predicted that the Chemicals and Metals and Engineering sectors would decline. In fact, the opposite occurred and Chemicals doubled its share of output and employment over the mid-1960s to 1978 period and Metals and Engineering substantially increased its share of employment from 17.6% to 23.1%, with moderate growth in output: these developments were due to strong FDI flows into these sectors (Barry and Hannan, 1996).

[46]    We deflate the FDI flows by the national investment deflators.

the size of the economy), while flows into Greece also showed no change, remaining at relatively low levels.[47]

**Table 6.3.    Sectors in which MNC employment in Ireland is substantial**

|  |  | NACE | Sector | M or I |
|---|---|---|---|---|
| S1 | S11 | 330 | Office & data-processing machinery | M |
|  |  | 344 | Telecommunications equipment | M |
|  |  | 341 | Insulated wires and cables | M |
|  | S12 | 421 | Cocoa, chocolate | I |
|  | S13 | 372 | Medical & surgical equipment | M |
| S2 | S21 | 251 | Basic industrial chemicals | I |
|  |  | 257 | Pharmaceuticals | M |
|  |  | 345 | Radios, TVs, etc. | M |
|  |  | 346 | Domestic electrical appliances | M |
|  |  | 351 | Motor vehicles | I |
|  |  | 428 | Soft drinks | M |
|  | S22 | 325 | Plant for mines, steel | M |
|  |  | 364 | Aerospace equipment | I |
|  |  | 413 | Dairy products | I |
|  |  | 427 | Brewing, malting | I |
|  | S23 | 247 | Glass & glassware | I |
|  |  | 322 | Machine tools | M |
|  |  | 323 | Textile machinery | M |
|  |  | 324 | Food, chemical machinery | M |
|  |  | 326 | Transmission equipment | M |
|  |  | 327 | Other machinery | M |
|  |  | 432 | Cotton industry | M |
|  |  | 481 | Rubber products | M |
|  |  | 491 | Jewellery | I |
|  |  | 494 | Toys & sports goods | I |
|  |  |  |  |  |
| D1 | D12 | 342 | Electrical machinery | M |
|  |  | 361 | Shipbuilding | I |
|  |  | 417 | Spaghetti, macaroni | I |
| D2 | D21 | 256 | Other chemical products | M |
|  |  | 321 | Agricultural machinery | M |
|  |  | 493 | Photographic labs | I |
|  | D22 | 431 | Wool industry | I |
|  |  | 453 | Clothing | I |
|  |  | 455 | Household textiles | I |
|  | D23 | 248 | Ceramic goods | I |
|  |  | 347 | Electric lamps | M |
|  |  | 438 | Carpets, floor coverings | M |
|  |  | 451 | Footwear | I |

*Note:* M represents multinational-dominated sectors, and I represents indigenous sectors.

On the basis of unpublished information supplied by the Irish Industrial Development Authority (IDA), the level of investment per job in Ireland is known to average around $ 150,000 at present. We assume for Spain, with its somewhat higher GDP per capita, a slightly higher investment-to-employment ratio, of $ 175,000 per job, and for Portugal a somewhat lower one of $ 125,000 per job. For Spain then, this apparent structural change in FDI inflows represents an extra 19,000 jobs per annum in manufacturing, and in Portugal an extra 1,500 jobs per annum. Little or no structural change is apparent in the cases of Ireland (where FDI inflows are already

---

[47]    We may be underestimating recent FDI inflows into Ireland and Greece, in that 1992 data (which is the most recent year for which data is available) shows a sharp increase in FDI inflows into Greece, while employment in the foreign-owned sector of Irish manufacturing has increased strongly in recent years. O'Malley (1992) argues that the SEM is likely to increase Ireland's attractiveness as a base for multinational investment still further.

very high) and Greece (where the inflows are rather low). It remains a moot point whether or not it was the SEM shock that caused the Portuguese and Spanish structural shift. If it did, then the FDI effect must be added to the other SEM effects. If it did not, then the FDI effect, although obviously related to Portuguese and Spanish accession in the late 1980s, is not strictly an SEM effect. We take both scenarios into account in the simulations reported in Chapter 8.

**Table 6.4.    FDI manufacturing flows into peripheral economies (US$ million)**

|      | Greece | | Ireland | | Portugal | | Spain | |
|------|---------|------|---------|------|----------|------|--------|------|
|      | Nominal | Real | Nominal | Real | Nominal | Real | Nominal | Real |
| 1982 |         |      |         |      | 60       | 222  | 1,150  | 1,990 |
| 1983 |         |      | 237     | 304  | 60       | 173  | 676    | 1,040 |
| 1984 |         |      | 198     | 237  | 61       | 145  | 878    | 1,235 |
| 1985 |         |      | 195     | 224  | 98       | 187  | 1,025  | 1,341 |
| 1986 |         |      | 244     | 280  | 68       | 114  | 1,758  | 2,180 |
| 1987 | 113     | 173  | 309     | 354  | 82       | 119  | 3,098  | 3,650 |
| 1988 | 93      | 127  | 223     | 237  | 222      | 278  | 2,674  | 2,979 |
| 1989 | 118     | 137  | 187     | 187  | 304      | 342  | 4,415  | 4,687 |
| 1990 | 136     | 136  | 194     | 194  | 428      | 428  | 6,250  | 6,250 |
| 1991 | 152     |      | 349     |      | 384      |      | 3,492  |      |

*Sources:*  OECD International Direct Investment Statistics Yearbook 1994, 1993, OECD, Paris.
Deflator of Investment in Manufacturing (Various National Accounts: Greece, Ireland, Portugal and Spain) used to calculate Real FDI Flows (1990 = 1).
IMF: International Financial Statistics, Yearbook 1994, for local/US$ exchange rates.

We wish to design a shock to represent these increased FDI flows, and this is illustrated in Figures 6.4 and 6.5. An extra 19,000 jobs per annum in Spanish manufacturing over a ten-year period represents an increase of 7% over the 1987 base level, while the extra jobs in Portugal over an equivalent time period represent an increase of 1.9%. We translate these numbers into combined output and productivity shocks.

Productivity in the modern (largely foreign-owned MNC) sectors of Irish manufacturing is over twice that in traditional (largely indigenous) industry. Using the Irish analogue, since employment in foreign-owned enterprises was low in both Portugal and Spain in 1987, we can assume that the productivity level associated with these new jobs is twice that in existing industry. Thus, an increase of 7% in Spanish employment translates to an increase of 14% in output and an increase of 7% in productivity. For Portugal, the increase of 1.9% in jobs translates to an increase of 3.8% in output and an increase of 1.9% in productivity (e.g. with output increasing from a base of 100 up to 103.8 and employment going from 100 to 101.9, productivity goes from 100 to 101.9).

The modifications to the static productivity effect are carried out as shown in Figures 6.4 and 6.5. Only for the cases of Portugal and Spain, where a structural shift in FDI flows is apparent, are the original Cecchini-motivated numbers modified. The two key assumptions made in constructing the FDI-modified shocks to output and productivity relate to the investment cost per new job and the extent to which the FDI-related jobs have a higher productivity. The Irish experience is drawn on to give initial guesses for these two assumptions, and these are modified in the light of what we know of the characteristics of the Portuguese and Spanish economies.

Taking these FDI effects into account alongside the static effects discussed earlier, then, the exogenous shocks we work with are shown in Table 6.5 below: columns 1 and 2 show the output shock, without and with the FDI modification, respectively. Columns 3 and 4 show the productivity shocks, where the 'no-FDI' numbers are taken from the original Cecchini research.

**Table 6.5.     Static output and productivity shocks**

|  | Net output shock (%) | | Productivity shock (%) | |
|---|---|---|---|---|
|  | No FDI | With FDI | No FDI | With FDI |
| Ireland | 8 | 8 | 5 | 5 |
| Portugal | -3 | 1 | 5 | 6.9 |
| Spain | -7 | 7 | 5 | 12 |
| Greece | -14 | -14 | 5 | 5 |
| *Source:* Own calculations. | | | | |

### 6.3.3.   The shift to greater trade orientation (shock (iv), in Figure 6.2)

Against the background of a fixed level of manufacturing output, another important effect of the SEM is to shift the economy towards a greater direct exposure to the world economy, i.e. to increase the share of tradables relative to non-tradables in the manufacturing sector. With the need to examine this kind of shock in mind, we imposed a uniform functional form structure on the output and producer price equations of the manufacturing sectors of all four HERMIN models.

Manufacturing output (OT) and output price (POT) are determined as follows:

$$\log(OT) = a_1 + a_2 \log(OW) + a_3 \log(FDOT)$$

$$+ a_4 \log(ULCT / POT) + a_5 \log(POT / PWORLD) + a_6 t$$

$$\log(POT) = b_1 + b_2 \log(PWORLD) + (1 - b_2) \log(ULCT)$$

where $OW$ represents world manufacturing output, $ULCT$ is (domestic) unit labour costs, $POT$ is the (domestic) output price, $FDOT$ is a weighted measure of domestic demand, and $PWORLD$ is the price of world manufacturing output.[48]

Free estimation of the output equation proved difficult, given the constrained formulation, the aggregate nature of the data, and the short time series available (e.g. only 1977 to 1990 for Portugal).[49] We make the admittedly strong assumption that goods sold on the home market can be identified as non-tradables. This is done because for several of the countries the ratio (for the manufacturing sector) of goods exported to sales on the home market is very close to the weight of world demand in the manufacturing output equation relative to domestic demand (a ratio of around 2 to 1 for Ireland). Goods exclusively dependent on domestic demand are by definition non-tradable.

---

[48]   The weighted measure of domestic demand assigns I-O weightings that represent the manufacturing output content of each expenditure component. The components included are private consumption (CONS), public consumption (G), and investment disaggregated into building and construction (IBC) and machinery and equipment (IME).

[49]   Clearly, further research is needed in the area of output determination at a disaggregated level in the manufacturing sector. In the Irish case, Bradley, Fitz Gerald and Kearney (1993) provide such a study, based on a three-way disaggregation of manufacturing into high-technology, food processing and other traditional. The HERMIN aggregate manufacturing output equation for Ireland is based on this disaggregated research.

**Figure 6.3.    Shift to greater tradable orientation for manufacturing output**

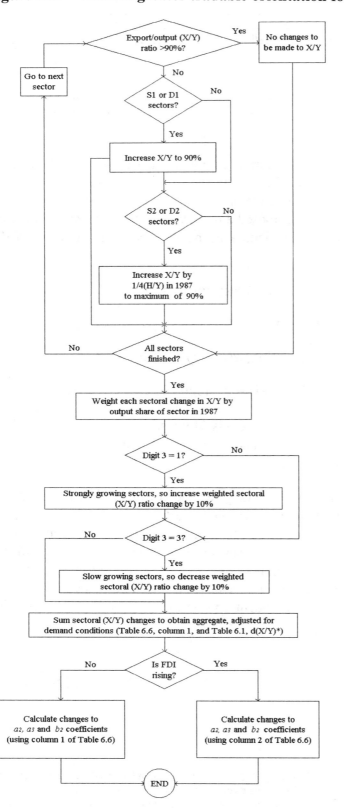

Consequently, we imposed constraints on the ratio of $a_2$ to $a_4$ (see Section 5.1.1), i.e. the estimated measure of within sample openness of the individual manufacturing sectors. For Ireland, the most open economy, the ratio 2 was imposed, reflecting the fact that two-thirds of output was initially dependent on world demand and one-third dependent on domestic demand. Greece and Portugal were intermediate cases, with the ratio 0.5 imposed; Spain, being the least open, had the ratio 0.33 imposed, reflecting the fact that a quarter of output was initially dependent on world demand and three quarters dependent on domestic demand.

The sequence of calculations required to quantify the way the SEM may influence the structure of the output and price equations in manufacturing is illustrated in a flow-chart in Figure 6.3. Each of the sectors in *European Economy* (1990) is examined. If the export/output ratio is already greater than 90%, no further changes are made to the ratio. Otherwise, for strongly affected sectors (S1 or D1) we increase the ratio to 90%; for weakly affected sectors, we increase it by a quarter of the initial home market orientation, to a maximum of 90%.

Each sector's export/output ratio is then weighted by its output share. For strongly growing sectors (according to the *European Economy* (1990) classification), we increase the ratio by a further 10%; for slow growing sectors, we decrease the ratio by 10%. Finally, an adjustment is made in the case where FDI inflows are rising since 1987 (i.e. for Portugal and Spain). The manner in which this is done is explained below and illustrated in Figure 6.3.

## 6.3.4.   Growth-dependent effects (shock (vii), Figure 6.2)

We must also recognize that the increased export orientation of the economy generates growth-dependent effects (i.e. any given increase in world demand will have more dramatic effects now that the economy is producing a higher proportion of tradable goods, and any increase in domestic demand will have less strong effects than before because the economy is now producing a smaller proportion of non-tradables, the output of which depends on domestic demand).

We have already explained in Figure 6.3 how the increased export/output ratio in each sector is calculated. For example, for the D1 sector 'Spaghetti and macaroni' we expect its sales on the home market to fall from 50% of output down to 10%, while for the S2 and D2 sectors 'Domestic electrical appliances' and 'Other chemical products', we expect home-market orientation to fall from 22% down to 16.5%, the former through increased exports and the latter through reduced home-market sales.

To work out the implications for the overall export/output ratio for manufacturing, we weight each percentage point change in the export/output share by its share of manufacturing output, Y/YM, and then make an adjustment for demand growth, since if the economy is specializing into sectors for which world demand is growing strongly, this will increase the elasticity of world demand in the domestic output equation still further.[50] (This adjustment entails factoring in data from the *European Economy* special issue on the state of demand for the output of individual sectors. For sectors for which EU demand is growing rapidly, the output-weighted percentage point change in the export/output ratio is multiplied by a factor 1.1; for average-growth sectors the numbers are unchanged, and for slow growth sectors the numbers are multiplied by a factor

---

[50]     Technically the percentage point change, which for the S2 and D2 sectors of Greece, Portugal and Ireland is $(1/4)(H/Y)$, is $d(X/Y)[Y/(Y+dY)]$.

0.9.) This yields the numbers presented in Table 6.1 and Appendix B in the columns entitled 'd(X/Y)*'.

We see that the total in the Irish case is around 6%, which indicates that the export orientation of Irish manufacturing we predict to rise from its current level of around 67% to about 73%. Our methodology entails embodying these structural changes into the HERMIN model through adjusting the coefficients in the output and pricing equations in line with these proportions. These changes are now described, developing on the basic model presented in Chapter 5.

## 6.4.    Implementing the SEM shocks in the HERMIN models

In most of the shocks illustrated in Figure 6.2, we simply have to alter an exogenous variable, such as world prices and costs (shock (ii)), public employment (shock (iii)), etc. In other shocks we only need to alter exogenous 'add-factors', such as in the case of shock (v) (manufacturing output), or shock (vi) (market services output). However, some of the more subtle shocks require us to alter the otherwise fixed coefficients of the model behavioural equations (e.g. shocks (iv) and (vii)). We turn to this latter category now.

## Figure 6.4.    Static productivity shock

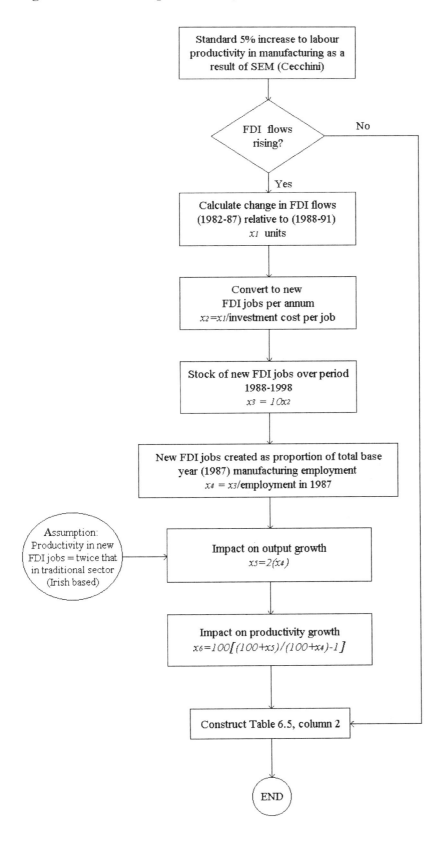

**Figure 6.5.     Static output shock (with, without FDI effect)**

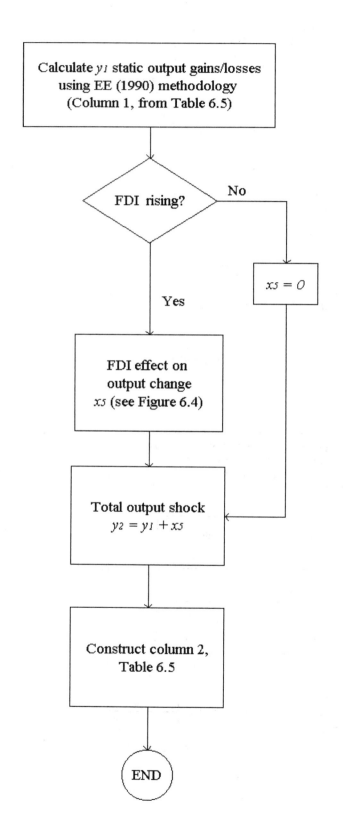

## 6.4.1. Manufacturing output equation alterations

The equation determining manufacturing output (OT) is a function of world demand (OW) and weighted domestic demand (FDOT), as well as cost and competitiveness terms (for simplicity, not shown explicitly below):

$$\log(OT) = a_1 + a_2 \log(OW) + a_3 \log(FDOT) + \text{relative price terms}$$

where $a_2$ and $a_3$ are the coefficients on the two variables respectively. The structural changes described above require altering the values of $a_2$ and $a_3$ to increase the dependence on OW and decrease the dependence on domestic demand FDOT. The adjustments to $a_2$ and $a_3$ are calculated as follows. For given levels of OW and FDOT, the changes in $a_2$ and $a_3$ should not affect OT. Therefore we require:

$$da_2 = -\left\{ \log(FDOT) / \log(OW) \right\}_{1987} da_3$$

where the shock is administered from the base year 1987. For this reason, we set indices so that the ratio of log(FDOT) to log(OW) for 1987 is unity.

The initial values of $a_2$ and $a_3$ were, for the Irish case, in the 2-to-1 ratio, reflecting the fact that 67% of initial output was initially dependent on world demand and one-third was initially dependent on domestic demand. We predict that this 67% will now rise by 6 percentage points to 73% of the sum of the initial values of $a_2$ and $a_3$. For Ireland, therefore, we need

$$da_2 = 6\% \text{ of } (a_2 + a_3).$$

while the other coefficient falls by an equal amount.

These calculations ensure that, for given levels of domestic and world demand, manufacturing output does not change. However, the increased export orientation of the economy after the introduction of the SEM means that the economy is now more reliant on world demand and less reliant on domestic demand.

## 6.4.2. Manufacturing output price equation alterations

The price of tradables (POT) is a function of world prices (PWORLD) and unit labour costs (ULCT), where price homogeneity is not rejected by the data:

$$\log(POT) = b_1 + b_2 \log(PWORLD) + (1 - b_2) \log(ULCT)$$

where $b_2$ (80%) and ($1-b_2$) (20%) are the coefficients on the two variables for Ireland respectively. In the Irish case, if the whole 33% of output which is initially non-traded switched to traded, then $b_2$ (the coefficient on PWORLD) would rise from 80% to 100%. So each 1% switch in the output equation requires the following change, $x$, to the coefficient on PWORLD in the pricing equation:

$$x = 20/33 = 0.606 \text{ points.}$$

Therefore, every percentage point switch from non-traded to traded means we add 0.606 points to $b_2$ and obviously subtract 0.606 points from ($1-b_2$). So a 6% switch out of the non-traded sector adds 3.6 points to the world price coefficient ($b_2$), increasing it to 83.6% and a drop in (1-$b_2$) to 16.4%.

### 6.4.3.  Implications for the other peripheral countries

We have carried out similar analyses for Greece, Spain and Portugal, and the equivalent results are listed in Table 6.6.

**Table 6.6.      Impact of the SEM: non-traded to traded shift (in output equations)**

|          | Without FDI increases | With FDI increases |
|----------|:---------------------:|:------------------:|
| Ireland  | 6%                    | 6%                 |
| Portugal | 13%                   | 16%                |
| Spain    | 9%                    | 18%                |
| Greece   | 14%                   | 14%                |

*Note:* The figures shown represent the proportions of the manufacturing sector that shift from being non-tradable to being tradable.
*Source*: Own calculations.

Thus, before taking the impact of increased FDI inflows into account, the Spanish export/output ratio for manufacturing would rise from 25% to 34%. Taking the increased FDI inflows into account, though, assuming they would be almost completely export-oriented, will add 14% to both the numerator and denominator of the export/output ratio, raising it from 25% to 34%; thus we add another 9% for the FDI-flow effect. The total change for Spain is therefore 9+9=18%.

The initial export/output ratio for Portugal is 33.3%. The increased FDI flows, which raise output by 3.8%, raise the export/output ratio to 35.8%, on the assumption that all this increased output is exported. This increase of some 2.5 percentage points must be added to the 13.5% calculation derived above to yield an overall change of 16%.

## 6.5.      Concluding comments on SEM methodology

Many of the effects of trade liberalization are ambiguous *a priori*. We view what we have done in this report as an attempt to put numbers on some of these effects. Our main methodological contribution is in the way we have taken likely structural changes into account, through a recognition that liberalization will make many heretofore non-tradable goods (and services) tradable. Some of these sectors will disappear, while others will prosper.

Finally, we suggest that the *European Economy* (1990) special issue, on which we have relied in our attempt to quantify these structural changes, may be overly pessimistic about the ability of some sectors in peripheral regions to prosper because it fails to recognize the enhanced ability of the periphery to attract FDI. This enhanced ability shows up clearly in the cases of Spain and Portugal, while there is no evidence that Ireland or Greece has suffered a reduced ability in this regard.

# 7. CSF impacts on the cohesion countries: methodology

Analysis of the impact and effectiveness of CSF-type policies can proceed at various levels. The essential difference between different levels of analysis is the extent to which the rest of the economy is assumed to remain unchanged while a specific CSF policy initiative is investigated. Using terminology somewhat loosely, these three stages could be conveniently called micro, mezzo, and macro evaluations. Since our focus in this paper is on the macro level of analysis, we only describe the other two levels briefly.[51]

In the most extreme case of an individual project (e.g. a particular stretch of road; a particular port extension; a specific local tourism initiative), a conventional cost-benefit analysis could be carried out. In cost-benefit analysis the rate of return to the project can be calculated as the internal discount rate which equates the discounted flow of benefits arising from the project to the costs involved in implementing it. Competing projects can then be ranked in terms of increasing internal rate of return. Such analysis, however, is undertaken in isolation from the rest of the economy, ignoring any other effects of the CSF, giving rise to difficulties in relation to the need to evaluate the impact of spillover effects and externalities in the context of the complete CSF.

Moving up the scale of aggregation, the totality of projects targeted at a general or systemic problem (say, long-term unemployment or industrial competitiveness) could be evaluated in terms of how successful they are in attaining the overall priority objective. In addition to the problems inherent in individual project cost-benefit analysis, extra issues and complications arise as a consequence of spillover effects and externalities, which may be difficult to quantify in isolation from the rest of the economy. Although such evaluations can be carried out informally, it is usually necessary to construct and use formalized sectoral economic models.

Finally, the effectiveness of the entire CSF can be evaluated as an aggregate. Given the size of the funding in relation to the economy, it is important to examine the impact of the CSF in this context. In this type of analysis, economy-wide feedbacks and interactions must be allowed for and an attempt must be made to account for spillover effects and externalities. Here it is almost essential to make use of formal models of the national or regional economy being studied.[52]

## 7.1.    Economic mechanisms and the CSF

To carry out the economic analysis of the effects of the Irish CSF 1989–93, an earlier methodology was developed and implemented in the large-scale HERMES model, which concentrated on the long-term implications of the different measures (Bradley, Fitz Gerald and Kearney, 1992). The channels through which the CSF would affect the supply side of the economy were identified, and, in some cases, the HERMES model was modified to facilitate quantification.

---

[51]    Of course, insights and results available from the micro and mezzo level of analysis often appear as inputs to the macro level of analysis. However, they are 'off model', in the sense of being pre-recursive to the model rather than being simultaneous.

[52]    A wide range of appropriate types of models exists, including macro-econometric, input-output (I-O), growth, computable general equilibrium (CGE), etc.

The ESRI study identified three channels through which the CSF investment will effect an economy's long-run supply potential:

(a)    through changes in human capital (the skills and education of the labour force);
(b)    through infrastructural investment;
(c)    through direct assistance to the private productive sector of the economy, reducing costs or increasing productivity.

The Irish HERMES model went a considerable distance towards allowing one to quantify the effects flowing through the third of these channels, basically through a careful definition of the cost of capital. However, considerable uncertainty surrounded the magnitude of the effects arising through the first two economic mechanisms, namely human capital and physical infrastructure.

## 7.1.1.  Human capital

An immediate impact of education and training schemes on the income-expenditure side of a model is fairly straightforward. A number of people (perhaps previously unemployed) are provided with full-time training, during which they are in receipt of an income supplement. A specified number of teachers/instructors also have to be hired and paid the going wage. Premises need to be built or rented, material and equipment needs to be purchased, other overheads need to be carried. All these aspects are 'inputs', and say little or nothing about the benefits of training schemes to individuals, firms or the economy at large.

Training and education schemes have a number of objectives. Firstly, they are designed to increase the skills of the labour force and thereby increase labour and total factor productivity. Secondly, they aim to improve the labour market participation of certain disadvantaged groups, such as the long-term unemployed and the disabled. Consequently, they will affect the supply potential of the economy through a range of different mechanisms.

To the extent that the additional people being trained or educated are taken out of the active labour force, the potential labour force will be reduced temporarily. This, in turn, will tend to reduce unemployment and emigration. Because of the Phillips curve effect, the reduction in unemployment will increase wage rates, with knock-on effects on unit labour costs. However, to the extent that those in training or education come from groups which are not active in seeking jobs although remaining in the labour force, such as the long-term unemployed, there may be less impact on wage bargaining.

The second way in which the increase in human capital will impact on the economy is through the increased supply of skilled labour. In this regard the first issue that arises is the extent to which the change in skill composition of the new labour force entrants affects migration. There is likely to be some leakage of skilled labour abroad. However, the Irish evidence suggests that in the past emigrants have had fairly diverse educational backgrounds and that the incidence of emigration is not concentrated purely on those with good skills (NESC, 1991). Thus, one expects that the training schemes will have a positive impact on the domestic supply of skilled labour, thereby reducing pressures in the labour market arising from skill shortages, and tending to reduce the rate of wage inflation below the baseline level. In addition, in so far as the schemes are successful in giving the long-term unemployed the skills and confidence to participate in the active labour force, they will reduce wage pressures at any given level of unemployment.

The third and most important effect of human capital on the productive capacity of the economy is the increase in efficiency and productivity which will arise from the greater skill and education of the labour force. The increase in productivity and efficiency reduces costs to existing firms, increasing the quality of output and may lead to new firms setting up to exploit this increased efficiency and productivity. This effect can be incorporated into a macro model (or rather grafted on) by the assumption of a rate of return to human capital investment that is in line with the limited empirical evidence. The assumption of a specific social rate of return to investment in human capital is crucial to any model-based quantitative analysis. However, the measurement of rates of return is fraught with difficulty.

### 7.1.2. Infrastructural investment

Infrastructural investment takes a number of different forms: increased expenditure on roads and ports; increased investment in sanitary services; developments in the telecommunications system; provision of advance factories. Generally, these investments will first impact on the economy through increased investment, thereby generating increased demand for building services. Most neo-Keynesian macromodels can handle these demand effects satisfactorily.

It is on the supply side that infrastructural investment can be expected to have the biggest impact and it is here that the greatest uncertainty arises. Infrastructural investment may have a highly non-linear effect on the economy. For example, a telephone system below a required standard may simply prevent any industrial investment of a high technology type. Once a threshold standard is passed it may then be possible for such high technology investment to take place, but any given standard of telecommunications will not guarantee such investment. In the case of roads, improvements may have little effect if they merely serve to shift traffic jams from one town to another. However, the completion of the final link on a major artery could have a very big effect on travel times and, thus, on industrial costs.

As with the measurement of the supply-side effects of investment in human capital, Bradley, Fitz Gerald and Kearney (1992) took an experimental approach to quantifying the effects of the infrastructural investment. While their macromodel allowed them to assess the impact on the industrial sector of a given percentage change in transport costs, it had no mechanism for measuring the potential impact on such costs of any given level of infrastructural investment. Indeed, little empirical evidence is available on this latter issue. In order to enter these cost savings into their model, the CSF peripherality programme was assumed to reduce transport costs by a specific amount, with an equal reduction in the unit costs of industrial production. Choice of the actual amount was influenced by the results of a micro-study. Within the model, a reduction in the cost of production increases competitiveness, leading to increased output and employment on a long-term basis.

### 7.1.3. Aid to the private sector

Aid to the private sector is generally given in the form of a grant or subsidy designed to encourage the private sector to undertake certain investments which are believed to be highly desirable, or of strategic importance. Such aid can take the form of incentives to expand or develop new industries; incentives for investment in forestry; incentives to agricultural investment; incentives and subsidies to increase the international marketing effort of firms and to encourage the greater use of research and development.

A key channel of influence for aid to the private sector is through the user cost of capital, and the crucial first step in assessing the impact of this aspect of the CSF is the quantification of the link between assistance and investment. Here, the micro-studies carried out for the Irish industrial and agricultural sectors helped fill this gap (Bradley, Fitz Gerald and Kearney, 1992). The effects of a change in the grant provision of the Irish Industrial Development Authority (IDA) on industrial investment and output in the long term were quantified within the macromodel. The same applied to some of the agricultural investment schemes. However, the quantification obtained was seen as imprecise because small changes in the terms or eligibility conditions, which might significantly affect behaviour, cannot be identified at a macroeconomic level.

Having quantified the impact of aid on investment behaviour, the macromodel provides a good tool for examining the long-term supply-side impact of the resulting increase in the productive potential of the economy. Reduced user cost of capital results in more capital intensive production techniques. However, if profitability is also increased, production will increase, and with it employment. The supply side of the Irish HERMES model, used by Bradley, Fitz Gerald and Kearney (1992), determines the production technology (i.e. factor proportions used in production) as a function of relative factor prices, i.e. cost of capital, wage rates, cost of energy, and cost of other material inputs. Also, output is driven by Irish cost competitiveness relative to a range of trading partners. Although the initial impact of the increase in investment is to disimprove the balance of payments since investment in machinery and equipment has a high component of imported capital goods, once the new capital stock is in place and productive, the effects on the balance of payments become positive.

### 7.1.4. Other issues related to aggregate and indirect effects of the CSF

CSF subventions from the European Commission require domestic co-financing, both public and private. Hence, the change in the balance of payments and government borrowing requirement, which will arise as by-products of the CSF, should not be ignored in any evaluation. The increase in growth and employment financed by the CSF will reduce certain aspects of government spending and increase tax revenue through buoyancy effects. The effects of these indirect changes could, over time, offset a considerable amount of the cost to the government of financing part of the CSF expenditure. Depending on how any remaining deficits to the balance of payments and the public sector balances are financed, they may reduce the benefits to the growth rate in the medium term.[53]

## 7.2.  The CSF and externalities: exploring growth mechanisms

Recent developments in endogenous growth theory have begun to provide a more adequate representation of the processes of economic growth by extending beyond the simple framework of the neo-classical theory of the firm to look at human capital, public capital and technology. The concept of a production externality is central to endogenous growth theory, where the essence of an externality is that its costs or benefits are not reflected in market prices. For example, Lucas (1988) sees human capital externalities as explaining migration flows and the role of cities; Romer (1990) views externalities associated with knowledge as

---

[53]    A similar issue of indirect additional effects arose in the Emerson-Cecchini study of the Single European Market where the benefits of 1992 were recycled as increased public investment (Cecchini, 1988; Emerson *et al.*, 1988, pp. 215-217).

being central to the creation of new technologies; Barro (1990) sees externalities associated with public infrastructure as having important effects on productivity.

Thus, when looking at the possible long-run growth effects of the CSF in the context of a specific national economy, it is useful to focus on externalities likely to be associated with public policy actions. Since externalities cannot be perceived by agents in their optimization behaviour, they can be exploited only through policy interventions. This highlights an important lesson for development policy analysts: in the presence of externalities, many of the simple policy rules emanating from the orthodox neo-classical growth theory are invalid. Policy rules aimed at minimizing static efficiency losses may miss potential gains arising from policy links to externalities. Indeed, de Melo and Robinson (1992) go further and assert that:

> If there appear to be externalities to be exploited, policy makers should pursue them aggressively and not worry too much about getting the instruments just right.

In the four peripheral country HERMIN models, we consider three types of externalities which could be associated with the CSF expenditures (Bradley, Herce and Modesto, 1995):

(a)   Factor productivity externalities: these refer to increases in productivity arising out of investment in human capital and public infrastructure. In some cases, total factor productivity is involved. In other cases, factor specific productivity may be relevant (e.g. in the case of human capital externalities).

(b)   Industrial composition externalities: these refer to the increasing sophistication of manufacturing due to increased foreign multinational investment that accompanies improvements in physical infrastructure and human capital.

(c)   Labour market externalities: these increase the efficiency of the labour market by enhancing skills, in particular those of the long-term unemployment and school-leavers.

## 7.2.1.   Factor productivity externalities

The factor productivity externality is associated with improved supply conditions in the economy as a result of the CSF investment in human capital and public infrastructure. These were incorporated into HERMIN by endogenizing the CES production function scale parameter, 'A', which is now modelled as a function of the stock of public and human capital. Increases in the value of 'A' imply that for a given amount of inputs, a higher level of output is produced.

Consider the production function

$$Q = A * f(L, I)$$

where $A$ is the scale parameter, which can be considered to represent the state of technology, and $L$ and $I$ are the labour and investment inputs, respectively.

Public infrastructural investment will increase the efficiency of the market services sector by cutting down on the costs of producing transport and other communication services, and by opening up greater opportunities for domestic competition to take place in the provision of non-traded goods. Unit labour costs in the market services sector of the HERMIN model have an impact on manufacturing sector price and cost competitiveness, so such cost reductions will also have a favourable supply-side effect on the exposed manufacturing sector.

The infrastructure factor productivity externality is incorporated into the production process as follows:

$$A_t = A_0 \left( KGINF_t \ / \ KGINF_0 \right)^{\eta}$$

where $A_0$ is the original estimated value of the scale parameter and $\eta$ is an unknown externality elasticity that can be assigned different numerical values in the empirical model; $KGINF$ is the stock of public infrastructure, computed as an accumulation of infrastructure investments (using the perpetual inventory method with a specified depreciation rate). The baseline stock of infrastructure, $KGINF_0$, is taken as the stock that would have been there in the absence of the CSF increases decided for the period under consideration.

Similarly, the CSF Social Fund programmes on education and training can be considered to promote the efficiency of the workforce in both manufacturing and services sectors and can give rise to a human capital externality. Incorporation of externality effects associated with the accumulation of human capital is not as straightforward as in the infrastructure case, since there is no readily available measure of the stock of human capital equivalent to the stock of infrastructure. One has a measure of the extra number of trainees funded by the CSF schemes. Hence, as a first approximation, one can use the inputs into training as a measure of the unknown outputs, although if the training courses are badly designed and poorly executed, the relationship between training and increased human capital will be tenuous.

We assume that, prior to the implementation of the CSF, the existing number of trained members of the labour force, $NTRAIN_0$, is known. If the CSF increases are used to fund an additional number of trainees, giving a total of $NTRAIN_t$ trained members of the labour force in year t, then the scale parameter in the production function is modified as follows:

$$A_t = A_0 \left( NTRAIN_t \ / \ NTRAIN_0 \right)^{\eta}$$

where $A_0$ is the original estimated value of the scale parameter. In the empirical model, this externality is incorporated into the treatment of both the manufacturing and service sectors.

### 7.2.2. Industrial composition externalities

This second type of externality is viewed as operating directly through the multinational and indigenous firm location and growth process that is so important in the case of the EU periphery. The treatment of the manufacturing sector in HERMIN posits a supply-side approach in which the share of the world's output being allocated to, or generated within, a peripheral country is determined by measures of international competitiveness (Bradley and Fitz Gerald, 1988).

However, this neglects the fact that many industries will require more than simply an appropriate level of, say, labour costs before they locate in, or grow spontaneously in, the periphery. Without an available labour force that is qualified to work in these industries, or without appropriate minimum levels of physical infrastructure, many firms simply may not even be able to consider the periphery as a location for production. Thus, a more realistic framework may be one which posits a two-stage process in which basic infrastructural and labour force quality conditions dictate the number of industries which could conceivably locate in the periphery, while competitiveness decides how many of the industries which can locate in the periphery actually do.

One simple way of describing this process is to link the growth of infrastructure and the increases in human capital to the HERMIN measure of world output, OWX, a key determinant of long-run domestic industrial output, in the following way:

$$OWX_t = OW_t * \left( KGINF_t \, / \, KGINF_0 \right)^{\eta_1} * \left( NTRAIN_t \, / \, NTRAIN_0 \right)^{\eta_2}$$

where output in the manufacturing sector (OT) is determined by the modified equation

$$\log(OT) = \ldots + a_1 \log(OWX) \ldots$$

ignoring all other driving (or dependent) variables on the right hand side of the equation.

Such a modification attempts to capture the notion that the periphery country can now attract a greater share of world mobile investment than it otherwise could in the absence of improved infrastructure and human capital. Another, demand-side, way of interpreting this externality could be to assume that the CSF may improve the quality of goods produced domestically and thus improve the demand for goods produced by firms already located in the country, whether foreign or indigenous.

## 7.2.3. Labour market externalities

A final externality mechanism which could be introduced into the model concerns the way in which the labour market functions. Many of the training programmes financed by the Social Fund component of the CSF are aimed at the long-term unemployed and school-leavers without qualifications. Empirical and theoretical work on hysteresis theories of the labour market has suggested that these social groupings are likely to have little influence on wage bargaining (Layard, Nickell and Jackman, 1991, pp. 173–213). Thus, one of the possible effects of the CSF human capital programmes could be to increase the number of active and influential labour market participants.

One way to model this effect would be to assume that the CSF expenditures increase the effect which the better trained long-term unemployed (i.e. the outsiders) have on wage bargaining. This would require the wage bargaining mechanism to become more responsive to unemployment, both short- and long-term, and can be modelled by increasing the size of the Phillips curve coefficient to represent a tightening of the labour market. Thus, the Phillips curve parameter in the wage bargaining equation could be adjusted to reflect this. Although this would seem to represent a theoretically attractive way of incorporating supply-side benefits of the CSF into the model, to do so would raise complex issues that have yet to be dealt with in the literature. In this report we do not implement any labour-market externality mechanism.

## 7.2.4. Externalities: choosing elasticity values

We have described an analytical approach to incorporating externality mechanisms into a macromodel, which augment the usual neo-Keynesian impact mechanisms with further supply-side mechanisms. The magnitude of the externality effects are related to the relative improvement in a stock (e.g. infrastructure, trained workers, or sectoral capital) and to an elasticity η. In order to operationalize the process within a model one needs to assign numerical values to these elasticities.[54]

*Physical infrastructure*

In the case of physical infrastructure, Aschauer (1989) showed that there was a significant relationship between public capital and private sector output, arguing that the fall in US productivity growth during the 1970s was precipitated by declining rates of public investment. Based on Aschauer's work, there have been many studies that have estimated regressions where the dependent variable is output and the independent variables are private capital, labour, public capital and a time trend to proxy technical progress (Munnell, 1992 and 1993). In such regressions the coefficient on public capital is generally significant, but varies over a wide range. [55]

Aschauer's early work was based on an aggregate Cobb-Douglas production function, and suggested that the impact of public capital on private sector output and productivity was very large, with the implication that an increase of 1% in public capital would give rise to an increase of about 0.40% in output. For the USA, given the size of public capital and output, this would mean that the marginal productivity of public capital was about 60%, as compared with a value of only 30% for private capital.

Various criticisms were made of this early work, ranging from econometric methodology (a need to use co-integration techniques), to a claim that causation ran in the opposite direction, i.e. from output to public capital. Furthermore, it was found that as the geographical focus narrows (from the whole nation, to states, to metropolitan areas in the USA), the elasticity falls because of leakages (i.e. it is impossible to capture all the benefits from an infrastructural investment within a small geographical area).

In a survey of econometric results, Munnell (1993) shows that the elasticity with respect to public capital ranges from an upper bound of 0.39 for the entire USA, through 0.20–0.15 for individual states, to lower bounds of 0.08–0.03 for individual metropolitan areas. In the empirical CSF 1994–99 analysis reported in Chapter 9 below, we examine the case where the externality elasticities are zero, and carry out a sensitivity analysis over the range of values indicated by the literature.

*Human resources*

There is much less corresponding literature examining the quantitative impact of human capital on growth but a vast literature examining the private and social returns to education and training, recently surveyed by Weale (1993) and Psacharopoulos (1994). Irish work in this area includes Callan (1993). Once again there is a wide range of estimates for the social rate of return, from high rates of 25% to lower rates of 5%. The international findings seem to imply that there is a law of diminishing returns: the social returns to education fall, by and large, as national income and aggregate spending on education rises.

---

[54]    As mentioned before, we do not treat the case of labour market (Phillips curve) externalities. These are examined in Bradley, Whelan and Wright (1993).

[55]    Draper and Herce (1994) have surveyed the relevant literature: Christodoulakis (1993) has analysed the Greek case and Bajo-Rubio and Sosvilla-Rivero (1993) together with Argimon *et al.* (1993) have treated the Spanish case.

Psacharopoulos (1994) found that, even for the richer OECD countries, the social rate of return for higher education (the least beneficial case) is over 8%. In the empirical CSF analysis reported in Chapter 9, we examine the case of zero human capital elasticities and carry out a sensitivity analysis over a likely range of values.

*Aid to the private sector*

While a good case can be made for externalities in the case of physical infrastructure and human resources, which, after all, are areas of predominantly public sector activity, only a weaker case can be made in the case of investment aid to the private sector. Here, there is likely to be crowding out of private sector activity and considerable dead-weight (i.e. state aided private investment that would have gone ahead on the basis of purely private sector finance in the absence of the state aids).

In the empirical CSF 1994–99 analysis reported in Chapter 9, we examine the zero elasticity case, and only allow for small positive elasticities of at most 2%.

## 7.2.5. Conclusions on externalities and growth

The three types of beneficial externalities described above are likely to enhance the standard neo-Keynesian impacts of well designed investment, training and aid policy initiatives. The first arises through the increased total or embodied factor productivity likely to be associated with improved infrastructure or a higher level of human capital associated with training and education. Of course, a side effect of increased factor productivity is that, in the restricted context of fixed output, labour is shed. This is particularly serious in economies like Ireland and Spain, where the recorded rate of unemployment is very high.

The second type of externality is likely to be associated with the role of improved infrastructure and training in attracting productive activities through foreign direct investment, and enhancing the ability of indigenous industries to compete in the international market-place. We have called this an industrial 'composition' externality, since it is well known that the range of products manufactured in developing countries changes during the process of development, and becomes more complex and technologically advanced.

The simulations described in Chapter 9 in our analysis of the combined effects of CSF 1989–93 and CSF 1994–99 for Greece, Ireland, Portugal and Spain, will indicate that the factor productivity externality is a two-edged process: industry and market services become more productive and competitive, but labour demand is weakened. The role of the industrial composition externality is more unambiguously beneficial: the higher it is, the faster the period of transitional growth to a higher income plateau. However, since it is attached only to the world demand variable in the equation determining industrial output, its power depends on the size of the estimated elasticity of world demand on output, i.e. on the openness of the economy in question.

A third type of possible beneficial externality is both the most controversial and, as it turns out from experimental simulations, the most beneficial to a country that badly needs to improve the operation of its labour market. In Bradley, Whelan and Wright (1993), exploratory simulations examined the effects of assuming that better training schemes might improve the process of wage bargaining by increasing the force with which unemployment dampens wage inflation. There are many interpretations of this effect, the most obvious being the blurring of the distinction between insiders and outsiders in the labour market. Trial simulations showed that even quite modest improvements in the efficiency of the labour market can yield very strong growth and employment effects, particularly when operating in combination with the first two types of externalities (Bradley, Whelan and Wright, 1993, pp. 138–155). However, this mechanism is still in the experimental stage and we do not incorporate it in this report.

## 7.3.    Incorporating the CSF into the HERMIN model

We have seen that there are three main economic channels through which the CSFs will impact on a peripheral economy's long-run supply potential:

(a)    through increased investment designed to improve physical infrastructure;
(b)    through increases in human capital (the skills and education of the labour force), brought about by investment in human resources;
(c)    through direct assistance to the private sector to stimulate investment, thus increasing factor productivity and reducing sectoral costs of production.

### 7.3.1.   Physical infrastructure

The HERMIN model assumes that any CSF-based expenditure, IGVCSFEC, on physical infrastructure that is directly financed by EU aid subvention is matched by a domestically financed expenditure of IGVCSFDP and a domestic privately financed component of IGVCSFPR. Hence, the total public and private CSF infrastructural expenditure is defined in the model as follows:

$$IGVCSF = IGVCSFEC + IGVCSFDP + IGVCSFPR$$

Inside the HERMIN model, these CSF-related expenditures are converted to real terms and added to existing (non-CSF) real infrastructural investment, determining total investment in infrastructure, IGINF. Using the perpetual inventory approach, these investments are accumulated into a notional 'stock' of infrastructure, KGINF:

$$KGINF = IGINF + (1-0.05) * KGINF(-1)$$

where a 5% rate of depreciation is assumed for all countries. This accumulated stock is divided by the (exogenous) baseline non-CSF stock ($KGINF_0$) to give the CSF-related relative improvement in the stock of infrastructure:

$$KGINFR = KGINF / KGINF_0$$

It is this ratio that enters into the calculation of any externalities associated with improved infrastructure, as described above.

As regards the public finance implications of the CSF, the total cost of the increased public expenditure on infrastructure (IGVCSF – IGVCSFPR) is added to the domestic public sector capital expenditure (GK). Of course, any increase in the domestic public sector borrowing requirement (GBOR) is reduced by the extent of EU CSF aid subventions (IGVCSFEC). Whether or not the post-CSF domestic borrowing requirement rises or falls relative to the no-CSF baseline will depend both on the magnitude of domestic co-financing and the stimulus imparted to the economy by the CSF shock. This differs from programme to programme.

In the absence of any externality mechanisms, the standard HERMIN model can only effectively calculate the Keynesian (mainly demand) effects of the CSF infrastructure programmes, the supply effects being only included to the very limited extent that they are captured by induced shifts in relative prices.

The HERMIN model introduces various externality effects to augment the demand-side impacts of the CSF infrastructure programmes in order to capture likely supply-side benefits. In each case, the strength of the externality effect is defined as a fraction of the improvement of the stock of infrastructure over and above the baseline (no-CSF) projected level, i.e.

Externality effect = $KGINFR^{\eta}$

where $\eta$ is the externality elasticity. The way in which the externality elasticity can be approximately calibrated numerically, drawing on the empirical growth theory research literature, was discussed above. In all the computations reported below, the externality effects are phased in linearly over a five-year period, reflecting the implementation stages of the CSF programmes and the fact that benefits from improved infrastructure are only slowly exploited by the private sector in terms of increased activity.

Externality effects associated with improved infrastructure are introduced into the following areas of the HERMIN model:

(a)    the influence of world activity on domestic manufacturing is enhanced, i.e. any given change in the level of world activity will give rise to a greater change in domestic manufacturing activity to the extent that the level of physical infrastructure is improved;

(b)    total factor productivity in the manufacturing and service sectors is increased.

The first type of externality is an unqualified benefit to the peripheral economy, and directly enhances its performance in responding to a given level of world demand. However, the second type could have a negative down-side, in that labour is shed as total factor productivity improves, unless output can be increased to offset this loss. Inevitably production will become less labour intensive in a way that may differ from the experience of more developed economies in the EU core.[56]

## 7.3.2.  Human resources

The HERMIN model assumes that any expenditure, GTRSFEC, on human resources directly financed by CSF aid subvention is matched by a domestically public financed expenditure of GTRSFDP, with perhaps some private finance, GTRSFPR. Hence, the total expenditure on human resources is defined in the model as follows:

GTRSF = GTRSFEC + GTRSFDP + GTRSFPR

As regards the domestic public finance implications, the total cost of the increased expenditure on human resources (GTRSFEC+GTRSFDP) is added to public expenditure on income

---

[56]    Barry *et al.* (1994) explore the different core-periphery labour market experiences and their policy implications in the context of the recent Commission White Paper on Growth, Competitiveness, Employment.

transfers (GTR). However, the increase in the domestic public sector borrowing requirement (GBOR) is reduced by the extent of CSF aid subventions (GTRSFEC).

Since the full institutional detail of the CSF human resource training and education programmes cannot be handled in a small macroeconomic model like HERMIN, we use the following method of approximation. Each trainee or participant in a training course is assumed to be paid an average annual income of WTRAIN, taken to be either a mark-up (TMUP) over the average rate of unemployment benefit or a mark-down on the average industrial wage. Each instructor is assumed to be paid the average annual wage appropriate to the market service sector (WN). We assume an overhead of 30% on total wage costs to take account of buildings, equipment, materials, etc. (OVERHD), and a trainee-instructor ratio of 15:1 (TRATIO). Hence, total CSF expenditure (GTRSF) can be written as follows:

GTRSF = (1+OVERHD) * (SFTRAIN*WTRAIN + LINS*WN)

where *SFTRAIN* is the number of trainees being supported and *LINS* is the number of instructors, defined as SFTRAIN/TRATIO. This formula is actually inverted in the HERMIN model and used to estimate the approximate number of extra trainees that can be funded by the CSF for a given total expenditure GTRSF on human resources, i.e.

SFTRAIN = (GTRSF/(1+OVERHD)) / (WTRAIN + WN/TRATIO)

The wage bill of the CSF programme (SFWAG) is as follows:

SFWAG = SFTRAIN*WTRAIN + LINS*WN

The CSF-funded trainees are accumulated in a perpetual inventory-like formula, with a 'depreciation' rate of 5%:

KSFTRAIN = SFTRAIN + (1-0.05) * KSFTRAIN(-1)

Existing survey information indicates that about 78% of the Spanish labour force has at least first and second level education, and about 70% of the Irish labour force. In the case of Portugal, it appears that the corresponding figure is lower and nearer 40%, and the same figure is applied to Greece. This information is used to calculate a projected baseline, no-CSF, stock of trained labour force, as follows:

$KTRAIN_0$ = FRACTED * (LT+LN+LA)

where *FRACTED* is the pre-CSF fraction of the labour force that is 'trained'. The accumulated stock of CSF trainees (KSFTRAIN) is added to the exogenous baseline stock of trained workers ($KTRAIN_0$) and is divided by the baseline stock to give the relative improvement in the proportion of trained workers associated with the CSF human resources programmes:

KTRNR = $(KTRAIN_0+KSFTRAIN)$ / $KTRAIN_0$

It is this ratio (KTRNR) that enters into the calculation of externalities associated with improved human resources.

In the absence of any externality mechanisms, the HERMIN model can only calculate the income-demand effects of the CSF human resource programmes. We have commented above that these effects can be limited in magnitude. In addition, a sizeable fraction of the CSF payments to trainees will simply replace existing unemployment transfers. The 'overhead' element of these programmes (equal to OVERHD*SFWAG) is assumed to boost non-wage public consumption directly.

The HERMIN model introduces externality effects to augment the demand-side impacts of the CSF human resource programmes. In each case, the strength of the externality effect is defined as a fraction of the improvement of the stock of 'trained' workers over and above the baseline (non-CSF) projected level, i.e.

Externality effect = $KTRNR^{\eta}$

where $\eta$ is the externality elasticity. See above for an examination of how the externality elasticities can be quantified.

Two types of eternality effects are introduced into the following areas of the model:

(a)    the influence of world activity on domestic manufacturing is enhanced, i.e. any given change in the level of world activity will give rise to a greater change in domestic manufacturing activity to the extent that a greater fraction of the labour force is trained;

(b)    labour embodied technical change in the manufacturing and service sectors is increased, where a given output can now be produced by less workers or where any increased level of sectoral output can become more skill intensive but less employment intensive.

A final change made to the HERMIN model to handle the CSF human resources programmes relates to the impact on the rate of unemployment of moving people out of the labour force and into temporary training schemes. As mentioned above, it is well known that untrained and/or unskilled workers compete in the labour market in a very ineffective way, and are much more likely to end up as long-term unemployed than are skilled/trained workers (Layard, Nickell and Jackman, 1991). For simplicity it is assumed in subsequent analysis of the CSF human resources investment impacts that all trainees are in the unskilled or semi-skilled category, and that their temporary removal from the labour force for the duration of their training scheme has almost no effect on wage bargaining behaviour through the Phillips curve 'pressure' effect in the HERMIN wage equation. This assumption is consistent with the stylized facts of the hysteresis in Irish and Portuguese labour markets (Bradley, Whelan and Wright, 1993; Modesto and das Neves, 1993). It is implemented in the HERMIN model by defining a 'corrected' measure (URP) of the unemployment rate (UR) for use in the Phillips curve.

### 7.3.3.    Production/investment aid to the private sector

Publicly financed expenditures in this category are targeted at three sectors: manufacturing, market services (in particular tourism) and agriculture. Unlike the categories of infrastructure and human resources, these aids are expected to induce very sizeable private sector co-financing responses.

In the HERMIN model, we assume that any public expenditure directly financed by EU aid subvention is matched by a domestically co-financed element of public expenditure. Hence, the total direct public expenditure in each of the three targeted sectors is defined in the model as follows:

TRIT = TRITEC + TRITDP + TRITPR
TRIN = TRINEC + TRINDP + TRINPR
TRIA = TRIAEC + TRIADP + TRIAPR

where *TRITEC*, *TRINEC* and *TRIAEC* are the EU-financed elements in the traded, non-traded and agriculture sectors, and where the domestic public sector co-financing elements carry the designation 'DP'. The private domestic components carry the designation 'PR'.

The real value of total CSF-related sectoral investment aid (i.e. the above totals deflated by the appropriate sectoral investment price) is added to the other – non-CSF – sectoral investments, determined behaviourally in the HERMIN factor demand equations. Sector specific capital stocks are generated within the model using the perpetual inventory formula. For the manufacturing and service sectors, these are as follows:

$$KT = IT + (1-0.08) * KT(-1)$$

$$KN = IN + (1-0.05) * KN(-1)$$

where an 8% rate of depreciation is assumed in the traded sector and a 5% rate in the non-traded.[57] These accumulated sectoral stocks are divided by the exogenous baseline no-CSF stocks ($KT_0$ and $KN_0$, respectively) to give the relative improvement in the sector-specific capital stock:

$$KTR = KT / KT_0$$

$$KNR = KN / KN_0$$

In the HERMIN model, these ratios for the manufacturing and service sectors enter into the calculation of externalities associated with improved sectoral capital stock.

As regards the domestic public finance implications of the CSF, the total public cost of the increased expenditure on sectoral productive/investment aids (i.e. the 'EC' and 'DP' components in the above equations) is added to public capital expenditure (GK). However, the increase in the domestic public sector borrowing requirement (GBOR) is reduced by the extent of EU aid transfers (TRITEC+TRINEC+TRIAEC).

In the absence of any externality mechanisms, the HERMIN model calculates the Keynesian demand effects of the CSF sectoral investment aid, the supply effects being only included to the limited extent that they are captured by induced shifts in unit labour costs and relative prices.

As regards externalities associated with the sectoral investment programmes, for the manufacturing (T) sector, the strength of the externality effect is defined as a fraction of the improvement of the stock of infrastructure over and above the baseline (non-CSF) projected level, i.e.

Externality effect = $KTR^{\eta}$

---

[57]    In the case of Spain, depreciation rates of 10% are assumed for both manufacturing and market services.

where $\eta$ is the externality elasticity. The influence of world activity is enhanced through this externality in exactly the same fashion as for infrastructure and human resources. In the case of the market service sector, no externality mechanism is assumed to operate and sectoral investment is simply augmented by the full amount of the CSF programme, public and private. The same approach is used in agriculture, where much of the aid programme is concerned with environmental improvements and quasi-income transfers.

## 7.3.4. Terminating the CSF after 1999

The HERMIN simulations of the CSF reported in Chapter 9 below are designed to handle both the Delors-I package (1989–93) and the follow-on Delors-II package (1994–99). In fact we phase both CSFs together into one continuous package that covers the full 10-year period, 1989–99.

The question arises as to how we should handle the terminal conditions after the year 1999. In the absence of information to the contrary, we are obliged to implement stylized terminal conditions along the following lines:

(a)    continue the CSF programmes unchanged at their 1999 levels for the year 2000 and thereafter;
(b)    wind down the CSF after 1999;
(c)    eliminate the CSF entirely immediately after 1999.

In the wind-down and elimination scenarios, it would be open to us to modify the EU subvention element alone, or both the EU and domestic elements together. Clearly, the different choices are likely to have very different impacts on the economy.

For simplicity, we only consider two options in the simulations presented in Chapter 9. The first case freezes all three elements of the CSF expenditures in nominal terms at their 1999 values (i.e. the EC subvention, the domestic public co-financing, and the domestic private co-financing). The alternative case eliminates all elements of the CSF expenditures immediately after the year 1999, i.e. all CSF-related EU subventions cease, and both domestic co-financing elements also cease. These two polar alternatives should serve to bracket the likely way in which the CSF will be gradually wound down for the existing periphery, paving the way for a transfer of structural aid to new Central and Eastern European members.

# 8.    The impact of the single market: simulation results

In this chapter we present a sequence of simulations designed to capture the effects of the impact of the single market. The simulations are carried out along the lines described in Chapter 6 above, i.e. as a sequence of shocks that explores the impacts of the different elements that make up the complete single market policy initiative. Section 8.1 reviews the nature of the sequence of shocks and describes the standardized method we use for presenting the simulation results.

To give an overview of the total impact of the single market, Section 8.2 presents the results of a simulation that incorporates all seven shocks. Section 8.3 focuses on a particularly interesting subset of the full set of shocks, namely the subset that most closely resembles those analysed in the Cecchini study for the core countries (Emerson, 1988).

Since these first two packages of shocks incorporate a complex series of different individual shocks, it is difficult to rationalize the pattern of economic responses for the different models without examining the impacts of each of the seven individual shocks in isolation. These individual shock results are presented in Section 8.4.

## 8.1.    The impact of the single market: introduction

The effects of the single market are handled by means of the following sequence of seven shocks, illustrated in a flow chart in Figure 6.2.

(a)    The first shock is to total factor productivity. This consists of a baseline 5% increase of the kind posited by Cecchini (Emerson, 1988, pp. 259–61; Catinat and Italianer, 1988), with extra increments associated with the projected increased FDI inflows that are likely to occur in Portugal and Spain. Details of the exact magnitude of the shocks for each of the four countries have been presented in Chapter 6, Table 6.5. They are implemented in the model by altering the scale parameter, 'A', in the CES production function for the manufacturing sector. There are two cases for this shock: the first ignores the productivity consequences of shifts in FDI flows for all four countries and the second includes the impact of changed FDI inflows on manufacturing productivity for Portugal and Spain, thus attributing them to an SEM effect.

(b)    The second shock involves a reduction of 6.4% in all external prices and costs. This comes from the original Cecchini study (Emerson, 1988, p. 264). Given the specification of the wage and price equations in all four models (where homogeneity is imposed), the real effects of this shock are quite modest for each model, and domestic wages, prices and costs all simply adjust to the changed world price environment.

(c)    The third shock implements a modest cut of 0.15% in public-sector employment for each country, reflecting primarily the abolition of border controls and consequential reductions in employment in the customs and excise branches of public administration.[58] In fact, this is a very minor shock and has negligible impact relative to the other shocks.

(d)    The fourth shock represents the effects of structural change on the manufacturing sector as production shifts from the non-traded to the traded goods categories, and was

---

[58]    The public employment shock is expressed as a percentage of total public employment, and is calibrated from the actual Irish changes.

described in detail in Sections 6.3.3 and 6.4 above. This shock is implemented through exogenous shifts to the behavioural coefficients in the model equations that determine manufacturing output and the price of output.

(e)     The fifth shock implements an exogenous change in manufacturing sector output, capturing static gains or losses as trade liberalization proceeds. This was described in Chapter 6, Table 6.5. There are two variations of this shock. In the first, we ignore the role of increased FDI inflows on the static gains to trade liberalization. In the second, we take into account the effects of the projected increased FDI inflows for Portugal and Spain, thus attributing them to SEM effects.

(f)     The sixth shock involves a modest exogenous cut of 1% in market services output and employment, designed to represent the rationalization of distribution channels and financial services in the periphery (see Bradley, Fitz Gerald and Kearney, 1992, pp. 28–38). There is great uncertainty about the magnitude of this shock, so we are obliged to carry out a sensitivity analysis in order to explore its consequences.

(g)     Finally, the seventh shock implements an increase in 'world' manufacturing output, superimposed on the structurally changed model (derived in shock (iv) above). We assign a value of 8% to this world output shock, which is consistent with the GDP effect within the range specified by Cecchini.[59] Basically, it represents the improvement in the EU and world economies that have been quantified by Cecchini as arising directly from the EU-wide benefits of the single market. In the context of our analysis, these EU-wide benefits are held to be pre-recursive to the periphery, i.e. the feedback effects from the periphery to the core are held to be negligible compared with the influence of the core on the periphery.

We now describe the individual effects of these seven shocks, as well as the total effect, for all four models. We also examine an intermediate case that is designed to capture the same kind of package of shocks as was analysed in the Cecchini Report for the core EU members. This intermediate case is a subset of the total package of seven shocks outlined above and, as we will see, it gives a rather incomplete picture of the SEM impacts on the cohesion countries.

We use a standardized format of table that shows the impacts on three groupings of model variables:[60]

(a)     The first grouping shows the impacts on sectoral output (manufacturing (OT), market services (ON) and total GDP at factor cost (GDPFC)). These are shown as percentage deviations from the no-SEM baseline projection for the period 1987 to 2010 inclusive. The year 1987 is the base year, and the single market shocks are phased in over a 10-year period to 1997, after which the exogenous shock is frozen at its full 1997 value.[61]

(b)     The second grouping shows the impacts on prices and wages (the deflator of GDP in manufacturing (POT), average annual earnings in manufacturing (WT), and the deflator

---

[59]    The SEM impacts on GDP estimated by Emerson, 1988 (p. 264), and Cecchini, 1988 (pp. 99-102), are consistent with a slightly higher impact on manufacturing.

[60]    A full set of simulation results is available on request.

[61]    We have imposed a common stylized phasing in pattern on all four countries, i.e. a constant incremental process over 10 years from 1988. In future work, we will seek better proxies, such as the actual implementation of the SEM directives in each country.

(c)     The third grouping shows the impacts on four measures of economic imbalance (the rate of unemployment (UR), the PSBR (GBORR) and the balance of trade (BPTR), measured as percentages of GDP or GNP, and the public debt/GDP ratio (RDEBT), also measured as a percentage of GDP). For this third set of variables, the results are shown as simple deviations from the baseline.

## 8.2.    Overall effects of the SEM

In this section, we report the overall effects of the SEM resulting from the combination of all the shocks discussed above. We characterize the SEM in terms of the totality of the above sequence of seven shocks. Thus, all the simulations are combined into one, noting, however, that the final shock (vii) already encompasses the structural change shock (iv). These are summarized in Table 8.1(a) for the case that excludes any FDI effect, and in Table 8.1(b) for the case where an additional FDI-related effect is incorporated for Portugal and Spain.

Turning first to Table 8.1(a), the case that excludes the FDI effects, it is perhaps not surprising, given the massive negative output shock with which we hit the Greek and Spanish economies (a net loss of manufacturing output of 14 and 7%, respectively, as shown in Chapter 6, Table 6.2), that Greece and Spain emerge furthest down the table in terms of GDP effects. In both cases, the reduction in GDP by 1995 is just over 1%, but this turns positive before 2010, the end of the simulation period. The effects on Ireland and Portugal are positive, rising from a boost of 5% in GDP by 1995 to just over 9% by 2010 (in the case of Ireland), and 2% rising to 7.5% (in the case of Portugal).

Turning to the disaggregated impacts on manufacturing and market services output, we see that big losses in manufacturing output are experienced by Greece and Spain, and large gains enjoyed by Ireland and Portugal. Both Greece and Spain experience deteriorations in their PSBR positions and, as a consequence, their debt/GDP ratios rise by 12 and 18 percentage points, respectively, relative to the baseline.[62] However, this only facilitates a modest rise in income transfers and market services output, resulting in net losses, or zero gains, in GDP. The net trade surplus moves in tandem with the PSBR, i.e. deteriorating in the cases of Greece and Spain, but improving in the cases of Ireland and Portugal.

Not surprisingly, Greece and Spain experience rises in their rates of unemployment of about 2 and 1 percentage points, respectively. In Ireland, the rate of unemployment falls initially by just under 1 percentage point, and in the long run, by just over 1.5 percentage points. The situation in Portugal is more dramatic, the initial fall also being just under 1 percentage point, but this becomes a fall of just over 5 percentage points in the long term. The difference in behaviour as between Ireland and Portugal can be explained by the openness of the Irish labour market and the fact that any economic improvement relative to the baseline will induce net inward migration flows, which will serve to increase the labour force, thus largely offsetting the decline in unemployment.

---

[62]     A number of the shocks reported have budgetary implications. To the extent that large government budget surpluses or deficits accumulate, this essentially entails combining an implicit fiscal policy shock with the other explicit shocks we wish to focus upon. We could correct for this by imposing a 'policy feedback rule' which attempts to stabilize the debt-to-GDP ratio.

## Table 8.1(a). Total SEM shock (no change in FDI)

| | | Greece | | | Ireland | | |
|---|---|---|---|---|---|---|---|
| | | **1995** | **2000** | **2010** | **1995** | **2000** | **2010** |
| % dif | GDPFC | -1.30 | -0.88 | 0.13 | 4.95 | 7.24 | 9.24 |
| | OT | -7.70 | -7.65 | -5.65 | 11.14 | 15.14 | 17.11 |
| | ON | 0.55 | 1.28 | 2.23 | 2.40 | 3.62 | 4.75 |
| | POT | -6.98 | -8.67 | -8.88 | -4.70 | -5.86 | -5.87 |
| | WT | -6.40 | -7.47 | -5.68 | 1.08 | 1.15 | 0.37 |
| | PC | -5.66 | -7.14 | -6.48 | -2.82 | -3.71 | -4.39 |

| | | Greece | | | Ireland | | |
|---|---|---|---|---|---|---|---|
| Dif | UR | 2.00 | 2.04 | 1.60 | -1.43 | -1.55 | -1.23 |
| | GBORR | 0.57 | 0.76 | 0.74 | -0.88 | -1.45 | -2.09 |
| | BPTR | -0.29 | -0.38 | -0.24 | 0.91 | 1.30 | 1.61 |
| | RDEBT | 8.47 | 11.61 | 12.28 | -5.51 | -11.06 | -21.62 |

| | | Portugal | | | Spain | | |
|---|---|---|---|---|---|---|---|
| | | **1995** | **2000** | **2010** | **1995** | **2000** | **2010** |
| % dif | GDPFC | 2.23 | 4.29 | 7.54 | -1.01 | -0.74 | 0.06 |
| | OT | 5.70 | 10.43 | 16.77 | -3.23 | -3.11 | -1.63 |
| | ON | 1.83 | 3.67 | 6.91 | -0.37 | 0.09 | 0.87 |
| | POT | -3.54 | -2.45 | 0.96 | -7.57 | -8.93 | -8.60 |
| | WT | -0.59 | 5.00 | 18.01 | -5.92 | -6.75 | -6.24 |
| | PC | -2.92 | -0.93 | 4.67 | -5.80 | -7.10 | -6.70 |

| | | Portugal | | | Spain | | |
|---|---|---|---|---|---|---|---|
| Dif | UR | -0.95 | -2.34 | -5.03 | 1.04 | 1.07 | 0.72 |
| | GBORR | -0.18 | -0.28 | -0.16 | 0.79 | 1.13 | 1.07 |
| | BPTR | 0.38 | 0.70 | 0.66 | -0.34 | -0.42 | -0.10 |
| | RDEBT | -0.43 | -1.97 | -0.55 | 7.08 | 12.48 | 17.92 |

*Legend*
| | |
|---|---|
| GDPFC | Gross domestic product at factor cost (real) |
| OT | GDP in manufacturing (real) |
| ON | GDP in market services (real) |
| POT | Deflator of GDP in manufacturing |
| WT | Average annual earnings in manufacturing |
| PC | Deflator of private consumption |
| UR | Unemployment rate |
| GBORR | Public sector borrowing requirement (% of GDP) |
| BPTR | Net trade surplus (% of GDP) |
| RDEBT | National debt (% of GDP) |

The impact of the SEM on price determination in the manufacturing sector (POT) is dominated initially by the imposed cuts in world prices and costs (shock (ii)). In all cases except Portugal, these price reductions endure into the long run. The case of Portugal is complicated because it experiences a significant increase in the level of wages (WT) that does not occur in any of the other country models. This effect operates mainly through the Phillips curve and, unlike Ireland, the permanent fall in the unemployment rate continues to exert upward pressure on wages into the long term. Both Greece and Ireland have somewhat similar Phillips curve semi-elasticities (see Chapter 5). However, the rise in Greek unemployment serves to depress wage levels relative to the baseline, and the upward pressure on wage levels in Ireland is diluted rapidly because of inward migration and the consequential high elasticity of labour supply.

Turning next to Table 8.1(b), here we attribute the increased FDI flows apparent in the data for Portugal and Spain to the SEM. Given the dramatic increase in inflows into Spain (documented in Chapter 6, Table 6.4), the overall SEM effect is substantially improved. Thus, in the long run the impact on Spanish GDP rises from 0.1% to 9.2%, while the impact on Portugal rises more modestly from 7.5% to 11.5%.

## Table 8.1(b).  Total SEM shock (increased FDI inflows in Portugal and Spain)

| | | Greece | | | | Ireland | | |
|---|---|---|---|---|---|---|---|---|
| | | 1995 | 2000 | 2010 | | 1995 | 2000 | 2010 |
| % dif | GDPFC | -1.30 | -0.88 | 0.13 | | 4.95 | 7.24 | 9.24 |
| | OT | -7.70 | -7.65 | -5.65 | | 11.14 | 15.14 | 17.11 |
| | ON | 0.55 | 1.28 | 2.23 | | 2.40 | 3.62 | 4.75 |
| | POT | -6.98 | -8.67 | -8.88 | | -4.70 | -5.86 | -5.87 |
| | WT | -6.40 | -7.47 | -5.68 | | 1.08 | 1.15 | 0.37 |
| | PC | -5.66 | -7.14 | -6.48 | | -2.82 | -3.71 | -4.39 |

| | | | | | | | | |
|---|---|---|---|---|---|---|---|---|
| Dif | UR | 2.00 | 2.04 | 1.60 | | -1.43 | -1.55 | -1.23 |
| | GBORR | 0.57 | 0.76 | 0.74 | | -0.88 | -1.45 | -2.09 |
| | BPTR | -0.29 | -0.38 | -0.24 | | 0.91 | 1.30 | 1.61 |
| | RDEBT | 8.47 | 11.61 | 12.28 | | -5.51 | -11.06 | -21.62 |

| | | Portugal | | | | Spain | | |
|---|---|---|---|---|---|---|---|---|
| | | 1995 | 2000 | 2010 | | 1995 | 2000 | 2010 |
| % dif | GDPFC | 3.81 | 6.90 | 11.47 | | 4.75 | 7.13 | 9.16 |
| | OT | 10.49 | 17.64 | 26.26 | | 12.71 | 18.18 | 22.01 |
| | ON | 2.63 | 5.29 | 9.96 | | 2.95 | 4.59 | 6.07 |
| | POT | -2.36 | -0.43 | 4.12 | | -7.96 | -8.99 | -8.33 |
| | WT | 3.70 | 13.15 | 32.93 | | -2.25 | -1.59 | -0.31 |
| | PC | -0.90 | 2.64 | 10.63 | | -4.03 | -4.22 | -3.44 |

| | | | | | | | | |
|---|---|---|---|---|---|---|---|---|
| Dif | UR | -1.88 | -3.97 | -7.73 | | -1.17 | -1.98 | -3.00 |
| | GBORR | -0.30 | -0.42 | -0.23 | | -0.77 | -1.61 | -2.77 |
| | BPTR | 0.82 | 1.18 | 0.86 | | 1.04 | 1.48 | 1.87 |
| | RDEBT | -2.06 | -4.08 | -1.55 | | -2.93 | -10.07 | -28.15 |

*Legend*
| | |
|---|---|
| GDPFC | Gross domestic product at factor cost (real) |
| OT | GDP in manufacturing (real) |
| ON | GDP in market services (real) |
| POT | Deflator of GDP in manufacturing |
| WT | Average annual earnings in manufacturing |
| PC | Deflator of private consumption |
| UR | Unemployment rate |
| GBORR | Public sector borrowing requirement (% of GDP) |
| BPTR | Net trade surplus (% of GDP) |
| RDEBT | National debt (% of GDP) |

## 8.3.  The 'Cecchini' single market shock

In the results reported above, we have included a number of channels over and above those taken into account in the original Cecchini analysis of Emerson *et al.*, 1988. In this section we compare our overall results (reported above) to those that would have emerged had we focused exclusively on the channels identified by Cecchini. The numerical simulation results are presented in Table 8.2. These channels are a subset of shocks (i) to (vii), and are as follows:

(a)   the *ex ante* flat rate increase in manufacturing productivity of 5% (shock (i) with no FDI effects);

(b)   the world price and cost reductions (shock (ii));

(c)   the modest reduction in public sector employment (shock (iii));
(d)   the reduction in output of market services (shock (vi));
(e)   the increase in world manufacturing output in the context of an unchanged model structure (i.e. shock (vii) with unchanged output and price elasticities).

From Table 8.2, we see that the impact on GDP is quite similar for each country, with Ireland leading slightly and Spain lagging slightly behind. Spain does relatively poorly because as the least open economy it benefits least from the SEM-generated expansion of world manufacturing. Ireland gains most, as we will show below, because of the competitiveness effect of the reduction in unit labour costs generated by the productivity increase in shock (i).

**Table 8.2.     Original 'Cecchini' effects for the periphery**

| | | Greece | | | Ireland | | |
|---|---|---|---|---|---|---|---|
| | | 1995 | 2000 | 2010 | 1995 | 2000 | 2010 |
| % dif | GDPFC | 1.70 | 2.48 | 3.04 | 1.87 | 2.64 | 3.21 |
| | OT | 1.87 | 2.38 | 2.44 | 3.84 | 4.89 | 5.06 |
| | ON | 2.75 | 3.97 | 4.65 | 1.23 | 1.89 | 2.58 |
| | POT | -3.67 | -4.10 | -3.59 | -5.23 | -6.48 | -6.49 |
| | WT | 4.04 | 6.86 | 8.74 | -1.74 | -2.11 | -2.18 |
| | PC | -1.13 | -0.42 | 0.47 | -3.80 | -4.76 | -4.88 |

| Dif | UR | -0.45 | -0.77 | -1.12 | -0.30 | -0.37 | -0.35 |
|---|---|---|---|---|---|---|---|
| | GBORR | 0.26 | 0.23 | 0.28 | -0.28 | -0.47 | -0.72 |
| | BPTR | -0.29 | -0.33 | -0.33 | 0.42 | 0.51 | 0.52 |
| | RDEBT | -0.78 | -1.59 | -0.14 | 0.34 | -1.58 | -6.18 |

| | | Portugal | | | Spain | | |
|---|---|---|---|---|---|---|---|
| | | 1995 | 2000 | 2010 | 1995 | 2000 | 2010 |
| % dif | GDPFC | 1.80 | 2.55 | 2.96 | 1.02 | 1.55 | 1.87 |
| | OT | 4.33 | 5.60 | 5.72 | 2.32 | 3.05 | 3.11 |
| | ON | 1.67 | 2.59 | 3.40 | 0.82 | 1.41 | 1.89 |
| | POT | -5.55 | -6.47 | -5.90 | -7.26 | -8.92 | -8.83 |
| | WT | -2.33 | -1.75 | -0.16 | -5.07 | -6.15 | -5.98 |
| | PC | -4.06 | -4.50 | -3.73 | -5.27 | -6.79 | -6.68 |

| Dif | UR | -0.60 | -0.96 | -1.31 | 0.01 | -0.10 | -0.24 |
|---|---|---|---|---|---|---|---|
| | GBORR | -0.13 | -0.21 | -0.27 | 0.09 | 0.17 | 0.04 |
| | BPTR | 0.09 | 0.18 | 0.23 | 0.16 | 0.12 | 0.30 |
| | RDEBT | 0.09 | -0.83 | -2.16 | 2.74 | 4.28 | 4.30 |

*Legend*
GDPFC          Gross domestic product at factor cost (real)
OT             GDP in manufacturing (real)
ON             GDP in market services (real)
POT            Deflator of GDP in manufacturing
WT             Average annual earnings in manufacturing
PC             Deflator of private consumption
UR             Unemployment rate
GBORR          Public sector borrowing requirement (% of GDP)
BPTR           Net trade surplus (% of GDP)
RDEBT          National debt (% of GDP)

As we will discuss later in our concluding Chapter 10, none of these GDP effects are as large as those predicted by the Cecchini Report for the core countries (i.e. all fall below the average impact of 4.5% in Emerson, 1988, Table B.5, p. 264).[63] Thus, in the absence of the additional channels which we have identified in Chapter 6, all the cohesion countries would have appeared to lose out relative to the core countries. The truth is likely to be more complex, as comparison of Tables 8.1 and 8.2 indicates.

## 8.4.   Decomposing the single market shocks

### 8.4.1.   Total factor productivity (shock (i))

The *ex ante* total factor productivity shock in manufacturing implemented for each country involves two different cases. The first, shown in Table 8.3(a), involves a baseline increase of 5% where no FDI effect is present (Greece and Ireland) or where the factor productivity implications of the FDI effect are ignored, i.e. not attributed to the SEM (Portugal and Spain). The second, shown in Table 8.3(b), involves a productivity shock for Portugal (6.9%) and Spain (12.0%) that is higher than the baseline shock, but involves only the baseline 5% shock for Greece and Ireland. In this second case, the effect of increased FDI inflows into the Iberian Peninsula are taken into account *and* attributed to the single market.

Some of the main qualitative effects of the productivity shock are likely to be as follows. For fixed manufacturing output, a rise in productivity will cause labour to be shed and unemployment to rise. But higher labour productivity will be associated with lower unit labour costs, increased international cost competitiveness, higher output and a rise in labour demand. To a limited extent, these two effects serve to offset each other.

Productivity shocks will also affect output pricing and wage bargaining. The more open the economy, the higher will be the extent of price taking, with a corresponding lower element of mark-up pricing. Thus, the Spanish model has a relatively high weight of 0.6 on unit labour costs, capturing the less open nature of the economy. At the other extreme, the Irish model has a weight of only 0.2 on unit labour costs, consistent with the very open nature of Irish manufacturing.

Higher productivity is also passed through to higher wage rates to some extent in all four models. At one extreme, all productivity is passed through to wages in Greece; about three quarters is passed through in Ireland; two thirds in Spain and only one third in Portugal. Consequently, we would expect the wage inflationary effects to be highest in Greece and lowest in Portugal, *ceteris paribus*. Of course, the Phillips curve parameter will heavily influence the actual outturn. We saw in Chapter 5 that Spain had a very low semi-elasticity of wages with respect to the unemployment rate, while all the other models had higher values.[64]

---

[63]   It should be noted that the Bradley *et al.* 1992 study of the impact of the single market on Ireland produced a result that was in line with the Cecchini estimates for the core countries. However, the characterization of the manufacturing sector in the version of the HERMES model used to carry out the simulations was one of total tradability, which served to exaggerate the impact of world growth.

[64]   Note that the Irish labour market is the only one modelled as being open, with a very elastic labour supply because of international migration flows.

We turn first to Table 8.3(a), the case of an *ex ante* flat 5% rise in total factor productivity in manufacturing. There are modest rises in real GDP in all cases, the strongest effect being in Ireland (about 0.5% in the long term), with lowest effects in Spain (about 0.25 in the long term). In all cases, the unemployment rate rises over the long term as labour is shed. In the Irish case, the unemployment rate converges to its baseline value as migration flows restore the baseline equilibrium situation. Manufacturing output increases in all models, the rise being smallest in the case of Greece (0.5% in the long term) and highest in the case of Portugal (1.5% in the long term).

Turning to wage and price effects, the shock results in significant wage and price deflation in Portugal (with reductions of between 2 and 3% in the long term). There are many reasons for this behaviour. First, the econometric results indicated that very little of the productivity increase feeds through to wages in Portugal. Second, wage bargaining in Portugal is characterized by a large Phillips curve effect, and has no migration mechanisms to dilute this effect over time (in contrast to the Irish case). Third, the weight attached to mark-up pricing in manufacturing is in the intermediate range of 0.4, above Ireland and Greece but below Spain.

The situation in Portugal contrasts strongly with the wage inflationary impact on Greece, where all productivity rises feed through to wages, but where prices are somewhat more anchored to world prices. Ireland and Spain are intermediate cases, where the almost complete absence of any Spanish Phillips curve effect influences the outturn.[65]

The consequences for movements in real unit labour costs (i.e. nominal unit labour costs deflated by the price of manufacturing output) differ between the four models. The results are summarized in Table 8.3(c). The largest reduction is for Portugal, where increased productivity reduces unit labour costs directly, since it does not feed through to wage demands. In Greece, the effect is essentially zero since all the increased productivity feeds through to wage demands, and Ireland and Spain are intermediate cases.

Turning now to Table 8.3(b), we see the effects of attributing the higher FDI inflows for Portugal and Spain to the SEM effect. The impact on real GDP increases by about one third in Portugal and more than doubles in Spain, relative to the flat 5% productivity shock. Basically this is due to the larger FDI inflow in Spain relative to Portugal. Note, however, that there is a deterioration in the public finances in Spain, with a rise in the debt/GDP ratio of over 8%. This comes about because the wage deflationary impacts on Portugal serve to reduce the public sector wage bill, which is a huge element in total public expenditure. No such wage deflation occurs in Spain, for reasons explained above.

---

[65]   Labour market closure can be forced by increasing the Phillips curve parameter in the wage bargaining equation. Although such behaviour seems inconsistent with past data, it might very well be consistent with the future policy imperatives of Spain's adjustment to the SEM.

## Table 8.3(a).  Labour productivity shock in manufacturing (no change in FDI)

| | | Greece | | | Ireland | | |
|---|---|---|---|---|---|---|---|
| | | **1995** | **2000** | **2010** | **1995** | **2000** | **2010** |
| % dif | GDPFC | 0.22 | 0.33 | 0.35 | 0.33 | 0.43 | 0.48 |
| | OT | 0.27 | 0.42 | 0.53 | 0.73 | 0.87 | 0.79 |
| | ON | 0.34 | 0.48 | 0.44 | 0.16 | 0.24 | 0.33 |
| | POT | 0.18 | 0.23 | 0.06 | -0.35 | -0.45 | -0.37 |
| | WT | 4.71 | 5.92 | 5.30 | 1.96 | 2.69 | 3.12 |
| | PC | 2.05 | 2.70 | 2.43 | 0.71 | 1.02 | 1.21 |

| | | | | | | | |
|---|---|---|---|---|---|---|---|
| Dif | UR | 0.61 | 0.77 | 0.89 | 0.33 | 0.29 | 0.15 |
| | GBORR | 0.17 | 0.19 | 0.27 | 0.22 | 0.26 | 0.28 |
| | BPTR | -0.05 | -0.06 | -0.06 | 0.08 | 0.10 | 0.05 |
| | RDEBT | -1.66 | -1.39 | 1.34 | -0.17 | 0.68 | 2.41 |

| | | Portugal | | | Spain | | |
|---|---|---|---|---|---|---|---|
| | | **1995** | **2000** | **2010** | **1995** | **2000** | **2010** |
| % dif | GDPFC | 0.29 | 0.34 | 0.30 | 0.17 | 0.27 | 0.27 |
| | OT | 1.27 | 1.58 | 1.51 | 0.80 | 1.01 | 1.01 |
| | ON | -0.11 | -0.22 | -0.36 | 0.01 | 0.04 | 0.02 |
| | POT | -2.31 | -3.02 | -3.21 | -2.53 | -3.16 | -3.20 |
| | WT | -2.12 | -3.02 | -3.56 | -0.43 | -0.55 | -0.61 |
| | PC | -1.32 | -1.84 | -2.13 | -0.78 | -1.03 | -1.10 |

| | | | | | | | |
|---|---|---|---|---|---|---|---|
| Dif | UR | 0.60 | 0.80 | 0.93 | 0.41 | 0.52 | 0.57 |
| | GBORR | -0.05 | -0.10 | -0.16 | 0.16 | 0.22 | 0.27 |
| | BPTR | 0.17 | 0.28 | 0.36 | 0.08 | 0.09 | 0.09 |
| | RDEBT | 0.27 | -0.11 | -1.26 | 1.02 | 2.01 | 3.65 |

*Legend*
GDPFC          Gross domestic product at factor cost (real)
OT             GDP in manufacturing (real)
ON             GDP in market services (real)
POT            Deflator of GDP in manufacturing
WT             Average annual earnings in manufacturing
PC             Deflator of private consumption
UR             Unemployment rate
GBORR          Public sector borrowing requirement (% of GDP)
BPTR           Net trade surplus (% of GDP)
RDEBT          National debt (% of GDP)

**Table 8.3(b).  Labour productivity shock in manufacturing (increased FDI inflows in Portugal and Spain)**

| | | Greece | | |
|---|---|---|---|---|
| | | 1995 | 2000 | 2010 |
| % dif | GDPFC | 0.22 | 0.33 | 0.35 |
| | OT | 0.27 | 0.42 | 0.53 |
| | ON | 0.34 | 0.48 | 0.44 |
| | POT | 0.18 | 0.23 | 0.06 |
| | WT | 4.71 | 5.92 | 5.30 |
| | PC | 2.05 | 2.70 | 2.43 |

| | | | | |
|---|---|---|---|---|
| Dif | UR | 0.61 | 0.77 | 0.89 |
| | GBORR | 0.17 | 0.19 | 0.27 |
| | BPTR | -0.05 | -0.06 | -0.06 |
| | RDEBT | -1.66 | -1.39 | 1.34 |

| Ireland | | |
|---|---|---|
| 1995 | 2000 | 2010 |
| 0.33 | 0.43 | 0.48 |
| 0.73 | 0.87 | 0.79 |
| 0.16 | 0.24 | 0.33 |
| -0.35 | -0.45 | -0.37 |
| 1.96 | 2.69 | 3.12 |
| 0.71 | 1.02 | 1.21 |

| | | |
|---|---|---|
| 0.33 | 0.29 | 0.15 |
| 0.22 | 0.26 | 0.28 |
| 0.08 | 0.10 | 0.05 |
| -0.17 | 0.68 | 2.41 |

| | | Portugal | | |
|---|---|---|---|---|
| | | 1995 | 2000 | 2010 |
| % dif | GDPFC | 0.39 | 0.47 | 0.41 |
| | OT | 1.73 | 2.14 | 2.05 |
| | ON | -0.15 | -0.29 | -0.48 |
| | POT | -3.11 | -4.05 | -4.31 |
| | WT | -2.83 | -4.04 | -4.74 |
| | PC | -1.78 | -2.47 | -2.84 |

| | | | | |
|---|---|---|---|---|
| Dif | UR | 0.81 | 1.08 | 1.25 |
| | GBORR | -0.07 | -0.14 | -0.21 |
| | BPTR | 0.22 | 0.38 | 0.49 |
| | RDEBT | 0.36 | -0.15 | -1.70 |

| Spain | | |
|---|---|---|
| 1995 | 2000 | 2010 |
| 0.46 | 0.63 | 0.64 |
| 1.83 | 2.34 | 2.33 |
| 0.04 | 0.10 | 0.06 |
| -5.65 | -7.03 | -7.11 |
| -0.95 | -1.21 | -1.35 |
| -1.75 | -2.29 | -2.45 |

| | | |
|---|---|---|
| 0.91 | 1.16 | 1.26 |
| 0.35 | 0.48 | 0.61 |
| 0.18 | 0.19 | 0.20 |
| 2.29 | 4.51 | 8.14 |

*Legend*
| | |
|---|---|
| GDPFC | Gross domestic product at factor cost (real) |
| OT | GDP in manufacturing (real) |
| ON | GDP in market services (real) |
| POT | Deflator of GDP in manufacturing |
| WT | Average annual earnings in manufacturing |
| PC | Deflator of private consumption |
| UR | Unemployment rate |
| GBORR | Public sector borrowing requirement (% of GDP) |
| BPTR | Net trade surplus (% of GDP) |
| RDEBT | National debt (% of GDP) |

**Table 8.3(c).  Labour productivity shock in manufacturing (percentage change in real unit labour costs from baseline)**

| | Shock i(a) (no FDI) | | |
|---|---|---|---|
| | 1995 | 2000 | 2010 |
| Greece | 0.42 | 0.53 | 0.13 |
| Ireland | -1.57 | -1.78 | -1.46 |
| Portugal | -3.70 | -4.82 | -5.14 |
| Spain | -1.77 | -2.22 | -2.24 |

| Shock i(b) (with FDI) | | |
|---|---|---|
| 1995 | 2000 | 2010 |
| 0.42 | 0.53 | 0.13 |
| -1.57 | -1.78 | -1.46 |
| -4.96 | -6.45 | -6.86 |
| -3.98 | -4.96 | -5.02 |

## 8.4.2.  External price and public-sector employment (shocks (ii) and (iii))

Given that all the models are largely homogeneous with respect to transmission of price effects, it comes as no surprise that the price shock has relatively minor real effects, as Table 8.4 reveals. There are, of course, real effects, which, in the case of Portugal, give rise to an increase in GDP of almost 0.5% in the long run. However, this arises mainly due to differences in the way price indexation of policy instruments is handled in the public sector. For example, current public expenditure is indexed mainly to wage inflation, but capital expenditure is fixed in nominal terms. Most elements of tax revenue are indexed to prices, usually consumer prices. In the cases of Greece and Spain, these effects result in a long-term build-up of public debt of between 7 and 8 percentage points of GDP.

The effects of the very small cut in public-sector employment are also relatively insignificant and are not shown in a separate table.

**Table 8.4.    Reductions in 'world' prices and costs (Cecchini)**

|       |       | Greece | | | Ireland | | |
|-------|-------|------|------|------|------|------|------|
|       |       | 1995 | 2000 | 2010 | 1995 | 2000 | 2010 |
| % dif | GDPFC | 0.24 | 0.25 | 0.17 | 0.06 | 0.07 | 0.05 |
|       | OT    | 0.05 | 0.07 | 0.05 | 0.00 | 0.01 | 0.02 |
|       | ON    | 0.46 | 0.45 | 0.28 | 0.14 | 0.15 | 0.10 |
|       | POT   | -4.90 | -6.16 | -6.23 | -5.13 | -6.38 | -6.39 |
|       | WT    | -4.30 | -5.60 | -5.83 | -5.05 | -6.30 | -6.38 |
|       | PC    | -4.68 | -6.02 | -6.13 | -5.02 | -6.35 | -6.38 |

| Dif | UR    | -0.16 | -0.17 | -0.12 | -0.04 | -0.04 | -0.01 |
|-----|-------|------|------|------|------|------|------|
|     | GBORR | 0.25 | 0.37 | 0.41 | -0.17 | -0.17 | -0.21 |
|     | BPTR  | -0.27 | -0.32 | -0.22 | 0.08 | 0.02 | -0.01 |
|     | RDEBT | 4.56 | 6.72 | 7.96 | 3.82 | 3.18 | 0.34 |

|       |       | Portugal | | | Spain | | |
|-------|-------|------|------|------|------|------|------|
|       |       | 1995 | 2000 | 2010 | 1995 | 2000 | 2010 |
| % dif | GDPFC | 0.49 | 0.60 | 0.48 | 0.28 | 0.45 | 0.33 |
|       | OT    | 0.55 | 0.70 | 0.57 | 0.18 | 0.32 | 0.24 |
|       | ON    | 0.82 | 1.01 | 0.81 | 0.40 | 0.64 | 0.46 |
|       | POT   | -4.62 | -5.68 | -5.78 | -5.03 | -6.24 | -6.28 |
|       | WT    | -3.68 | -4.41 | -4.71 | -4.96 | -6.13 | -6.19 |
|       | PC    | -4.50 | -5.51 | -5.63 | -4.71 | -6.18 | -6.23 |

| Dif | UR    | -0.39 | -0.49 | -0.42 | -0.15 | -0.22 | -0.17 |
|-----|-------|------|------|------|------|------|------|
|     | GBORR | 0.03 | 0.01 | -0.01 | 0.10 | 0.30 | 0.39 |
|     | BPTR  | -0.37 | -0.45 | -0.36 | -0.06 | -0.20 | -0.15 |
|     | RDEBT | 1.25 | 1.22 | 0.67 | 2.71 | 4.87 | 7.38 |

*Legend*
GDPFC    Gross domestic product at factor cost (real)
OT       GDP in manufacturing (real)
ON       GDP in market services (real)
POT      Deflator of GDP in manufacturing
WT       Average annual earnings in manufacturing
PC       Deflator of private consumption
UR       Unemployment rate
GBORR    Public sector borrowing requirement (% of GDP)
BPTR     Net trade surplus (% of GDP)
RDEBT    National debt (% of GDP)

### 8.4.3.  Structural change (shock (iv))

In these shocks changes are made to parameters in the output and pricing equations of the manufacturing sector, but no other changes are made to exogenous variables relative to the benchmark. In Chapter 6 we explained the methodological rationale for this shock, and in Table 6.6 we gave the data needed to calculate the values of the shifts to the parameters. Thus, in the case where FDI effects are ignored, there will be shifts of varying magnitude in the four countries. In Greece, about 14% of manufacturing is likely to shift from non-tradable to tradable. Portugal is similar at 13%, with Spain at 9%. Ireland, being the most open and having experienced a much earlier transition to free trade, is likely to have a shift of only 6% from non-tradable to tradable. In the cases of Portugal and Spain, the magnitude of these shifts increase, to 16 and 18% respectively, when the likely increases in FDI inflows are attributed to the SEM effect (see Table 6.6).

Having made the necessary changes to the behavioural coefficients in the manufacturing output and price equations (see Section 6.4 for details), Tables 8.5(a) and (b) give the simulation results for the no-FDI and with-FDI cases.

In all cases there are positive impacts on real GDP. These are greatest for Portugal, where even in the no-FDI case (Table 8.5(a)), real GDP rises by almost 5.5% in the long term. However, this is accompanied by upward pressure on wage and price levels. In the long term, nominal wage levels increase by almost a quarter relative to benchmark levels, and real wage levels increase by some 12%, mainly due to a falling rate of unemployment (down by over 4.5 percentage points in the long term) in conjunction with a relatively strong Phillips curve effect in the wage bargaining equation.

Although the shock which is administered to the Greek model is of the same size as that applied to Portugal, its effects are much smaller. This is because the Greek economy is less influenced by world growth than is the Portuguese economy to begin with, and so the equiproportionate increase in the elasticity with respect to world output implies an absolute increase of smaller magnitude.[66]

The effects of including the projected increase in FDI inflows for Portugal and Spain are to increase further the already large boost to the Portuguese economy and to double the positive, but more modest, boost to the Spanish economy (Table 8.5(a)).

---

[66]     Thus, the elasticity of manufactured output (OT) with respect to world output (OW) is 0.25 for Greece and 0.37 for Portugal. The absolute shifts in these elasticities are 0.105 for Greece and 0.145 for Portugal.

## Table 8.5(a). Shift to greater proportion of tradables in manufacturing (no change in FDI)

| | | Greece | | | Ireland | | |
|---|---|---|---|---|---|---|---|
| | | 1995 | 2000 | 2010 | 1995 | 2000 | 2010 |
| % dif | GDPFC | 0.39 | 0.98 | 1.68 | 0.28 | 0.64 | 1.32 |
| | OT | 1.27 | 3.18 | 5.02 | 0.65 | 1.41 | 2.60 |
| | ON | 0.28 | 0.67 | 1.27 | 0.11 | 0.26 | 0.51 |
| | POT | -0.33 | -0.22 | 0.02 | 0.13 | 0.23 | 0.40 |
| | WT | 1.28 | 3.54 | 7.69 | 0.35 | 0.69 | 1.05 |
| | PC | 0.47 | 1.39 | 3.29 | 0.15 | 0.28 | 0.38 |

| | | Greece | | | Ireland | | |
|---|---|---|---|---|---|---|---|
| Dif | UR | -0.33 | -0.86 | -1.65 | -0.12 | -0.22 | -0.30 |
| | GBORR | -0.01 | -0.03 | -0.04 | -0.05 | -0.14 | -0.31 |
| | BPTR | -0.06 | -0.11 | -0.27 | 0.05 | 0.11 | 0.25 |
| | RDEBT | -0.95 | -2.58 | -4.36 | -0.55 | -1.30 | -3.08 |

| | | Portugal | | | Spain | | |
|---|---|---|---|---|---|---|---|
| | | 1995 | 2000 | 2010 | 1995 | 2000 | 2010 |
| % dif | GDPFC | 1.09 | 2.57 | 5.48 | 0.36 | 0.77 | 1.42 |
| | OT | 3.26 | 6.98 | 13.16 | 0.97 | 2.02 | 3.59 |
| | ON | 0.57 | 1.66 | 4.26 | 0.21 | 0.47 | 0.86 |
| | POT | 2.85 | 5.32 | 8.70 | -0.06 | 0.22 | 0.59 |
| | WT | 4.22 | 10.34 | 22.94 | 0.04 | 0.44 | 1.03 |
| | PC | 2.36 | 5.34 | 10.82 | -0.03 | 0.27 | 0.70 |

| | | Portugal | | | Spain | | |
|---|---|---|---|---|---|---|---|
| Dif | UR | -0.89 | -2.10 | -4.61 | -0.19 | -0.40 | -0.78 |
| | GBORR | -0.10 | -0.12 | 0.07 | -0.09 | -0.26 | -0.60 |
| | BPTR | 0.43 | 0.63 | 0.44 | 0.07 | 0.16 | 0.29 |
| | RDEBT | -1.36 | -2.09 | 0.75 | -0.41 | -1.80 | -6.04 |

*Legend*

| | |
|---|---|
| GDPFC | Gross domestic product at factor cost (real) |
| OT | GDP in manufacturing (real) |
| ON | GDP in market services (real) |
| POT | Deflator of GDP in manufacturing |
| WT | Average annual earnings in manufacturing |
| PC | Deflator of private consumption |
| UR | Unemployment rate |
| GBORR | Public sector borrowing requirement (% of GDP) |
| BPTR | Net trade surplus (% of GDP) |
| RDEBT | National debt (% of GDP) |

### 8.4.4. Tradable sector output (shock (v))

This shock is implemented in the models as an exogenous change to manufacturing output, and is designed to capture the static gains or losses to trade liberalization. The actual magnitudes of the exogenous changes involved were shown in Table 6.5. We see that the impact on Greece, Portugal and Spain are negative when the increased FDI inflows are ignored. However, it becomes positive for Portugal and Spain when the benefits of FDI effects are taken into account.[67] Thus, in the case of Spain, an *ex ante* fall of 7% in manufacturing output is transformed into an *ex ante* rise of 7% if FDI inflows are taken into account.

---

[67] Barry (1996) shows that the adverse effects highlighted in the Krugman-Venables analysis have shown up in Ireland for indigenous industry, but these effects have been dominated by the increased inflows of foreign direct investment. A similar process seems to be operating in the present case in the Iberian Peninsula, but not in Greece.

**Table 8.5(b). Shift to greater proportion of tradables in manufacturing (increased FDI inflows in Portugal and Spain)**

|  |  | Greece | | | Ireland | | |
|---|---|---|---|---|---|---|---|
|  |  | 1995 | 2000 | 2010 | 1995 | 2000 | 2010 |
| % dif | GDPFC | 0.39 | 0.98 | 1.68 | 0.28 | 0.64 | 1.32 |
|  | OT | 1.27 | 3.18 | 5.02 | 0.65 | 1.41 | 2.60 |
|  | ON | 0.28 | 0.67 | 1.27 | 0.11 | 0.26 | 0.51 |
|  | POT | -0.33 | -0.22 | 0.02 | 0.13 | 0.23 | 0.40 |
|  | WT | 1.28 | 3.54 | 7.69 | 0.35 | 0.69 | 1.05 |
|  | PC | 0.47 | 1.39 | 3.29 | 0.15 | 0.28 | 0.38 |

|  |  | Greece | | | Ireland | | |
|---|---|---|---|---|---|---|---|
| Dif | UR | -0.33 | -0.86 | -1.65 | -0.12 | -0.22 | -0.30 |
|  | GBORR | -0.01 | -0.03 | -0.04 | -0.05 | -0.14 | -0.31 |
|  | BPTR | -0.06 | -0.11 | -0.27 | 0.05 | 0.11 | 0.25 |
|  | RDEBT | -0.95 | -2.58 | -4.36 | -0.55 | -1.30 | -3.08 |

|  |  | Portugal | | | Spain | | |
|---|---|---|---|---|---|---|---|
|  |  | 1995 | 2000 | 2010 | 1995 | 2000 | 2010 |
| % dif | GDPFC | 1.34 | 3.18 | 6.83 | 0.71 | 1.53 | 2.86 |
|  | OT | 4.02 | 8.62 | 16.34 | 1.92 | 4.03 | 7.24 |
|  | ON | 0.70 | 2.07 | 5.38 | 0.42 | 0.93 | 1.72 |
|  | POT | 3.44 | 6.35 | 10.36 | -0.13 | 0.33 | 0.93 |
|  | WT | 5.19 | 12.84 | 29.09 | 0.07 | 0.77 | 1.80 |
|  | PC | 2.89 | 6.55 | 13.43 | -0.06 | 0.45 | 1.19 |

|  |  | Portugal | | | Spain | | |
|---|---|---|---|---|---|---|---|
| Dif | UR | -1.10 | -2.60 | -5.75 | -0.37 | -0.80 | -1.56 |
|  | GBORR | -0.11 | -0.14 | 0.10 | -0.18 | -0.51 | -1.17 |
|  | BPTR | 0.52 | 0.74 | 0.45 | 0.14 | 0.32 | 0.57 |
|  | RDEBT | -1.65 | -2.50 | 1.12 | -0.81 | -3.49 | -11.65 |

| *Legend* | |
|---|---|
| GDPFC | Gross domestic product at factor cost (real) |
| OT | GDP in manufacturing (real) |
| ON | GDP in market services (real) |
| POT | Deflator of GDP in manufacturing |
| WT | Average annual earnings in manufacturing |
| PC | Deflator of private consumption |
| UR | Unemployment rate |
| GBORR | Public sector borrowing requirement (% of GDP) |
| BPTR | Net trade surplus (% of GDP) |
| RDEBT | National debt (% of GDP) |

The simulation results are shown in Table 8.6(a) for the no-FDI case, and in Table 8.6(b) for the case where FDI effects are included for Portugal and Spain. The results are rather straightforward in the light of the magnitude of the shocks imposed that were shown in Table 6.5. In the no-FDI case (Table 8.6(a)), Greece fares worst, followed by Spain and Portugal, while Ireland improves. Taking the Portuguese and Spanish FDI inflows into account, Spain improves considerably while Portugal experiences a more moderate improvement.

Other things being equal, these effects have fiscal consequences. Thus, the impact on the debt/GDP ratio in each case is inversely related to the impact on the real economy. Consequently, the Greek fiscal position deteriorates while the Irish one improves.

## Table 8.6(a).  Shock to manufacturing output (no change in FDI)

| | | Greece | | | Ireland | | |
|---|---|---|---|---|---|---|---|
| | | 1995 | 2000 | 2010 | 1995 | 2000 | 2010 |
| % dif | GDPFC | -3.45 | -4.33 | -4.46 | 2.61 | 3.60 | 4.21 |
| | OT | -11.14 | -13.55 | -13.33 | 6.19 | 8.02 | 8.44 |
| | ON | -2.45 | -3.21 | -3.38 | 1.00 | 1.33 | 1.47 |
| | POT | -3.52 | -5.19 | -6.09 | 0.49 | 0.51 | 0.30 |
| | WT | -11.50 | -16.60 | -19.21 | 2.50 | 2.58 | 1.51 |
| | PC | -5.12 | -7.98 | -9.52 | 0.91 | 0.88 | 0.20 |

| | | | | | | | |
|---|---|---|---|---|---|---|---|
| Dif | UR | 2.90 | 3.79 | 4.40 | -0.97 | -0.91 | -0.55 |
| | GBORR | 0.33 | 0.58 | 0.52 | -0.53 | -0.82 | -1.04 |
| | BPTR | 0.07 | 0.06 | 0.37 | 0.43 | 0.67 | 0.84 |
| | RDEBT | 10.71 | 16.67 | 17.81 | -5.16 | -7.96 | -12.20 |

| | | Portugal | | | Spain | | |
|---|---|---|---|---|---|---|---|
| | | 1995 | 2000 | 2010 | 1995 | 2000 | 2010 |
| % dif | GDPFC | -0.86 | -1.20 | -1.41 | -2.40 | -3.04 | -3.19 |
| | OT | -2.53 | -3.25 | -3.42 | -6.51 | -8.08 | -8.14 |
| | ON | -0.49 | -0.79 | -1.08 | -1.44 | -1.80 | -1.88 |
| | POT | -1.19 | -1.73 | -2.05 | -0.95 | -1.22 | -1.32 |
| | WT | -3.05 | -4.43 | -5.28 | -1.63 | -2.09 | -2.28 |
| | PC | -1.56 | -2.24 | -2.64 | -1.08 | -1.50 | -1.60 |

| | | | | | | | |
|---|---|---|---|---|---|---|---|
| Dif | UR | 0.71 | 0.98 | 1.19 | 1.26 | 1.61 | 1.76 |
| | GBORR | 0.07 | 0.07 | 0.07 | 0.82 | 1.32 | 1.75 |
| | BPTR | -0.23 | -0.24 | -0.13 | -0.58 | -0.76 | -0.74 |
| | RDEBT | 1.15 | 1.44 | 1.33 | 5.14 | 11.05 | 21.72 |

*Legend*
| | |
|---|---|
| GDPFC | Gross domestic product at factor cost (real) |
| OT | GDP in manufacturing (real) |
| ON | GDP in market services (real) |
| POT | Deflator of GDP in manufacturing |
| WT | Average annual earnings in manufacturing |
| PC | Deflator of private consumption |
| UR | Unemployment rate |
| GBORR | Public sector borrowing requirement (% of GDP) |
| BPTR | Net trade surplus (% of GDP) |
| RDEBT | National debt (% of GDP) |

**Table 8.6(b).  Shock to manufacturing output (increased FDI inflows in Portugal and Spain)**

| | | Greece | | | Ireland | | |
|---|---|---|---|---|---|---|---|
| | | 1995 | 2000 | 2010 | 1995 | 2000 | 2010 |
| % dif | GDPFC | -3.45 | -4.33 | -4.46 | 2.61 | 3.60 | 4.21 |
| | OT | -11.14 | -13.55 | -13.33 | 6.19 | 8.02 | 8.44 |
| | ON | -2.45 | -3.21 | -3.38 | 1.00 | 1.33 | 1.47 |
| | POT | -3.52 | -5.19 | -6.09 | 0.49 | 0.51 | 0.30 |
| | WT | -11.50 | -16.60 | -19.21 | 2.50 | 2.58 | 1.51 |
| | PC | -5.12 | -7.98 | -9.52 | 0.91 | 0.88 | 0.20 |

| | | Greece | | | Ireland | | |
|---|---|---|---|---|---|---|---|
| Dif | UR | 2.90 | 3.79 | 4.40 | -0.97 | -0.91 | -0.55 |
| | GBORR | 0.33 | 0.58 | 0.52 | -0.53 | -0.82 | -1.04 |
| | BPTR | 0.07 | 0.06 | 0.37 | 0.43 | 0.67 | 0.84 |
| | RDEBT | 10.71 | 16.67 | 17.81 | -5.16 | -7.96 | -12.20 |

| | | Portugal | | | Spain | | |
|---|---|---|---|---|---|---|---|
| | | 1995 | 2000 | 2010 | 1995 | 2000 | 2010 |
| % dif | GDPFC | 0.21 | 0.29 | 0.34 | 2.59 | 3.34 | 3.50 |
| | OT | 0.60 | 0.78 | 0.82 | 6.99 | 8.85 | 8.93 |
| | ON | 0.12 | 0.19 | 0.27 | 1.56 | 1.99 | 2.07 |
| | POT | 0.28 | 0.42 | 0.50 | 1.02 | 1.33 | 1.45 |
| | WT | 0.74 | 1.09 | 1.32 | 1.77 | 2.31 | 2.52 |
| | PC | 0.37 | 0.54 | 0.65 | 1.16 | 1.64 | 1.76 |

| | | Portugal | | | Spain | | |
|---|---|---|---|---|---|---|---|
| Dif | UR | -0.17 | -0.24 | -0.29 | -1.34 | -1.75 | -1.90 |
| | GBORR | -0.02 | -0.01 | -0.02 | -0.83 | -1.35 | -1.79 |
| | BPTR | 0.05 | 0.06 | 0.03 | 0.59 | 0.78 | 0.75 |
| | RDEBT | -0.27 | -0.33 | -0.30 | -5.14 | -11.12 | -22.01 |

*Legend*
GDPFC      Gross domestic product at factor cost (real)
OT         GDP in manufacturing (real)
ON         GDP in market services (real)
POT        Deflator of GDP in manufacturing
WT         Average annual earnings in manufacturing
PC         Deflator of private consumption
UR         Unemployment rate
GBORR      Public sector borrowing requirement (% of GDP)
BPTR       Net trade surplus (% of GDP)
RDEBT      National debt (% of GDP)

### 8.4.5.  Non-tradable sector output (shock (vi))

This shock also exerts a multiplier effect, so that non-traded sector output falls by more than the initial exogenous 1% negative shock (Table 8.7).

## Table 8.7.    Exogenous shock to output of market services

| | | Greece | | | Ireland | | |
|---|---|---|---|---|---|---|---|
| | | 1995 | 2000 | 2010 | 1995 | 2000 | 2010 |
| % dif | GDPFC | -0.47 | -0.56 | -0.48 | -0.34 | -0.40 | -0.35 |
| | OT | -0.01 | -0.01 | -0.01 | 0.06 | 0.02 | -0.06 |
| | ON | -0.95 | -1.10 | -0.86 | -0.84 | -0.96 | -0.78 |
| | POT | -0.35 | -0.53 | -0.47 | -0.11 | -0.09 | -0.02 |
| | WT | -1.33 | -1.80 | -1.58 | -0.53 | -0.45 | -0.12 |
| | PC | -0.57 | -0.82 | -0.73 | -0.26 | -0.24 | -0.08 |

| | | | | | | | |
|---|---|---|---|---|---|---|---|
| Dif | UR | 0.32 | 0.38 | 0.33 | 0.21 | 0.16 | 0.04 |
| | GBORR | 0.05 | 0.08 | 0.08 | 0.11 | 0.16 | 0.16 |
| | BPTR | 0.00 | -0.01 | 0.01 | -0.03 | -0.04 | -0.03 |
| | RDEBT | 1.25 | 1.81 | 1.70 | 1.14 | 1.59 | 2.07 |

| | | Portugal | | | Spain | | |
|---|---|---|---|---|---|---|---|
| | | 1995 | 2000 | 2010 | 1995 | 2000 | 2010 |
| % dif | GDPFC | -0.41 | -0.52 | -0.48 | -0.66 | -0.78 | -0.68 |
| | OT | -0.06 | -0.12 | -0.17 | -0.20 | -0.24 | -0.21 |
| | ON | -0.96 | -1.20 | -1.12 | -1.06 | -1.25 | -1.10 |
| | POT | -0.57 | -0.76 | -0.75 | -0.23 | -0.28 | -0.26 |
| | WT | -1.52 | -2.01 | -1.99 | -0.40 | -0.48 | -0.45 |
| | PC | -0.79 | -1.03 | -1.01 | -0.31 | -0.40 | -0.37 |

| | | | | | | | |
|---|---|---|---|---|---|---|---|
| Dif | UR | 0.34 | 0.43 | 0.43 | 0.31 | 0.37 | 0.34 |
| | GBORR | 0.04 | 0.04 | 0.05 | 0.23 | 0.36 | 0.44 |
| | BPTR | -0.11 | -0.10 | -0.03 | -0.23 | -0.27 | -0.23 |
| | RDEBT | 0.59 | 0.72 | 0.80 | 1.44 | 3.00 | 5.57 |

*Legend*
GDPFC          Gross domestic product at factor cost (real)
OT             GDP in manufacturing (real)
ON             GDP in market services (real)
POT            Deflator of GDP in manufacturing
WT             Average annual earnings in manufacturing
PC             Deflator of private consumption
UR             Unemployment rate
GBORR          Public sector borrowing requirement (% of GDP)
BPTR           Net trade surplus (% of GDP)
RDEBT          National debt (% of GDP)

## 8.4.6.   World output combined with structural change (shock (vii))

In this shock we include a Cecchini-inspired world output shock of 8% combined with all the structural changes to the manufacturing sector output and price equations that were examined in the simulation of shock (iv) above. To understand the outcome of this shock, we need to apply the insights obtained in Chapter 5 from the effects of altering world output in isolation (Table 5.7), and combine them with the known impacts of the structural changes in isolation (shown in shock (iv) above). The results of this combination of shocks are shown in Tables 8.8(a) and (b).

**Table 8.8(a).  Influence of higher world growth on manufacturing through greater share of tradables (no change in FDI)**

| | | Greece | | | Ireland | | |
|---|---|---|---|---|---|---|---|
| | | 1995 | 2000 | 2010 | 1995 | 2000 | 2010 |
| % dif | GDPFC | 2.23 | 3.61 | 4.86 | 2.21 | 3.35 | 4.56 |
| | OT | 3.11 | 5.44 | 7.12 | 3.89 | 5.73 | 7.30 |
| | ON | 3.28 | 4.96 | 6.26 | 1.93 | 2.79 | 3.52 |
| | POT | 1.02 | 1.92 | 2.78 | 0.48 | 0.60 | 0.63 |
| | WT | 7.04 | 13.48 | 21.06 | 2.46 | 2.96 | 2.53 |
| | PC | 2.86 | 5.78 | 9.19 | 1.00 | 1.20 | 0.84 |

| | | Greece | | | Ireland | | |
|---|---|---|---|---|---|---|---|
| Dif | UR | -1.67 | -2.78 | -4.06 | -0.97 | -1.06 | -0.86 |
| | GBORR | -0.18 | -0.35 | -0.39 | -0.50 | -0.86 | -1.26 |
| | BPTR | -0.09 | -0.14 | -0.43 | 0.32 | 0.53 | 0.77 |
| | RDEBT | -5.72 | -10.58 | -13.72 | -4.90 | -8.19 | -13.98 |

| | | Portugal | | | Spain | | |
|---|---|---|---|---|---|---|---|
| | | 1995 | 2000 | 2010 | 1995 | 2000 | 2010 |
| % dif | GDPFC | 2.85 | 5.35 | 9.19 | 1.62 | 2.55 | 3.56 |
| | OT | 6.60 | 11.83 | 18.79 | 2.73 | 4.37 | 6.09 |
| | ON | 2.73 | 5.30 | 9.60 | 1.67 | 2.55 | 3.48 |
| | POT | 4.90 | 8.65 | 13.46 | 0.31 | 0.73 | 1.23 |
| | WT | 10.78 | 22.19 | 41.57 | 0.76 | 1.44 | 2.28 |
| | PC | 5.53 | 10.74 | 18.74 | 0.48 | 1.02 | 1.64 |

| | | Portugal | | | Spain | | |
|---|---|---|---|---|---|---|---|
| Dif | UR | -2.34 | -4.39 | -7.79 | -0.81 | -1.29 | -1.88 |
| | GBORR | -0.20 | -0.22 | 0.03 | -0.50 | -0.98 | -1.66 |
| | BPTR | 0.80 | 0.94 | 0.42 | 0.43 | 0.67 | 0.87 |
| | RDEBT | -3.33 | -4.35 | -0.17 | -2.86 | -7.44 | -18.25 |

*Legend*

| | |
|---|---|
| GDPFC | Gross domestic product at factor cost (real) |
| OT | GDP in manufacturing (real) |
| ON | GDP in market services (real) |
| POT | Deflator of GDP in manufacturing |
| WT | Average annual earnings in manufacturing |
| PC | Deflator of private consumption |
| UR | Unemployment rate |
| GBORR | Public sector borrowing requirement (% of GDP) |
| BPTR | Net trade surplus (% of GDP) |
| RDEBT | National debt (% of GDP) |

Thus, the direct strength of the 8% rise in world output, considered in isolation, will depend on two factors. First, the size of the elasticity of domestic manufacturing output on world output. Here, Ireland has the highest elasticity (at 0.51), Spain the lowest at 0.18, and Greece and Portugal are at intermediate values. Second, the strength of the direct effect of world output on market services, where Greece and Portugal have the highest elasticities (in the region of 0.2), and Ireland the lowest.[68]

---

[68]  It should be noted that in using the multiplier results from Chapter 5 to deconstruct shock (vi), there is an additional component that is included in the simulations reported in Tables 8.7(a) and 8.7(b), i.e. the fact that the elasticity of OT with respect to OW will change as a result of shock (iv).

## Table 8.8(b). Influence of higher world growth on manufacturing through greater share of tradables (increased FDI inflows in Portugal and Spain)

| | | Greece | | | Ireland | | |
|---|---|---|---|---|---|---|---|
| | | 1995 | 2000 | 2010 | 1995 | 2000 | 2010 |
| % dif | GDPFC | 2.23 | 3.61 | 4.86 | 2.21 | 3.35 | 4.56 |
| | OT | 3.11 | 5.44 | 7.12 | 3.89 | 5.73 | 7.30 |
| | ON | 3.28 | 4.96 | 6.26 | 1.93 | 2.79 | 3.52 |
| | POT | 1.02 | 1.92 | 2.78 | 0.48 | 0.60 | 0.63 |
| | WT | 7.04 | 13.48 | 21.06 | 2.46 | 2.96 | 2.53 |
| | PC | 2.86 | 5.78 | 9.19 | 1.00 | 1.20 | 0.84 |

| | | | | | | | |
|---|---|---|---|---|---|---|---|
| Dif | UR | -1.67 | -2.78 | -4.06 | -0.97 | -1.06 | -0.86 |
| | GBORR | -0.18 | -0.35 | -0.39 | -0.50 | -0.86 | -1.26 |
| | BPTR | -0.09 | -0.14 | -0.43 | 0.32 | 0.53 | 0.77 |
| | RDEBT | -5.72 | -10.58 | -13.72 | -4.90 | -8.19 | -13.98 |

| | | Portugal | | | Spain | | |
|---|---|---|---|---|---|---|---|
| | | 1995 | 2000 | 2010 | 1995 | 2000 | 2010 |
| % dif | GDPFC | 3.18 | 6.12 | 10.80 | 2.06 | 3.46 | 5.18 |
| | OT | 7.54 | 13.82 | 22.42 | 3.93 | 6.80 | 10.20 |
| | ON | 2.92 | 5.85 | 11.04 | 1.93 | 3.10 | 4.44 |
| | POT | 5.47 | 9.67 | 15.20 | 0.19 | 0.74 | 1.45 |
| | WT | 12.02 | 25.53 | 49.92 | 0.76 | 1.72 | 2.99 |
| | PC | 6.15 | 12.21 | 21.99 | 0.42 | 1.15 | 2.05 |

| | | | | | | | |
|---|---|---|---|---|---|---|---|
| Dif | UR | -2.60 | -5.01 | -9.15 | -1.03 | -1.76 | -2.75 |
| | GBORR | -0.22 | -0.23 | 0.08 | -0.61 | -1.27 | -2.27 |
| | BPTR | 0.89 | 1.03 | 0.38 | 0.52 | 0.85 | 1.16 |
| | RDEBT | -3.64 | -4.73 | 0.43 | -3.34 | -9.35 | -24.25 |

*Legend*
GDPFC     Gross domestic product at factor cost (real)
OT     GDP in manufacturing (real)
ON     GDP in market services (real)
POT     Deflator of GDP in manufacturing
WT     Average annual earnings in manufacturing
PC     Deflator of private consumption
UR     Unemployment rate
GBORR     Public sector borrowing requirement (% of GDP)
BPTR     Net trade surplus (% of GDP)
RDEBT     National debt (% of GDP)

In the case of Portugal, the already strong positive GDP effect of shock (iv) (i.e. 5.5%) rises to 9.2% in the long run for shock (vii). Hence, the 8% increase in world output has added an extra 3.7% increase to GDP. The multiplier in Table 5.7 would suggest that an 8% rise in OW would lead to a 2.7% increase in OT. The difference of 1% (i.e. between 3.7 and 2.7) is accounted for by the increase in the elasticity coefficient that results from shock (iv).

In the case of Ireland, the weak but positive GDP effect of shock (iv) (i.e. 1.3%) rises to 4.6% in the long run for shock (vii). Hence, the 8% increase in world output has added an extra 3.3% increase to GDP, which is just 0.1% above what we would have expected on the basis of the multiplier in Table 5.7. Since the change in the elasticities is very small for Ireland, the effects are almost additive.

## 8.5.    Summary on the single market simulations

In this chapter we have presented a simulation analysis of the impacts of the single market in isolation from the role of the Community Support Framework. We started with the full effects as studied in Chapter 6, and then showed the effects of a subset of the full set of shocks, designed to reproduce the more limited channels of influence studied in the original Cecchini project. We concluded with a set of simulations that gave the effects of each of the individual components of the full single market shock, but in isolation from each other.

In our concluding Chapter 10 we will return to a wider evaluation of the above simulations, taken together with the likely impacts of the CSF (to be examined in isolation in the next chapter). However, a few key conclusions should be briefly noted here.

First, if our analysis of Chapter 6 is correct, and if we have correctly identified channels of influence that were not taken into account in the Cecchini analysis of the core countries, then the 'Cecchini' subset of our full set of seven shocks will present a misleading picture of the likely impact of the single market on the cohesion countries.

Second, the issue of whether or not the projected increase in FDI inflows is counted as a single market effect, is crucial for the cases of Portugal and Spain. In the case of Spain, if FDI effects are not included, the overall impact of the single market on GDP is effectively zero. If they are included, then the overall impact suggests a rise of over 9% in the long run.

Third, we suggest that there is little evidence for a structural shift in FDI inflows in the case of Greece. If this is, indeed, the case, then the Greek economy seems set to lose out as a result of the single market, even though the previous 'Cecchini' methodology would indicate otherwise.

Fourth, the manner in which wage bargaining and price setting is handled in the four HERMIN models is crucial to the transmission of the individual single market shocks. This was illustrated in Table 8.3(a) for the transmission of the shock to total factor productivity, which was price deflationary for Portugal and inflationary for Greece.

Finally, two of the seven shocks proved to be of major importance in terms of their impacts on GDP, namely the shift to a greater proportion of tradables in manufacturing and the knock-on effect on the cohesion countries of the higher level of manufacturing activity in the rest of the EU.

# 9. The impact of the CSF: simulation results

## 9.1. Introduction

We have implemented the CSF methodology described in Chapter 7 for all four models. CSF expenditure data was taken from the official EU Community Support Framework documents (European Commission, 1990a, 1990b, 1989, 1990c, for CSF 1989–93, and European Commission, 1994a, 1994b, 1994c and 1994d, for CSF 1994–99). All expenditures in ECU were converted to national currencies using the following exchange rates:

*CSF 1989–93*

Greece:    178.841 Drachmas per ECU
Ireland:   0.7769 Irish pounds per ECU
Portugal:  173.388 Escudos per ECU
Spain:     130.357 Pesetas per ECU

*CSF 1994–99*

Greece:    288.034 Drachmas per ECU
Ireland:   0.7935 Irish pounds per ECU
Portugal:  196.905 Escudos per ECU
Spain:     158.903 Pesetas per ECU

The Delors I and II packages were negotiated between the Commission and the national authorities and implemented separately as two distinct CSFs, even though they form a logical 10-year continuous programme of EU-assisted investment planning in the periphery. In our simulations, we combine both CSFs into one policy shock that starts in the year 1989 and continues to 1999, the terminal year of the Delors II CSF.

Since the externality effects described earlier in Chapter 7 are not yet well defined or quantifiable, we restrict ourselves initially to the more straightforward standard (or neo-Keynesian) impacts (i.e. we set the externality elasticities to zero). This means that any build-up of stocks of infrastructure or of stocks of trained labour do not have additional impacts over and above the standard neo-Keynesian ones reported in the first set of simulations.

Having examined the standard (or neo-Keynesian) impacts of the CSF, we then introduce positive values for the externalities that are associated with increases in the stocks of physical infrastructure and human capital. Since we are quite ignorant of the exact values to be assigned to these elasticities, we examine the impact of low values and high values and compare these to the case of zero values.

Finally, we explore the case where the CSFs are terminated after the year 1999. It would have been open to us to simulate a wide range of termination paths, ranging from the case of permanent finance (i.e. no termination) to the abrupt and complete termination of all CSF-related activities after the year 1999. For simplicity, we only present results for this latter case, since any intermediate case would be a weighted average of the permanent and the abrupt termination cases.

As in the case of reporting the single market simulations, we again use a standardized format of table that shows the impacts on three groupings of model variables:[69]

(a)    The first grouping shows the impacts on sectoral output (manufacturing (OT), market services (ON) and total GDP at factor cost (GDPFC)). These are shown as percentage deviations from the no-CSF baseline projection for the period 1988 to 2010 inclusive. The year 1988 is the base year, and the CSF shocks are implemented over a 10-year period to 1999.

(b)    The second grouping shows the impacts on prices and wages (the deflator of GDP in manufacturing (POT), average annual earnings in manufacturing (WT), and the deflator of private consumption expenditures (PC)). These are also shown as percentage deviations from the no-SEM baseline.

(c)    The third grouping shows the impacts on four measures of economic imbalance (the rate of unemployment (UR), the PSBR (GBORR) and the balance of trade (BPTR), measured as percentages of GDP or GNP, and the public debt/GDP ratio (RDEBT), also measured as a percentage of GDP). For this third set of variables, the results are shown as simple deviations from the baseline.

In order to give an impression of the size of the CSF relative to GDP, Table 9.1 shows the values generated from the model simulations. In this table, the measure of the size of the CSF includes all elements of the CSF, i.e. EU financial aid, domestic public co-finance and private domestic co-finance. The measure of GDP is the *ex post* value, i.e. it includes the impact of the CSF. In the case of Ireland GNP is used.

We present the results of five different simulations, designed to explore the role of externalities and the consequences of termination of the CSFs after the year 1999. These simulations are as follows:

(a)    In this case we assume that the CSF funding, from the EU, the domestic public co-finance and the private finance, is frozen at its 1999 value and continues indefinitely. We term this 'infinite EU finance'. In addition, we assume that the externality elasticities are zero. Thus, only the standard neo-Keynesian mechanisms operate. We refer to this as 'permanent CSF finance with no externalities'.

(b)    This case is identical to case (a) with the exception that the externality elasticities take on positive, but small, values. Thus, the externality elasticities associated with public infrastructure and human capital that operate directly on manufacturing output, are set at 5%, and all other elasticities are set at 2%. We refer to this as 'permanent CSF finance with low externalities'.

(c)    This case is identical to case (b) with the exception that the externality elasticities take on larger values. Thus, the externality elasticities associated with public infrastructure and human capital that operate directly on manufacturing output, are set at 10%, and all other elasticities are set at 4%. We refer to this as 'permanent CSF finance with high externalities'.

---

[69]    A full set of simulation results is available from the Consultant on request.

(d)    This is identical to case (c), but all the CSF expenditures are terminated after the year 1999. We refer to this as 'temporary CSF finance with high externalities'.

(e)    This case is identical to case (d) above, but all the CSF expenditures are terminated after the year 1999 and with the externality elasticities now set once again to zero. We refer to this as 'temporary CSF finance with no externalities'.

**Table 9.1.    CSF as a percentage of *ex post* GDP[1]**

|       | Greece | Ireland | Portugal | Spain |
|-------|--------|---------|----------|-------|
| 1989  | 4.74   | 5.56    | 6.24     | 0.84  |
| 1990  | 4.12   | 4.80    | 6.53     | 0.88  |
| 1991  | 4.24   | 4.97    | 6.71     | 0.95  |
| 1992  | 4.38   | 5.30    | 7.19     | 1.02  |
| 1993  | 4.52   | 5.73    | 7.83     | 1.10  |
| 1994  | 7.21   | 3.44    | 7.04     | 1.92  |
| 1995  | 7.15   | 3.99    | 7.33     | 1.99  |
| 1996  | 8.27   | 4.05    | 7.07     | 2.07  |
| 1997  | 8.21   | 4.21    | 7.06     | 2.16  |
| 1998  | 8.45   | 4.45    | 7.45     | 2.25  |
| 1999  | 8.76   | 4.63    | 7.59     | 2.34  |
| 2000  | 8.49   | 4.41    | 7.25     | 2.26  |
| 2001  | 8.26   | 4.21    | 6.98     | 2.18  |
| 2002  | 8.02   | 4.01    | 6.71     | 2.10  |
| 2003  | 7.75   | 3.83    | 6.46     | 2.03  |
| 2004  | 7.47   | 3.65    | 6.21     | 1.95  |
| 2005  | 7.19   | 3.47    | 5.96     | 1.88  |
| 2006  | 6.94   | 3.31    | 5.71     | 1.81  |
| 2007  | 6.71   | 3.15    | 5.47     | 1.74  |
| 2008  | 6.49   | 2.99    | 5.23     | 1.68  |
| 2009  | 6.27   | 2.85    | 5.00     | 1.61  |
| 2010  | 6.05   | 2.70    | 4.77     | 1.55  |

[1]    These projections differ from the 'official' ones supplied by the Commission, since the HERMIN model-generated projections for GDP are different to the implicit ones used in the Commission's calculations.

## 9.2.    The CSF simulations: description

We have implemented the CSF shocks in the HERMIN national models along the lines described in Chapter 7. Thus, the total CSF expenditures are considered under three headings:

(a)    expenditures on physical infrastructure;
(b)    expenditure on human resources;
(c)    production/investment aid to the private sector.

Within each of these three economic categories we consider three sources of funding:

(a)    EU transfers in the form of subventions to the domestic public authorities;
(b)    domestic public sector co-financing as set out in the CSF treaties;
(c)    domestic private sector co-financing as set out in the CSF treaties.

A full understanding of how the CSF shocks influence the economies would require a detailed disaggregation of the individual components of the CSF along the above lines. Details of these individual shocks are available from the Consultant on request. However, we restrict ourselves here to a presentation of the aggregate impacts of the CSF and examine the influence of different assumptions on the values of externality elasticities and on the termination conditions.

## 9.3.   The CSF simulations: results

### 9.3.1.   Permanent CSF finance with no externalities

We show the standard set of results for this case in Table 9.2. Here there is a sharp distinction between the relatively strong effects on Greece and Portugal and the weaker effects on Ireland and Spain. The impact on Portuguese GDP is strongest, for two reasons: first, since the CSF funds represent a high proportion of GDP (see Table 9.1 above), and second, since the Portuguese public investment multiplier is quite strong (see Table 5.9 in Chapter 5).

Even though CSF funds represent a larger proportion of GDP for Greece, the lower public investment multiplier there ensures that the overall GDP effects are weaker. Spanish CSF funds as a proportion of GDP are the lowest of all four countries, but the fact that its public investment multiplier is larger than Ireland's results in the overall GDP effects also being somewhat larger than is the case for Ireland.

A somewhat worrying feature of this simulation is that the CSF programme is seen to give rise to fiscal imbalances in all four economies, for several reasons. The co-financing requirements tend to be proportional to the size of the EU injection of finance, and this bears most heavily on Greece and Portugal. This is exacerbated by the inflationary impact on wages and consequently on the public-sector wage bill in Greece and Portugal.

The unemployment effects for Portugal and Greece are also very large, and in fact unrealistically so. They arise because of the high employment impact of the CSF, whether through direct employment creation in building and construction (a sub-sector of market services), or indirectly through the funding of training schemes that have the effect of reducing the ranks of the unemployed. In each table, we also show a corrected measure of the unemployment rate, URP, which can be interpreted as the effect on unemployment when the trainees are assumed to be new entrants to the labour force, rather than being drawn from the ranks of the existing unemployed. This measure of the unemployment rate was designed for use in the Phillips curve, since the effect of training schemes is arguably to increase the effective pool of labour (and so bid down wages), rather than to reduce the effective pool and bid up wages.

**Table 9.2.     Delors I and II combined (permanent CSF finance with no externalities)**

| | | Greece | | | | Ireland | | |
|---|---|---|---|---|---|---|---|---|
| | | 1995 | 2000 | 2010 | | 1995 | 2000 | 2010 |
| % dif | GDPFC | 6.16 | 8.00 | 5.74 | | 1.65 | 1.88 | 1.21 |
| | OT | 2.75 | 3.28 | 2.35 | | 0.88 | 1.03 | 0.94 |
| | ON | 11.52 | 14.46 | 9.54 | | 3.09 | 3.52 | 1.98 |
| | POT | 6.35 | 9.39 | 7.08 | | 0.27 | 0.29 | -0.10 |
| | WT | 23.28 | 35.67 | 26.15 | | 1.35 | 1.47 | -0.50 |
| | PC | 9.72 | 16.03 | 12.13 | | 0.74 | 0.74 | -0.25 |

| | | | | | | | | |
|---|---|---|---|---|---|---|---|---|
| Dif | UR | -9.87 | -11.76 | -8.95 | | -2.13 | -1.96 | -0.58 |
| | URP | -4.66 | -5.96 | -4.48 | | -0.58 | -0.47 | 0.20 |
| | GBORR | 2.29 | 2.33 | 3.05 | | 0.96 | 1.20 | 1.43 |
| | BPTR | -6.85 | -8.47 | -6.17 | | -3.00 | -3.36 | -1.63 |
| | RDEBT | -0.96 | 0.28 | 28.84 | | 5.08 | 9.02 | 17.79 |

| | | Portugal | | | | Spain | | |
|---|---|---|---|---|---|---|---|---|
| | | 1995 | 2000 | 2010 | | 1995 | 2000 | 2010 |
| % dif | GDPFC | 8.15 | 9.10 | 7.14 | | 1.94 | 2.08 | 1.33 |
| | OT | 7.42 | 8.36 | 6.96 | | 1.79 | 1.94 | 1.26 |
| | ON | 15.03 | 16.96 | 13.18 | | 2.60 | 2.78 | 1.75 |
| | POT | 13.20 | 15.30 | 12.26 | | 0.43 | 0.45 | 0.27 |
| | WT | 38.74 | 45.80 | 35.95 | | 0.75 | 0.77 | 0.46 |
| | PC | 18.56 | 21.44 | 16.92 | | 0.55 | 0.64 | 0.38 |

| | | | | | | | | |
|---|---|---|---|---|---|---|---|---|
| Dif | UR | -12.01 | -13.27 | -10.16 | | -1.88 | -2.14 | -1.53 |
| | URP | -6.97 | -7.88 | -6.46 | | -0.57 | -0.59 | -0.35 |
| | GBORR | 2.63 | 3.07 | 3.05 | | 0.24 | 0.35 | 0.63 |
| | BPTR | -6.00 | -6.37 | -4.95 | | -1.13 | -1.20 | -0.78 |
| | RDEBT | 12.07 | 22.39 | 38.73 | | 0.14 | 1.07 | 5.51 |

*Legend*
| | |
|---|---|
| GDPFC | Gross domestic product at factor cost (real) |
| OT | GDP in manufacturing (real) |
| ON | GDP in market services (real) |
| POT | Deflator of GDP in manufacturing |
| WT | Average annual earnings in manufacturing |
| PC | Deflator of private consumption |
| UR | Unemployment rate |
| GBORR | Public sector borrowing requirement (% of GDP) |
| BPTR | Net trade surplus (% of GDP) |
| RDEBT | National debt (% of GDP) |

### 9.3.2.   Permanent CSF finance with low externalities

The standard set of simulation results for this case are shown in Table 9.3. The effects of the CSF on GDP, unsurprisingly, are larger than in the previous case where externality elasticities were set at zero. Portuguese GDP now rises by 9.3% above the baseline, as compared to 7% in the previous scenario. Greece and Ireland experience an extra 1 percentage point increase in GDP, while Spain experiences a more modest increase of 0.4%. Ireland now surpasses Spain in terms of effects on GDP, since the most important externality mechanism operates by enhancing the beneficial impact of the world economy, a channel which operates particularly strongly in the Irish case (see Table 5.7).

**Table 9.3.    Delors I and II combined (permanent CSF finance with low externalities)**

| | | Greece | | | Ireland | | |
|---|---|---|---|---|---|---|---|
| | | 1995 | 2000 | 2010 | 1995 | 2000 | 2010 |
| % dif | GDPFC | 6.53 | 8.63 | 6.52 | 2.16 | 2.66 | 2.26 |
| | OT | 4.17 | 5.90 | 6.01 | 2.15 | 2.82 | 3.10 |
| | ON | 11.69 | 14.71 | 9.68 | 3.25 | 3.75 | 2.30 |
| | POT | 5.85 | 8.31 | 5.37 | 0.19 | 0.19 | -0.20 |
| | WT | 23.01 | 34.31 | 23.36 | 1.63 | 1.93 | 0.22 |
| | PC | 9.13 | 14.40 | 9.46 | 0.58 | 0.51 | -0.49 |

| | | Greece | | | Ireland | | |
|---|---|---|---|---|---|---|---|
| Dif | UR | -9.42 | -11.00 | -7.81 | -2.04 | -1.86 | -0.51 |
| | URP | -4.22 | -5.17 | -3.28 | -0.50 | -0.38 | 0.26 |
| | GBORR | -2.37 | 2.54 | 3.42 | 1.00 | 1.26 | 1.51 |
| | BPTR | -7.45 | -8.81 | -6.57 | -3.20 | -3.28 | -1.48 |
| | RDEBT | -1.54 | 2.32 | 34.05 | 6.61 | 9.16 | 18.41 |

| | | Portugal | | | Spain | | |
|---|---|---|---|---|---|---|---|
| | | 1995 | 2000 | 2010 | 1995 | 2000 | 2010 |
| % dif | GDPFC | 9.33 | 10.81 | 9.26 | 2.07 | 2.34 | 1.70 |
| | OT | 11.12 | 13.58 | 13.30 | 2.12 | 2.57 | 2.16 |
| | ON | 15.55 | 17.68 | 13.89 | 2.69 | 2.96 | 1.99 |
| | POT | 11.75 | 13.21 | 9.69 | 0.15 | -0.07 | -0.47 |
| | WT | 36.77 | 42.81 | 32.34 | 0.64 | 0.59 | 0.19 |
| | PC | 16.79 | 18.88 | 13.84 | 0.24 | 0.06 | -0.48 |

| | | Portugal | | | Spain | | |
|---|---|---|---|---|---|---|---|
| Dif | UR | -11.80 | -12.98 | -9.73 | -1.80 | -1.99 | -1.30 |
| | URP | -6.70 | -7.49 | -5.95 | -0.48 | -0.44 | -0.13 |
| | GBORR | 2.61 | 3.02 | 2.93 | 0.28 | 0.45 | 0.83 |
| | BPTR | -6.16 | -6.46 | -4.89 | -1.17 | -1.29 | -0.90 |
| | RDEBT | 12.36 | 22.56 | 38.12 | 0.38 | 1.79 | 7.59 |

*Legend*
| | |
|---|---|
| GDPFC | Gross domestic product at factor cost (real) |
| OT | GDP in manufacturing (real) |
| ON | GDP in market services (real) |
| POT | Deflator of GDP in manufacturing |
| WT | Average annual earnings in manufacturing |
| PC | Deflator of private consumption |
| UR | Unemployment rate |
| GBORR | Public sector borrowing requirement (% of GDP) |
| BPTR | Net trade surplus (% of GDP) |
| RDEBT | National debt (% of GDP) |

### 9.3.3.  Permanent CSF finance with high externalities

The standard set of simulation results are shown in Table 9.4. Doubling the elasticities in this case serves simply to accentuate the processes discussed in the previous simulation. Thus the effect on the level of Portuguese GDP as we move from zero through low to high elasticities is 7.1, 9.3 and 11.6% respectively. In the case of Ireland, the corresponding impacts are 1.2, 2.3 and 3.4% respectively.

The research literature in this area is such that it is difficult to select values of the externality elasticities with any degree of precision. In the above three cases, we have selected a range of values, ranging from zero to 10%. The survey of research findings in Chapter 7 indicated that for infrastructure, these elasticities could be in the higher range. However, there is considerable doubt if the value of some of the expenditures on training will generate any positive elasticities, i.e. if it will have any long-term benefit. Hence, our simulations serve to bracket the probable range of possibilities. The (unknown) actual impacts are probably greater than in the zero elasticity case, but lower than in the high elasticity case, but nothing very precise can be said using macroeconometric models in the absence of detailed microeconomic research.

**Table 9.4.    Delors I and II combined (permanent CSF finance with high externalities)**

| | | Greece | | | Ireland | | |
|---|---|---|---|---|---|---|---|
| | | 1995 | 2000 | 2010 | 1995 | 2000 | 2010 |
| % dif | GDPFC | 6.90 | 9.31 | 7.38 | 2.68 | 3.45 | 3.35 |
| | OT | 5.62 | 8.61 | 9.86 | 3.43 | 4.64 | 5.32 |
| | ON | 11.86 | 14.95 | 9.86 | 3.40 | 3.99 | 2.63 |
| | POT | 5.36 | 7.27 | 3.75 | 0.11 | 0.08 | -0.30 |
| | WT | 22.77 | 33.10 | 20.96 | 1.91 | 2.41 | 0.95 |
| | PC | 8.55 | 12.86 | 7.01 | 0.43 | 0.29 | -0.73 |

| Dif | UR | -8.98 | -10.23 | -6.66 | -1.96 | -1.76 | -0.45 |
|---|---|---|---|---|---|---|---|
| | URP | -3.78 | -4.40 | -2.10 | -0.42 | -0.30 | 0.31 |
| | GBORR | 2.44 | 2.74 | 3.79 | 1.03 | 1.32 | 1.59 |
| | BPTR | -7.61 | -9.14 | -6.94 | -2.91 | -3.19 | -1.32 |
| | RDEBT | -0.97 | 4.28 | 39.07 | 5.02 | 9.28 | 18.95 |

| | | Portugal | | | Spain | | |
|---|---|---|---|---|---|---|---|
| | | 1995 | 2000 | 2010 | 1995 | 2000 | 2010 |
| % dif | GDPFC | 10.58 | 12.66 | 11.62 | 2.20 | 2.61 | 2.08 |
| | OT | 15.03 | 19.24 | 20.32 | 2.47 | 3.22 | 3.08 |
| | ON | 16.10 | 18.46 | 14.73 | 2.78 | 3.14 | 2.23 |
| | POT | 10.33 | 11.19 | 7.27 | -0.14 | -0.58 | -1.21 |
| | WT | 34.92 | 40.11 | 29.30 | 0.54 | 0.41 | -0.08 |
| | PC | 15.09 | 16.46 | 11.01 | -0.07 | -0.53 | -1.35 |

| Dif | UR | -11.61 | -12.72 | -9.36 | -1.71 | -1.84 | -1.08 |
|---|---|---|---|---|---|---|---|
| | URP | -6.44 | -7.14 | -5.50 | -0.40 | -0.29 | 0.10 |
| | GBORR | 2.58 | 2.96 | 2.78 | 0.33 | 0.55 | 1.03 |
| | BPTR | -6.30 | -6.52 | -4.77 | -1.21 | -1.37 | -1.02 |
| | RDEBT | 12.60 | 22.62 | 37.23 | 0.62 | 2.52 | 9.70 |

*Legend*
GDPFC       Gross domestic product at factor cost (real)
OT          GDP in manufacturing (real)
ON          GDP in market services (real)
POT         Deflator of GDP in manufacturing
WT          Average annual earnings in manufacturing
PC          Deflator of private consumption
UR          Unemployment rate
GBORR       Public sector borrowing requirement (% of GDP)
BPTR        Net trade surplus (% of GDP)
RDEBT       National debt (% of GDP)

## 9.3.4.  Temporary CSF finance with high externalities

In this case we terminate all CSF-related expenditures after the year 1999. Thus, all CSF-related grants from the EU, together with domestic co-financing public expenditure and domestic private expenditure, are cut off from the year 2000, and revert to their pre-1989 zero values. However, we leave in place the high values of the elasticities that were examined in the previous, no-termination case.

## Table 9.5.    Delors I and II combined (temporary CSF finance with high externalities)

| | | Greece | | | Ireland | | |
|---|---|---|---|---|---|---|---|
| | | 1995 | 2000 | 2010 | 1995 | 2000 | 2010 |
| % dif | GDPFC | 6.90 | 2.94 | 0.54 | 2.68 | 1.42 | 0.90 |
| | OT | 5.62 | 3.82 | 2.93 | 3.43 | 3.40 | 2.05 |
| | ON | 11.86 | 4.34 | 0.00 | 3.40 | 0.32 | 0.06 |
| | POT | 5.36 | 4.66 | -1.34 | 0.11 | -0.33 | -0.27 |
| | WT | 22.77 | 21.80 | -1.77 | 1.91 | 0.12 | -0.26 |
| | PC | 8.55 | 10.08 | -1.87 | 0.43 | -0.45 | -0.69 |
| Dif | UR | -8.98 | 0.19 | 1.03 | -1.96 | 1.28 | 0.37 |
| | URP | -3.78 | 0.19 | 1.03 | -0.42 | 1.28 | 0.37 |
| | GBORR | 2.44 | 0.44 | 1.82 | 1.03 | 0.90 | 0.86 |
| | BPTR | -7.61 | -1.05 | -0.08 | -2.91 | 0.51 | 0.50 |
| | RDEBT | -0.97 | 11.63 | 37.49 | 5.02 | 11.69 | 14.78 |

| | | Portugal | | | Spain | | |
|---|---|---|---|---|---|---|---|
| | | 1995 | 2000 | 2010 | 1995 | 2000 | 2010 |
| % dif | GDPFC | 10.58 | 5.69 | 2.31 | 2.20 | 0.43 | 0.20 |
| | OT | 15.03 | 11.74 | 6.42 | 2.47 | 1.09 | 0.59 |
| | ON | 16.10 | 6.25 | 1.23 | 2.78 | 0.28 | 0.08 |
| | POT | 10.33 | 5.57 | -1.47 | -0.14 | -0.89 | -0.57 |
| | WT | 34.92 | 21.82 | -0.52 | 0.54 | -0.31 | -0.24 |
| | PC | 15.09 | 8.24 | -1.44 | -0.07 | -0.78 | -0.68 |
| Dif | UR | -11.61 | -1.44 | 0.10 | -1.71 | 0.26 | 0.20 |
| | URP | -6.44 | -1.44 | 0.10 | -0.40 | 0.26 | 0.20 |
| | GBORR | 2.58 | 0.95 | 0.71 | 0.33 | 0.08 | 0.50 |
| | BPTR | -6.30 | -1.26 | -0.07 | -1.21 | -0.08 | -0.06 |
| | RDEBT | 12.60 | 24.36 | 22.97 | 0.62 | 3.85 | 7.08 |

*Legend*

| | |
|---|---|
| GDPFC | Gross domestic product at factor cost (real) |
| OT | GDP in manufacturing (real) |
| ON | GDP in market services (real) |
| POT | Deflator of GDP in manufacturing |
| WT | Average annual earnings in manufacturing |
| PC | Deflator of private consumption |
| UR | Unemployment rate |
| GBORR | Public sector borrowing requirement (% of GDP) |
| BPTR | Net trade surplus (% of GDP) |
| RDEBT | National debt (% of GDP) |

### 9.3.5.  Temporary CSF finance with no externalities

As would be expected, the withdrawal of CSF-related expenditures produces an abrupt and large fall in GDP. Thus, in the case of Greece, the impact on GDP falls from 9.31% (in the infinite finance case of Table 9.4) to 2.9% in the present case (Table 9.5). The impacts on the other countries are also quite dramatic: from 3.5 to 1.4 for Ireland; from 12.7 to 5.7 for Portugal; and from 2.1 to 0.2 for Spain.

The other feature in Table 9.5 is that the impact of the CSF falls to small but positive values by the year 2010. There is a major reason for this: the stocks of CSF-related physical infrastructure 'decay' at set depreciation rates (2% per year for infrastructure and 5% per year for human capital). Thus, if the CSF-related expenditures are cut off after the year 1999, the externality elasticities will operate on a declining incremental stock.

**Table 9.6.    Delors I and II combined (temporary CSF finance with no externalities)**

| | | Greece | | | | Ireland | | |
|---|---|---|---|---|---|---|---|---|
| | | **1995** | **2000** | **2010** | | **1995** | **2000** | **2010** |
| % dif | GDPFC | 6.16 | 1.96 | -0.04 | | 1.65 | 0.02 | -0.01 |
| | OT | 2.75 | -0.66 | -0.01 | | 0.88 | 0.18 | 0.19 |
| | ON | 11.52 | 4.17 | -0.02 | | 3.09 | -0.10 | -0.22 |
| | POT | 6.35 | 6.59 | -0.02 | | 0.27 | -0.14 | -0.20 |
| | WT | 23.28 | 24.26 | -0.06 | | 1.35 | -0.72 | -1.01 |
| | PC | 9.72 | 12.98 | -0.04 | | 0.74 | -0.06 | -0.52 |

| | | Greece | | | | Ireland | | |
|---|---|---|---|---|---|---|---|---|
| Dif | UR | -9.87 | -1.18 | 0.01 | | -2.13 | 1.16 | 0.36 |
| | URP | -4.66 | -1.18 | 0.01 | | -0.58 | 1.16 | 0.36 |
| | GBORR | 2.29 | 0.11 | 1.49 | | 0.96 | 0.79 | 0.76 |
| | BPTR | -7.29 | -0.63 | 0.07 | | -3.00 | 0.37 | 0.36 |
| | RDEBT | -2.13 | 7.35 | 31.78 | | 5.08 | 11.40 | 13.70 |

| | | Portugal | | | | Spain | | |
|---|---|---|---|---|---|---|---|---|
| | | **1995** | **2000** | **2010** | | **1995** | **2000** | **2010** |
| % dif | GDPFC | 8.15 | 2.84 | 0.46 | | 1.94 | -0.02 | -0.06 |
| | OT | 7.42 | 2.57 | 0.68 | | 1.79 | -0.01 | -0.06 |
| | ON | 15.03 | 5.36 | 0.74 | | 2.60 | -0.02 | -0.08 |
| | POT | 13.20 | 9.11 | 0.71 | | 0.43 | -0.01 | -0.03 |
| | WT | 38.74 | 26.30 | 1.88 | | 0.75 | -0.01 | -0.04 |
| | PC | 18.56 | 12.27 | 0.88 | | 0.55 | 0.28 | -0.04 |

| | | Portugal | | | | Spain | | |
|---|---|---|---|---|---|---|---|---|
| Dif | UR | -12.01 | -2.17 | -0.42 | | -1.88 | 0.01 | 0.03 |
| | URP | -6.97 | -2.17 | -0.42 | | -0.57 | 0.01 | 0.03 |
| | GBORR | 2.63 | 1.13 | 0.91 | | 0.24 | -0.11 | 0.29 |
| | BPTR | -6.00 | -1.37 | -0.30 | | -1.13 | 0.08 | 0.03 |
| | RDEBT | 12.07 | 24.22 | 24.58 | | 0.14 | 2.43 | 4.49 |

*Legend*

| | |
|---|---|
| GDPFC | Gross domestic product at factor cost (real) |
| OT | GDP in manufacturing (real) |
| ON | GDP in market services (real) |
| POT | Deflator of GDP in manufacturing |
| WT | Average annual earnings in manufacturing |
| PC | Deflator of private consumption |
| UR | Unemployment rate |
| GBORR | Public sector borrowing requirement (% of GDP) |
| BPTR | Net trade surplus (% of GDP) |
| RDEBT | National debt (% of GDP) |

This last case is identical to the previous case, with one exception: the externality elasticities are set at zero. The simulation results are shown in Table 9.6, where it is seen that the long-term impacts decline to zero. This merely illustrates a Keynesian withdrawal of expenditure, where the CSF leaves no long-term positive impact. However, because of the domestic co-financing requirement during the years 1989–99, the public debt has risen as a percentage of GDP.

## 9.4.  Conclusions on the CSF

We have examined the impact of the CSF under different assumptions about externality elasticities and under different termination conditions. Some general conclusions can be drawn.

First, focusing on the purely neo-Keynesian impacts of the CSF (i.e. under the assumption of zero externalities), the effects are broadly in line with the known multiplier properties of the models, as previously discussed in Chapter 5. Thus, the public investment multipliers are largest for Portugal (in the range 1.5) and smallest for Ireland (in the range 1.0). On the other hand, the multipliers associated with human resource programme transfer payments are less than unity for all models.

Second, we have presented the impacts on gross domestic product (GDP). However, the CSF grant allocations coming from the European Commission will also contribute directly to 'national resources', (i.e. GNDI plus capital transfers from abroad). These will be additional to the GDP effects, but will vanish when the CSF is terminated.

Third, increasing the size of the externality elasticities will boost the impact of the CSF programmes. This is most dramatically illustrated by the Irish case, where the GDP impact is tripled in the case of high elasticities relative to the zero elasticity case.

Fourth, the beneficial impacts of the CSF programmes decay after the termination of the CSF, since the incremental stocks of infrastructure and human capital also decay. However, there are modest positive effects in the long run.

Finally, if the CSF is terminated and there are no beneficial externality effects, then there are no long-term benefits from the CSF. Thus, the withdrawal of the CSF simply reverses the previous Keynesian expansion.

# 10.  Summary and conclusions

## 10.1. Conclusions

To arrive at a definitive answer to the question of the combined effects of the single market and the CSF programmes requires choosing amongst a range of scenarios, for example: are the increased FDI flows into Spain and Portugal to be attributed to the SEM? Is the CSF funding temporary or permanent? Are the economic mechanisms that generate long-run supply responses to CSF programmes strong or weak? In the light of the most recent research, we do not yet have definitive answers to these difficult questions.

Table 10.1 reproduces the overall effects of the SEM and CSF shocks, and the sum of these, for each of the peripheral countries. Since we have examined various kinds of SEM and CSF shocks, we need to define the nature of the combined shock presented in these tables.

The SEM variant presented in the table below consists of the complete set of seven shocks detailed in Section 8.1, but excludes the effects of the increased FDI inflows into Portugal and Spain, on the assumption that they cannot be ascribed to the SEM. Thus, the data for the simulations is taken from Table 8.1(a).

The CSF shock consists of the combined Delors I and II packages, with Delors II phased in to take over from Delors I in 1994. This table is based on the assumption that all CSF expenditures will remain fixed in nominal terms after the terminal year of Delors II (i.e. the year 1999). Thus, we use the permanent finance case in this table. We have examined in Chapter 9 the consequences of terminating the CSF after 1999, but this case is not used here. Furthermore, in this table we assume that there are no externalities associated with the CSF expenditures. The consequences of alternative assumptions on externality effects have also been explored in Chapter 9. The data for the CSF simulations are taken from Table 9.2.

As previously noted, we report the outcomes for the following variables: GDP at factor cost (GDPFC); manufacturing sector output (OT); output of building, construction, utilities and market services (ON); the manufacturing sector wage (WT) and the consumer price index (PC); the unemployment rate (UR) and a corrected unemployment rate (URP) that takes into account the fact that the training programmes associated with the CSF, while technically reducing the labour force, do not in fact increase labour market tension; the government borrowing requirement as a proportion of GDP (GBORR); the net trade surplus as a proportion of GDP (BPTR); and the national debt/GDP ratio (RDEBT).

As discussed in Chapter 8, the SEM effects, taken alone, are strongest for Ireland. Then, in descending order come Portugal, Greece and Spain. The reason for this order is that Ireland and Portugal have been found to have the largest shares of employment and output in the sectors in which these individual countries are expected to benefit from the SEM, relative to those in the (country-specific) sectors which are expected to be adversely affected.

We saw in Chapter 8 that Portugal and Spain, in addition, experienced large increases in FDI inflows as a result of EU accession-cum-SEM. Ireland, in contrast, although continuing to do well in terms of attracting FDI flows, has not experienced any substantial increase in its relative attractiveness in recent times.[70] However, these FDI effects are not included in the summary Table 10.1.

For Spain and Greece, output and employment are at present concentrated in sectors in which these individual countries are not expected to do very well as a result of the single market. To that extent, a tremendous amount of restructuring is required, which imparts substantial negative shocks to manufacturing output and employment in the early stages of the SEM process.

This is the case particularly for Greece. Spain requires somewhat less restructuring, and the negative shocks are substantially ameliorated by increased inflows of FDI, which, as we have seen, occurred for Portugal also. FDI inflows into Greece remain low at present, meaning that the whole massive burden of adjusting to the adverse shocks is thrown onto indigenous Greek industry.

Only after the year 2000 do the effects of the SEM on Greek GDP become positive. This reversal in sign occurs for two reasons: firstly, through the classical adjustment mechanism of a downward adjustment of real wages in response to the adverse shocks, and secondly, and most importantly, because of the 'growth-dependent effects' we have identified. As the Greek and other economies become more integrated with the rest of Europe, they benefit more than previously from growth in the European core.

Appropriately enough, since Greece is found to benefit least substantially from the SEM, it, along with Portugal, is found to benefit most substantially from the CSF. The effects on Ireland and Spain are very much less.[71]

The relative size of these effects is due both to the relative sizes of the CSF shocks and to the endogenous response of each economy to the shocks. Although Ireland does well in per capita terms from the CSF allocations, for example, its relatively large GDP means that the CSF shocks as a ratio of GDP are smaller than the equivalent ratios for Greece and Portugal (see Tables 9.1 and 10.2).

It should be noted again, with respect to the CSF shocks, that the results presented in Tables 9.2, 9.3, 9.4, 9.5 and 9.6 take account mainly of the expenditure side of these programmes. We have left aside many of the crucial supply-side effects which are, of course, the primary *raison d'être* of the CSF programmes. These supply-side effects would generate extra benefits, and some of these have been discussed and explored in Chapter 9. Our reason for not including them here is that there is little agreement on the empirical magnitudes of the externality mechanisms through which these programmes affect the supply side of the economy. In our discussion of the CSF impacts in Chapter 9, we argued that these externality mechanisms could well prove to be quite substantial.

---

[70]    Ireland in fact experienced an equivalent substantial increase in inflows upon its accession to the EU in 1972.

[71]    Note that the proportion of the CSF allocations coming from the European Commission contribute directly to 'national resources' (i.e. GNDI plus capital transfers). The GDP effects reported in Tables 10.1 to 10.4 are additional to these effects.

## Table 10.1.    SEM and CSF effects: no FDI, permanent CSF finance, no externalities

| Greece | | | | | | | | | | |
|---|---|---|---|---|---|---|---|---|---|---|
| | | 1995 | | | 2000 | | | 2010 | | |
| | | SEM | CSF | TOTAL | SEM | CSF | TOTAL | SEM | CSF | TOTAL |
| % dif | GDPFC | -1.30 | 6.16 | 4.86 | -0.88 | 8.00 | 7.12 | 0.13 | 5.74 | 5.87 |
| | OT | -7.70 | 2.75 | -4.95 | -7.65 | 3.28 | -4.37 | -5.65 | 2.35 | -3.30 |
| | ON | 0.55 | 11.52 | 12.07 | 1.28 | 14.46 | 15.74 | 2.23 | 9.54 | 11.77 |
| | POT | -6.98 | 6.35 | -0.63 | -8.67 | 9.39 | 0.72 | -8.88 | 7.08 | -1.80 |
| | WT | -6.40 | 23.28 | 16.88 | -7.47 | 35.67 | 28.20 | -5.68 | 26.15 | 20.42 |
| | PC | -5.66 | 9.72 | 4.06 | -7.14 | 16.03 | 8.89 | -6.48 | 12.13 | 5.65 |
| Dif | UR | 2.00 | -9.87 | -7.87 | 2.04 | -11.76 | -9.72 | 1.60 | -8.95 | -7.35 |
| | URP | 2.00 | -4.66 | -2.66 | 2.04 | -5.96 | -3.92 | 1.60 | -4.48 | -2.88 |
| | GBORR | 0.57 | 2.29 | 2.86 | 0.76 | 2.33 | 3.09 | 0.74 | 3.05 | 3.79 |
| | BPTR | -0.29 | -6.85 | -7.14 | -0.38 | -8.47 | -8.85 | -0.24 | -6.17 | -6.41 |
| | RDEBT | 8.47 | -0.96 | 7.51 | 11.61 | 0.28 | 11.89 | 12.28 | 28.84 | 41.12 |

| Ireland | | | | | | | | | | |
|---|---|---|---|---|---|---|---|---|---|---|
| | | 1995 | | | 2000 | | | 2010 | | |
| | | SEM | CSF | TOTAL | SEM | CSF | TOTAL | SEM | CSF | TOTAL |
| % dif | GDPFC | 4.95 | 1.65 | 6.60 | 7.24 | 1.88 | 9.12 | 9.24 | 1.21 | 10.45 |
| | OT | 11.14 | 0.88 | 12.02 | 15.14 | 1.03 | 16.17 | 17.11 | 0.94 | 18.05 |
| | ON | 2.40 | 3.09 | 5.49 | 3.62 | 3.52 | 7.14 | 4.75 | 1.98 | 6.73 |
| | POT | -4.70 | 0.27 | -4.43 | -5.86 | 0.29 | -5.57 | -5.87 | -0.10 | -5.97 |
| | WT | 1.08 | 1.35 | 2.43 | 1.15 | 1.47 | 2.62 | 0.37 | -0.50 | -0.13 |
| | PC | -2.82 | 0.74 | -2.08 | -3.71 | 0.74 | -2.97 | -4.39 | -0.25 | -4.64 |
| Dif | UR | -1.43 | -2.13 | -3.56 | -1.55 | -1.96 | -3.51 | -1.23 | -0.58 | -1.81 |
| | URP | -1.43 | -0.58 | -2.01 | -1.55 | -0.47 | -2.02 | -1.23 | 0.20 | -1.03 |
| | GBORR | -0.88 | 0.96 | 0.08 | -1.45 | 1.20 | -0.25 | -2.09 | 1.43 | -0.66 |
| | BPTR | 0.91 | -3.00 | -2.09 | 1.30 | -3.36 | -2.06 | 1.61 | -1.63 | -0.02 |
| | RDEBT | -5.51 | 5.08 | -0.43 | -11.06 | 9.02 | -2.04 | -21.62 | 17.79 | -3.83 |

| Portugal | | | | | | | | | | |
|---|---|---|---|---|---|---|---|---|---|---|
| | | 1995 | | | 2000 | | | 2010 | | |
| | | SEM | CSF | TOTAL | SEM | CSF | TOTAL | SEM | CSF | TOTAL |
| % dif | GDPFC | 2.23 | 8.15 | 10.38 | 4.29 | 9.10 | 13.39 | 7.54 | 7.14 | 14.68 |
| | OT | 5.70 | 7.42 | 13.12 | 10.43 | 8.36 | 18.79 | 16.77 | 6.96 | 23.73 |
| | ON | 1.83 | 15.03 | 16.86 | 3.67 | 16.96 | 20.63 | 6.91 | 13.18 | 20.09 |
| | POT | -3.54 | 13.20 | 9.66 | -2.45 | 15.30 | 12.85 | 0.96 | 12.26 | 13.22 |
| | WT | -0.59 | 38.74 | 38.15 | 5.00 | 45.80 | 50.80 | 18.01 | 35.95 | 53.96 |
| | PC | -2.92 | 18.56 | 15.64 | -0.93 | 21.44 | 20.51 | 4.67 | 16.92 | 21.59 |
| Dif | UR | -0.95 | -12.01 | -12.96 | -2.34 | -13.27 | -15.61 | -5.03 | -10.16 | -15.19 |
| | URP | -0.95 | -6.97 | -7.92 | -2.34 | -7.88 | -10.22 | -5.03 | -6.46 | -11.49 |
| | GBORR | -0.18 | 2.63 | 2.45 | -0.28 | 3.07 | 2.79 | -0.16 | 3.05 | 2.89 |
| | BPTR | 0.38 | -6.00 | -5.62 | 0.70 | -6.37 | -5.67 | 0.66 | -4.95 | -4.29 |
| | RDEBT | -0.43 | 12.07 | 11.64 | -1.97 | 22.39 | 20.42 | -0.55 | 38.73 | 38.18 |

| Spain | | | | | | | | | | |
|---|---|---|---|---|---|---|---|---|---|---|
| | | 1995 | | | 2000 | | | 2010 | | |
| | | SEM | CSF | TOTAL | SEM | CSF | TOTAL | SEM | CSF | TOTAL |
| % dif | GDPFC | -1.01 | 1.94 | 0.93 | -0.74 | 2.08 | 1.34 | 0.06 | 1.33 | 1.39 |
| | OT | -3.23 | 1.79 | -1.44 | -3.11 | 1.94 | -1.17 | -1.63 | 1.26 | -0.37 |
| | ON | -0.37 | 2.60 | 2.23 | 0.09 | 2.78 | 2.87 | 0.87 | 1.75 | 2.62 |
| | POT | -7.57 | 0.43 | -7.14 | -8.93 | 0.45 | -8.48 | -8.60 | 0.27 | -8.33 |
| | WT | -5.92 | 0.75 | -5.17 | -6.75 | 0.77 | -5.98 | -6.24 | 0.46 | -5.78 |
| | PC | -5.80 | 0.55 | -5.25 | -7.10 | 0.64 | -6.46 | -6.70 | 0.38 | -6.32 |
| Dif | UR | 1.04 | -1.88 | -0.84 | 1.07 | -2.14 | -1.07 | 0.72 | -1.53 | -0.81 |
| | URP | 1.04 | -0.57 | -0.57 | 1.07 | -0.59 | 0.48 | 0.72 | -0.35 | 0.37 |
| | GBORR | 0.79 | 0.24 | 1.03 | 1.13 | 0.35 | 1.48 | 1.07 | 0.63 | 1.70 |
| | BPTR | -0.34 | -1.13 | -1.47 | -0.42 | -1.20 | -1.62 | -0.10 | -0.78 | -0.88 |
| | RDEBT | 7.08 | 0.14 | 7.22 | 12.48 | 1.07 | 13.55 | 17.92 | 5.51 | 23.43 |

**Table 10.2.    CSF shock as % of GDP**

|          | 1995 | 2000 | 2010 |
|----------|------|------|------|
| Greece   | 8.29 | 11.4 | 10.1 |
| Ireland  | 3.91 | 4.32 | 2.68 |
| Portugal | 7.93 | 8.25 | 6.15 |
| Spain    | 2.17 | 2.44 | 1.73 |

*Source:* Model simulations.

Whereas the SEM effects operate primarily on the manufacturing sector (OT), with positive but generally smaller knock-on effects on the services sector (which includes building and construction) (ON), the effects of the CSF shocks operate primarily through ON.

Shocks with the same quantitative effects on GDP, but which operate through ON rather than OT, have larger employment effects, given the labour intensity of services (e.g. compare the employment effects of the SEM and CSF shocks for Ireland in 1995). Thus, a country like Greece, with a large CSF shock combined with a relatively adverse SEM shock, experiences high employment growth, while Ireland, with a strongly beneficial SEM shock combined with a relatively small CSF shock, experiences much lower employment growth.

Thus, the Greek unemployment rate, corrected, comes down 3% by 2010 while Ireland's comes down only 1% (though, of course, the reduction in net out-migration from Ireland – not shown separately – contributes to this relatively small reduction in unemployment).

The small overall effects on Spanish and Irish unemployment rates means that real wage growth is moderate (at around 4% by 2010) in these countries, compared to the situation in Greece and Portugal where the large drop in (corrected) unemployment rates (of 3% and 11% respectively) brings both economies close to full employment relative to their baselines, and results in substantial real wage growth (of 15% and 32% respectively). In the case of Greece and Portugal, the reduction in the unemployment rate is unrealistically large and would call into question the modelling assumptions made in the labour markets in these two HERMIN models. This clearly should be the subject of further research.

The overall government borrowing requirement is up by about 4% in Greece and 3% in Portugal, while it is largely unchanged in the other two economies, indicating that the output and employment effects for Greece and Portugal, in a balanced budget environment, would be less favourable. A mirror image of this fiscal overspending is, of course, a deterioration in a country's net trade surplus. Thus, both Greece and Portugal suffer some deterioration in their trade surpluses, but the net trade surpluses of Ireland and Spain are largely unaffected by the combined shocks.

Portugal, we see, is the only economy to experience overall price increases of any magnitude. These, of course, come primarily through the stimulation of the non-traded (ON) sector due to the large CSF shocks. For Greece, which also experiences large CSF shocks, the inflationary effects are largely offset by the price reductions associated with the single market. For Portugal, though, the SEM effects are so strong that they, too, generate inflation. For Ireland and Spain, the CSF shocks are relatively moderate, and so no strong inflationary impulses are imparted to the system.

We can now compare our results for the SEM shock and the combined SEM/CSF shocks for the year 2010 to the medium-term effects emerging from the Cecchini Report and the subsequent analysis of Baldwin (1989). This is done in Table 10.3 below, where in this table, in contrast to Table 10.1 above, we have included the FDI effects as SEM-related for Portugal and Spain. Although we excluded the FDI effects from Table 10.1, a case could be made that the FDI effects are SEM-related, rather than related to accession.

**Table 10.3.    Results compared to Cecchini[72]**

|  | Spain | | Portugal | | Ireland | | Greece | | Cecchini |
|---|---|---|---|---|---|---|---|---|---|
|  | SEM | Total | SEM | Total | SEM | Total | SEM | Total | SEM |
| GDP | 9.16 | 10.49 | 11.47 | 18.61 | 9.24 | 10.45 | 0.13 | 5.87 | 4.5 |
| PC | -3.44 | -3.06 | 10.63 | 27.55 | -4.39 | -4.64 | -6.48 | 5.65 | -6.1 |
| GBORR | -2.77 | -2.14 | -0.23 | 2.82 | -2.09 | -0.66 | 0.74 | 3.79 | -2.2 |
| BPTR | 1.87 | 1.09 | 0.86 | -4.09 | 1.61 | -0.02 | -0.24 | -6.41 | 1.0 |

Leaving the most important effect, on GDP, until last, let us focus first on consumer prices. Cecchini predicts a fall in prices; and this result emerges from our analysis also, for all countries except Portugal. For Ireland, by far the most open of the economies, the explanation is clear-cut: the dominant price effect is the fall in international prices that we have taken directly from Cecchini. For Portugal, though, these effects are offset by the growth in domestic demand that results from economic expansion: there is still a good degree of price-cost marking up. For Greece and Spain, which are also relatively closed, the expansionary effects of the SEM shock are not as strong as in Portugal, and so the imported reduction in prices dominates.

With regard to the government borrowing requirement, the SEM results for Ireland, Portugal and Spain are reasonably close to the Cecchini estimates, resulting from the relatively strong output effects of the SEM for these countries. Greece does not benefit so strongly from the SEM according to our analysis, however, and so their budgetary position also remains less buoyant.

The results for the net trade surplus effects are all quite close to Cecchini, with the exception of that for Greece and, to a lesser extent, Portugal; the deterioration in the former, however, appears simply to reflect the deterioration in the Greek budgetary position.

Now we come to the GDP effects. Here we find that Greece comes in below the Cecchini estimates while Ireland, Spain and Portugal come in above. Note that we have included the FDI effects as SEM-related for Portugal and Spain. In fact, all our results are outside the Cecchini range, which runs from 3.2% to 5.7%. It is perhaps not so surprising that Greece comes in below the Cecchini estimates, since part of the rationale for the CSF programmes was that just such an eventuality was possible.

How do we explain the strong performance of Ireland, Spain and Portugal relative to the Cecchini estimates? An answer to this question is, of course, only worthwhile attempting on the assumption that our methodology, if applied to the whole EU, would reveal the periphery economies coming out ahead of the average. This does appear to be the case, however, since Ireland and Portugal appear to be well positioned in terms of revealed comparative advantage

---

[72]    Note that the SEM impacts include the FDI effects for Portugal and Spain.

in the sectors deemed likely to be affected by the SEM, while both Portugal and Spain appear to be attracting strongly increased FDI inflows which that analysis largely ignores.

In the main body of our analysis we made a good deal of use of the country studies contained in the special edition of *European Economy* (1990), which looked at both static and dynamic indicators of competitiveness in the affected sectors. The only relevant data that the special edition provides for all EU countries is, unfortunately, based solely on the static indicators (pp. 34–37). The charts presented there, however, reveal that Portugal is as well positioned in these sectors as the leaders, Germany and Italy, while both Ireland and Portugal appear well ahead of the other large EU economies, France and the UK. Thus, on the basis of our methodology, both would appear to come out ahead of the EU average. Spain and particularly Greece appear more vulnerable than the average.

We have argued, though, that Spain's proven ability to attract increased FDI flows dominates the vulnerability of its existing industry. Of the countries studied, Greece appears to lag far behind the others in terms of its ability to attract FDI. Our feeling is that this is a consequence of the unsettled nature of Greek macroeconomic policy, rather than an inherent characteristic of the economy, and so if the macroeconomic problems could be overcome, the Greek position in our analysis would appear much more favourable.

Finally, it is worth pointing out that our estimates of the growth effects of the SEM for Ireland, Spain and Portugal are within the bounds of the range predicted by Baldwin (1989), who argued that the medium-term growth bonus (resulting from increased investment) which Cecchini ignored, would more than double the range of predicted GDP effects presented in that report.

## 10.2. Remaining issues

Preliminary analysis of our results has identified a number of issues that remain to be dealt with in future research.

The first of these concerns the Greek model. We have constructed this model from scratch, though we have included references to the Greek literature to support the assumptions we adopted in constructing the model. We are encouraged by the fact that the properties of the model appear very similar to those of the two-sector SOE model of Greece due to Alogoskoufis (1990b).

The second issue concerns our treatment of the implications of the SEM for the services sector. Our treatment in this report has, in fact, been minimal. On the strength of the literature reviewed in Appendix C on this issue, however, there appears to be relatively little work done on quantification of the implications of the SEM for this sector. It should be possible, however, to incorporate the interest-rate effects of the integration of financial services, as was done in an earlier Irish study (Bradley, Fitz Gerald and Kearney, 1992).

The third issue concerns the wage bargaining mechanism in Portugal and Greece, where up to now we have assumed an inelastic labour supply in the context of fairly strong Phillips curve effects. An implication of this modelling approach is that shocks to the Portuguese and Greek models can produce large changes to the real wage. In the case of Ireland, on the other hand, the moderately large Phillips curve parameter occurs in the context of an extremely open labour market. In the case of Spain, the Phillips curve effect was found to be very small. It remains to be investigated whether, in the case of Greece and Portugal, the existence of rural-urban migration might play a similar role to the international migration mechanism.

The fourth issue concerns our treatment of the CSF shocks. We have seen that the implications of the structural changes wrought by the SEM are in some cases quite dramatic. The consequences of the CSF shocks within the context of the structurally changed models could be explored in future work.

Finally, and perhaps most importantly, we suspect that even temporary CSF programmes can have stronger permanent effects than those identified here. These 'industrial composition externalities' have been identified in recent work by authors such as Romer (1986) and Krugman (1987). The essential idea here is that of 'learning-by-doing', in which the economy's stock of knowledge is modelled as a function either of cumulative output or of cumulative gross investment. By increasing these, programmes such as the CSF can have permanent hysteresis-type effects on the structure of the economy, with implications for long-run growth prospects. To capture these would require that we would extend the HERMIN model to take on the characteristics of an endogenous growth model. These effects could well prove to be much more profound than those emerging from the incorporation of the externality elasticities explored in the present study.

APPENDIX A

# The analytics of regional and small-open-economy macro-models

Versions of the small open economy model provide the framework for most macroeconomic debates in Ireland and other small economies. This appendix offers a unified treatment of the simple analytics of such models.

## A.1. Introduction

With the demise of the Keynesian demand-driven view of the world, attention came to be focused on cost competitiveness as the most important ingredient in output determination, in highly open economies at least. This view was encapsulated in the one-sector small-open-economy model, in which all goods were internationally tradable. Recognition that domestic demand continued to play some role lead to an increasing interest in the two-sector small-open-economy (SOE) model, in which some goods were recognized to be non-(internationally-) tradable.

Although the model is variously denoted the 'Australian' or the 'Scandinavian' model, its popularity is probably primarily due to the works of Dornbusch published in the 1970s and collected in Dornbusch (1980). Many authors, such as Helpman (1977), Neary (1980), Calmfors and Viotti (1982) and Cuddington and Viñals (1986a, 1986b), subsequently made important contributions to the model's development.

Surprisingly, however, given that the model provides the corner-stone for most discussions of the macroeconomy of Ireland, for example, there is no unified treatment of the simple analytics of how the model operates.[73] This appendix provides such a unified framework. It also shows how relatively simple versions of the model can be used to structure many of the debates that take place over macroeconomic issues in small open economies.

The appendix is structured as follows. The next section presents the basic one-sector SOE model, illustrating how, though highly oversimplified, it provides the easiest means by which the interrelatedness of macroeconomic aggregates, such as output, employment, investment, inflation and interest rates, can be grasped. Some of the difficulties that the model encounters in explaining aspects of the macroeconomy are then pointed out, and it is shown how these can be overcome by moving to the two-sector model. The latter, of course, allows Keynesian elements to be introduced quite easily.

For the most part, inter-temporal issues are not dealt with, as they increase the complexity of the model considerably. They have been dealt with recently in some detail by Barry and Devereux (1995) who present a two-period version of the two-sector model presented here.

---

[73]   The model does not appear explicitly, for example, in any of the three most popular textbooks on the Irish macroeconomy: O'Hagan (1995), Leddin and Walsh (1995), and Norton (1994), though the latter discusses it informally.

## A.2.  The one-sector small-open-economy model

In this model all goods are assumed to be internationally tradable, and all firms in the SOE are perfect competitors. This has two implications; first, that goods produced domestically are perfect substitutes for goods produced elsewhere so that prices (mediated through the exchange rate) cannot deviate from world levels, and second, that firms are able to sell as much as they desire to produce at going world prices. The latter is arguably an undesirable implication, and will be further discussed later. Note that it rules out Keynesian phenomena right from the start.

The 'law of one price', operating through goods arbitrage, therefore ensures:

$$(1) \qquad\qquad\qquad\qquad p_t = e p_t^*$$

where $e$ is the price of foreign currency and $p_t^*$ is the world price. Under a fixed exchange rate this means that domestic inflation is determined abroad. In the pre-1979 period when the Irish pound was linked one-for-one with sterling, Irish and UK inflation were indeed equal, and it was widely felt that breaking the link with sterling and tying to the DM would bring Irish inflation down quite rapidly to the much lower German level.

The second implication of perfect competition is that the SOE faces an infinitely elastic world demand function for its output, and an infinitely elastic world supply function for whatever it wishes to purchase. This is marked World D/S in Figure A.1 below at the initial price level $p_{t0}$ (where, for simplicity, we assume zero world inflation).

**Figure A.1.    The traded goods sector**

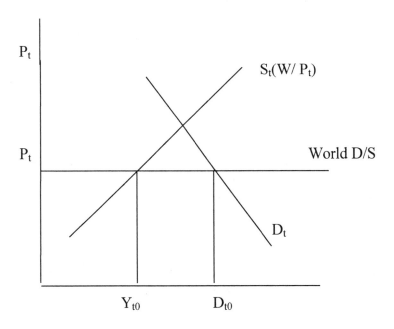

Output is determined by firms choosing labour inputs and a level of investment ($I_t$) that maximizes profits $\pi_t$:

(2)
$$\pi_t = p_t Y_t - r^* p_t (K_0 + I + bI^2) - wL_t$$

where $Y_t = F(K_0 + I + L_t)$ is the firm's constant returns to scale production function, the second term is the cost to the firm of borrowing for its capital investments, $bI^2$ is a capital-adjustment cost term which ensures that firms do not adjust instantaneously to their desired long-run capital stock, as is common in the theory of the firm, and the final term on the right is the wage bill.

Optimization yields the following labour demand and investment functions:

(3)
$$F_{Lt} = w / p_t$$

and

(4)
$$I_t = I(F_{Kt} / r^*)$$

With constant returns to scale, the marginal products of capital and labour depend only on the capital labour ratio, which, as (3) reveals, is determined by the real product wage.

With capital fixed at a point in time, a disequilibrating increase in real wages will lead to labour shedding in the short run, and will lead to reduced investment and further labour shedding over time. Higher world interest rates, for a given real wage, will also lead to reduced investment and a decrease in employment over time.

This simple model therefore reveals that output is determined by real wages and interest rates. As interest rate effects take time to impact on output, let us concentrate for the moment on the role of real wages in output determination.

The supply of output depends on the real wage (w/p$_t$), which is graphed as S$_t$ in Figure A.1. A rise in wage demands shifts the supply curve to the left, and output is reduced.

So much for output, employment, inflation and interest rates. What of the trade balance? The trade deficit is determined by the excess of expenditure *(C+I+G)* over income (Y$_t$). If expenditure is as drawn in Figure A.1, represented by D$_t$, there is a trade deficit of $D_{t0} - Y_{t0}$.

Now consider the impact of fiscal and exchange rate policies in this model. Ignoring taxation (so that it may be realistic to assume that nominal wages are not affected), an increase in government spending raises D$_t$ but leaves Y$_t$ unchanged. Its only effect therefore is to worsen the trade balance. When it comes to be financed by taxation, however, it is reasonable to suppose that wage demands will rise to some extent in an attempt to compensate, so output and employment will fall. This reveals the extremely non-Keynesian nature of the model.

Now consider a devaluation. The increase in the exchange rate (i.e. the price of foreign currency) raises domestic prices and shifts the world supply/demand line upwards. If domestic wages do not respond, then output and employment are increased and the trade deficit reduced. If real wages are rigid, on the other hand, so that wage demands rise in line with inflation, the domestic supply curve will shift upwards in the same proportion, and there will be no real effects. The devaluation will have generated inflation without raising employment or output.[74]

### A.3. Defects of the one-sector SOE model

That this very simple model dominated policy-making for at least one short period in recent Irish economic history is attested to by Honohan (1988) who writes that

> One oversimplified view enjoyed an early vogue, and was, I believe, influential in determining the course of policy between 1981 and 1984. According to this view the Government's overspending was closely matched by national overspending, as reflected in the balance of international payments, which has increased in line with the Government's borrowing. Accordingly the task facing the Government was a mechanical one with limited adverse consequences: if the Government's overspending could be reduced - by whatever means - the impact would be on national spending, and not on production. It was held by many that the expansion of the Government's deficit had created jobs abroad rather than at home. If so, then by an argument of symmetry, the elimination of that deficit need have little effect on jobs at home.

We now need to take note of the weaknesses of the model as a description of economic reality for even as open an economy as Ireland's.

One weakness is that the assumption (implied by perfect competition) that firms can sell all they desire to produce at going world prices is patently unrealistic. As long ago as 1981 Honohan showed that contrary to the predictions of the model, world demand exerted an impact on Irish output independent of its impact on price. Kennedy and Foley (1978) explored one way out of this dilemma using the kinked-oligopoly-curve model. A more satisfactory solution, however, has been provided by Bradley and Fitz Gerald (1990). They propose a model in which all tradable-sector production is done by internationally footloose companies (MNCs); pricing decisions are therefore independent of the SOE's factor costs. When world output expands MNCs expand production at all their production locations. The proportion of MNC investment located in any individual SOE, however, depends on the relative competitiveness of the SOE in question. This allows SOE output to be determined both by domestic factor costs and by world demand. Since SOE demand is tiny relative to world demand, it plays no role in the MNCs' output decisions.

There are two further weaknesses, however, that drive one in the direction of the two-sector SOE model. The first is that purchasing power parity (PPP), to the extent to which it is valid, is known to break down for substantial periods of time. PPP holds that the relationship between domestic and foreign price levels (rather than the prices of traded goods only) can be described as:

$$(5) \qquad\qquad\qquad p_t = ep^*$$

If all goods are tradable and if arbitrage ensures that the law of one price holds, then this relationship clearly must hold. If some goods are non-(internationally-)tradable, however, then arbitrage does not occur; PPP will hold in this case only if all shocks are nominal shocks (i.e.

---

[74]     Kouri (1979) shows that devaluations in Finland typically had real effects lasting several years before the competitiveness gain was lost through increased wage demands.

monetary or exchange rate shocks), and even then only in the long run (if there are some nominal rigidities such as wage stickiness that apply in the short run but disappear over time).

In a model with non-tradables, one does not expect PPP to hold in the face of real shocks, such as government expenditure or taxation changes or disequilibrating movements in wages. As Purvis (1982) puts it: 'PPP should be interpreted as a comparative static result arising from a monetary disturbance and embodying the essential feature of monetary neutrality.'

Labour market hysteresis would, however, invalidate PPP since nominal shocks in this scenario can exert real long-run effects (Barry, 1994).

The other weakness of the one-sector SOE model is that, as already noted, government spending is precluded from having any positive effects. Yet most studies of Irish employment and unemployment conclude that the debt-financed fiscal expansion of the late-1970s did indeed boost employment and reduce unemployment (albeit at the expense of requiring very contractionary policies over the course of the whole 1980s) (Walsh (1987), and Barry and Bradley (1991)).

## A.4. The two-sector small-open-economy model

Let us therefore add an extra sector, the non-tradable (NT) sector, to the model. Output and employment in tradables continues to be determined as before, while the NT sector operates more like a closed economy model. The interactions between the two sectors prove interesting, however.

The price of NTs is determined by the interaction of supply and demand for these goods, as in Figure A.2.

Analogous to the situation with tradables, the supply of non-tradables depends on real product wages in that sector ($w/p_n$), while the demand for NTs, $D_n$, depends on relative prices and on real expenditure as follows:

$$(7) \qquad D_n = D_n\big[p_n / p_t; Y_t + (p_n / p_t)Y_n\big]$$

The first derivative is negative, of course, and the second is positive.

As before, the results depend very much on whether nominal wages or real wages are rigid.

Consider nominal wage rigidity first of all. An increase in government spending on non-tradables raises the demand for non-tradables and shifts $D_n$ to the right in Figure A.2, raising prices and the output level in that sector. With no effect on wages the output of tradables is not affected, so the policy has unambiguously positive effects on aggregate output and employment, and adverse effects on the price level. The trade balance is also adversely affected, as before. To see this note that, in line with (7), expenditure on tradables is

$$(8) \qquad D_t = D_t\big[p_n / p_t; Y_t + (p_n / p_t)Y_n\big]$$

where both derivatives in this case are positive. The increase in the relative price of NTs and the increase in NT-sector output both raise the demand for tradables, shifting the $D_t$ line to the right in Figure A.1, which worsens the trade deficit.

**Figure A.2.    The non-traded goods sector**

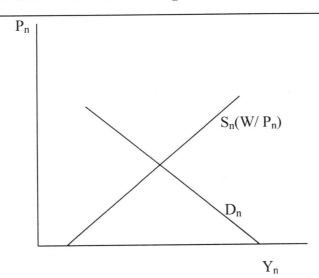

A devaluation once again pushes up the world D/S line and expands $Y_t$. This output effect alongside the increase in the relative price of tradables expands the demand for non-tradables, and leads to a knock-on expansion in this sector.

The devaluation of the Irish pound in 1986, at a time when unemployment was at an all time high, appeared to have had such unambiguously positive effects on output and employment, which were not then inflated away through wage catch-up (Giavazzi and Pagano (1990), Barry (1991)).[75]

If wages do catch up with policy-generated inflation, however, the effects can be substantially different. This case, of real wage rigidity, can be written:

(9)                                    $$w = \phi( p_n, p_t )$$

where $\Phi()$ is a linearly homogenous function.

Now, with no nominal rigidities in the system, a nominal shock such as a devaluation can have no real effects. An increase in $e$ will simply give rise to equiproportionate increases in $p_t$, $p_n$ and $w$, and employment and output levels will be unchanged.

There is a possible non-homogeneity in response to devaluation, however. Barry (1994) argues that if nominal wages are sticky in the short run, becoming more flexible over time, but if the labour market is characterized by hysteresis as appears to be the case in Ireland, then the increased pool of insiders created by a devaluation will exert downward pressure on wage demands in the longer term, so that the rise in employment may be sustained. This may account

---

[75]    The fact that they were not inflated away, though, could possibly be an effect of the fiscal contraction which began in 1987.

for the success of the strong Irish devaluation of 1986 (Leddin and Walsh, 1995), and Barry (1994) adopts this hypothesis in arguing that the devaluation of January 1993 should have been more substantial.

Even with wage demands linearly homogenous in prices, however, a fiscal shock will still have real effects. We now turn to an analysis of these effects.

With the exchange rate fixed in the SOE model, $p_t$ remains constant, so any increase in $p_n$ gives rise to a less-than-proportionate increase in $w$ (which follows from the linear homogeneity of equation (8)). An increase in government spending on non-tradables in this scenario, then, pushes up $D_n$ and $p_n$ as before. Since $w$ rises less than $p_n$, the fall in the real product wage stimulates output and employment in the NT sector. The wage shock, however, gets transmitted to the tradable goods sector, so $w/p_t$ rises, and $Y_t$ and $L_t$ are reduced.

The T and NT sectors therefore move in opposite directions in response to a government expenditure shock, when real wages are rigid.

The impact on aggregate employment, $L$, can be calculated from

(10)
$$L = L_n(p_n/w) + L_t(p_t/w)$$

and the wage equation (9).

The effect of a fiscal expansion is positive, zero or negative, then, depending on whether the following expression is greater than, equal to, or less than 1:

(11)
$$[\varepsilon(L_n; p_n/w)/\varepsilon(L_t; p_t/w)][\varepsilon(w; p_t)/\varepsilon(w; p_n)][L_n/L_t]$$

The functions on the left-hand side are the elasticities of sectoral labour demands and of wage demands. Total employment is therefore more likely to rise in response to increased government expenditure on non-tradables, the greater the elasticity of labour demand and the initial level of employment in that sector, and the lower the influence of non-tradable goods prices on the nominal wage, the latter obviously being related to the share of these goods in private consumption. This is a standard condition in the literature (see Barry and Devereux, 1995 and the references cited there), and is usually considered to hold.

If one believes that the Irish economy is characterized by such classical (high wage) constraints rather than Keynesian demand constraints, then the results of Barry and Bradley (1991) and Walsh (1987) alluded to earlier would suggest that the expansion in non-tradable employment generated by the Irish fiscal expansion of the late 1970s more than dominated the contraction in tradable sector employment induced by increased wage demands. This indeed suggests that the elasticities condition above is likely to be greater than 1.

Adopting the long-run condition that the return to capital be equalized across sectors will, of course, tie down prices in the SOE, as the following equations reveal:

(12)
$$p_n = a_{Ln}w + a_{Kn}r$$

$$p_t = a_{Lt}w + a_{Kt}r$$

since both $w$ and $p_t$ are fixed, yielding two equations in two unknowns, $p_n$ and $r$ ($a_{ij}$ represents units of factor $i$ per unit output of good $j$).

For wage stickiness to be possible as an equilibrium in this model, $r$ must be endogenous to the region/SOE (since $p_t$, $w$ and $r$ cannot all be exogenous), i.e. the stock located there must be related to the gap between regional (or SOE) and national (or international) required rates of return.[76] While it may at first seem implausible that these required rates of return could differ, not allowing them to differ would require that the own price elasticity for capital should be infinite. Bradley and Fitz Gerald (1990), however, are able to model Ireland's share of world output as dependent on relative profitability levels, and show that the own price elasticity of capital, when domestic output is allowed to adjust, is of the order of -0.4.

The empirical evidence for Ireland suggests then that the appropriate long-run condition on rates of profitability should be:

(13)                                    $$K = K(r - r^*)$$

rather than r = r$^*$, where $K$ is the domestic capital stock and $r^*$ is the international rate of profitability. Combining this with equations (12) above then gives us a system of three equations in three unknowns, when wages are rigid, and the model can then generate an equilibrium.

Allowing the return to capital to be determined endogenously in this way, a fiscal contraction in the wage-rigidity case reallocates capital from the NT sector to the T sector; capital-labour ratios remain unchanged in each sector, and the impact on employment then depends on the relative factor intensities of the two sectors (Helpman, 1976).

Besides generating more realistic fiscal policy effects, one of the other advantages of introducing a non-tradable goods sector is that deviations from PPP are more easily analysed in this context. Purchasing power parity (PPP) holds that a relationship such as that depicted in equation (5) holds not just for traded goods prices but also for price levels. This will hold, however, only if relative prices (i.e. the ratio of non-traded to traded goods prices or the real exchange rate) are constant. As noted above, this will apply only if shocks hitting the economy are monetary in nature (since real shocks will change equilibrium relative prices), and even then, given some short-run nominal rigidities, PPP would only be expected to hold in the long run.

Given the existence of NTs, it would have been completely wrong of policy-makers in 1979 to expect that simply because Irish inflation closely matched UK inflation in the pre-1979 period, it would come quickly down to German levels regardless of domestic conditions if the currency were tied to the DM.

What kind of factors would have led to an overvalued currency in the post-1979 period? Amongst the real shocks that would cause this are fiscal expansion and excessive wage growth,

---

[76]   This is in fact similar to applying an Armington assumption to the financial sector, an assumption which does not, of course, apply to goods markets in the SOE model.

since both would push $p_n$ up relative to $p_t$.[77] According to this view, Ireland would have been susceptible to overvaluation against sterling pre-1979 if fiscal policy had been very expansionary or if wage agreements had far exceeded the exogenous component of productivity growth.

In the post-1979 period, wage demands, fuelled by fiscal stimulation, rose at a rate that was inconsistent with the exchange rate target, so PPP was violated (i.e. $p_n/p_t$ rose relative to the country's trading partners). While fiscal retrenchment began in 1982, it proceeded at first through tax increases which exerted further upward pressure on wages, thereby worsening the overvaluation.[78]

The problem did appear to be brought substantially under control, however, by the large devaluations of 1986 and 1993, combined as they were with policies which achieved fiscal retrenchment through tight controls on government spending (with concomitant effects on expected taxes) rather than through further increases in taxation.

These deviations from PPP can be seen by looking either at hourly earnings in a common currency relative to one's trading partners, or by graphing relative output prices against the exchange rate. Each method tells the same qualitative story, with slight differences in timing. The cost competitiveness measure is depicted in Table A.1 (where a decline in the index represents a depreciation of the real exchange rate and an improvement in competitiveness).

**Table A.1.    A measure of cost competitiveness**

| 1979 | 1981 | 1983 | 1985 | 1987 | 1989 | 1991 | 1993 | 1995 |
|------|------|------|------|------|------|------|------|------|
| 96   | 95   | 101  | 104  | 115  | 109  | 112  | 110  | 110  |

A.4.1. Introducing Keynesian phenomena

Another advantage of introducing a non-tradable goods sector is that Keynesian phenomena are also more easily analysed. Given the intense competition assumed to prevail in the international marketplace, as well as the possibility of arbitrage, it is difficult to envisage long-lasting deviations from the law of one price. The possibility of non-tradable prices remaining at disequilibrium levels for some period of time is less controversial however (Neary, 1980).

The requirements for a Keynesian recession are that nominal wages and some output prices be sticky (Neary, 1990).[79] Thus, if a fall in demand for non-tradables occurs, this sector will contract without any stimulus towards the expansion of the tradable sector being imparted. Under

---

[77]    Note though that if the 'elasticities condition' is satisfied, an overvaluation due to the spending effects of fiscal expansion (as opposed to the effects of the associated present or anticipated future tax increases) is associated with employment gains, while an overvaluation due to excessive costs is associated with unemployment.

[78]    Econometrically, labour costs seem to exert a stronger influence on Irish prices than do domestic demand factors. The tax aspects of fiscal policy may therefore be more important for the extent of overvaluation than the level of government spending. Accordingly, one could argue that the fiscal expansion of 1977–82 induced some overvaluation of the real exchange rate, which was worsened by the tax increases thereafter. This overvaluation is frequently interpreted as an indication that the commitment to the exchange rate target was not credible. It is hard to believe, however, that the response of wage demands to these fiscal shocks would have been different under any alternative exchange rate regime.

[79]    Thus, Neary writes that 'it is the interaction of such failures (e.g. a sticky price of the non-traded good, or an export sales constraint) with the rigid wage in the labour market which gives rise to Keynesian phenomena'.

Keynesian conditions, therefore, a decline in government spending will have large effects on output and employment whether real or nominal wages are rigid.

Short-run stickiness in the price of non-traded goods means that a devaluation of the nominal exchange rate translates into a real exchange rate depreciation. The resulting fall in the real product wage in the traded goods sector induces that sector to expand, while the knock-on effects seen in equation (7) are likely to cause the other sector to expand also.

Both fiscal and exchange rate policies are therefore likely to have strong positive short-run effects in conditions of Keynesian recession. A similar result applies to monetary policy, even under fixed exchange rates, as will be clear from the discussion above of the monetary approach to the balance of payments. In line with Dornbusch (1976), similar effects will arise under flexible exchange rates, as with sticky nominal wages and non-traded goods prices the real exchange rate depreciates temporarily in response to a monetary expansion.

Accordingly, the British monetary contraction of the early 1980s would have caused a *real* appreciation of sterling in the early 1980s, which would have pushed Irish inflation above UK levels, leading to a competitiveness loss for Ireland *vis-à-vis* Germany, and a gain against the UK. This is, in fact, exactly what occurred (Leddin and Walsh, 1995).

## A.5.  Concluding comments

Appendix A has demonstrated the broad range of issues that can be tackled in the context of the small-open-economy model. The model yields insights into the macroeconomic impact of policies such as devaluation and government spending programmes, as well as exogenous shocks such as disequilibrating wage movements.

We have suggested that the two-sector version, embodying non-tradable goods as well as tradables, is a more useful tool of analysis than the model that assumes that all goods are tradable, and that there may be benefits to be gained from recognizing that Keynesian assumptions may sometimes be appropriate (i.e. the recognition that prices as well as wages may not move perfectly flexibly to their equilibrium levels).

We saw that this relatively simple model can give a reasonable account of the response of the Irish economy to the macroeconomic shocks of recent decades.

APPENDIX B

# Classification of the sectors to be affected by the SEM for Greece, Ireland, Portugal and Spain

## Table B.1.    Greece: Classification of the sectors to be affected by the SEM (employment weighted)

| | | NACE | Sector | X/Y | H/Y | L/LM | dX/LM | d(X/Y)* |
|---|---|---|---|---|---|---|---|---|
| S1 | S11 | 341 | Insulated wires and cables | 18.48 | 81.52 | 0.6 | | 0.47 |
| | S11 | 351 | Motor vehicles | 3.78 | 96.22 | 0.7 | | 0.66 |
| | S12 | 453 | Clothing | 71.87 | 28.13 | 8.1 | | 1.47 |
| S2 | S21 | 417 | Spaghetti, macaroni | 10.44 | 89.56 | 0.4 | | 0.10 |
| | S21 | 436 | Knitting mills | 100.00 | 0.00 | 4.5 | | 0.00 |
| | S21 | 471 | Pulp and paper manuf. | 10.03 | 89.97 | 1.5 | | 0.37 |
| | S22 | 431 | Wool industry | 13.04 | 86.96 | 1.0 | | 0.22 |
| | S22 | 432 | Cotton industry | 28.89 | 71.11 | 7.1 | | 1.26 |
| | S23 | 224 | Prod. of non-ferrous metal | 47.47 | 52.53 | 2.1 | | 0.25 |
| | S23 | 481 | Rubber products | 16.67 | 83.33 | 0.8 | | 0.15 |
| Total | | | | | | 26.80 | 8.93 | |
| | | | | | | | -dH/LM | |
| D1 | D11 | 251 | Basic industrial chemicals | 9.38 | 90.62 | 2.3 | -2.06 | 2.04 |
| | D11 | 344 | Telecommunications equipment | 41.83 | 58.17 | 0.6 | -0.32 | 0.32 |
| | D11 | 442 | Leather industry | 56.67 | 43.33 | 0.1 | -0.04 | 0.04 |
| | D12 | 256 | Other chemical products | 85.77 | 14.23 | 0.4 | -0.02 | 0.02 |
| | D12 | 315 | Boilermaking | 3.92 | 96.08 | 0.2 | -0.19 | 0.17 |
| | D12 | 342 | Electrical machinery | 25.40 | 74.60 | 1.2 | -0.86 | 0.78 |
| | D12 | 427 | Brewing, malting | 0.47 | 99.53 | 1.0 | -0.99 | 0.90 |
| | D12 | 451 | Footwear | 59.00 | 41.00 | 1.9 | -0.65 | 0.59 |
| | D12 | 455 | Household textiles | 100.00 | 0.00 | 0.2 | 0.02 | 0.00 |
| | D13 | 248 | Ceramic goods | 14.98 | 85.02 | 1.8 | -1.50 | 1.22 |
| D2 | D21 | 255 | Paints, varnishes & inks | 3.40 | 96.60 | 0.4 | -0.35 | 0.11 |
| | D21 | 257 | Pharmaceuticals | 17.07 | 82.93 | 2.0 | -1.10 | 0.46 |
| | D21 | 347 | Electric lamps | 21.38 | 78.62 | 0.1 | -0.05 | 0.02 |
| | D21 | 352 | Car bodies, trailers, caravans | 50.89 | 49.11 | 0.2 | -0.04 | 0.03 |
| | D21 | 411 | Manuf. of veg. & oils | 22.19 | 77.81 | 0.6 | -0.28 | 0.13 |
| | D21 | 428 | Soft drinks | 1.18 | 98.82 | 1.1 | -1.05 | 0.30 |
| | D21 | 441 | Leather tan & fin | 17.91 | 82.09 | 0.4 | -0.21 | 0.09 |
| | D21 | 483 | Plastic products | 12.16 | 87.84 | 2.5 | -1.61 | 0.60 |
| | D22 | 222 | Steel tubes | 37.53 | 62.47 | 0.7 | -0.21 | 0.11 |
| | D22 | 247 | Glass & glassware | 15.11 | 84.89 | 0.5 | -0.29 | 0.11 |
| | D22 | 316 | Tools, fin. metal goods | 11.28 | 88.72 | 4.1 | -2.72 | 0.91 |
| | D22 | 325 | Plant for mines, steel | 37.18 | 62.82 | 0.1 | -0.3 | 0.02 |
| | D22 | 328 | Other mach. & equipment | 28.50 | 71.50 | 1.0 | -0.39 | 0.18 |
| | D22 | 346 | Domestic electrical appliances | 2.67 | 97.33 | 1.4 | -1.26 | 0.34 |
| | D22 | 412 | Slaughtering prep. meat | 32.84 | 67.16 | 0.8 | -0.27 | 0.13 |
| | D22 | 413 | Manuf. of dairy products | 5.77 | 94.23 | 1.4 | -1.12 | 0.33 |
| | D22 | 419 | Bread & flour confectionery | 9.87 | 90.13 | 1.1 | -0.76 | 0.25 |
| | D22 | 472 | Processed paper | 15.84 | 84.16 | 1.2 | -0.68 | 0.25 |
| | D22 | 494 | Manuf. of sports goods and toys | 8.15 | 91.85 | 0.3 | -0.22 | 0.07 |
| | D23 | 314 | Structural metal products | 8.95 | 91.05 | 0.9 | -0.65 | 0.18 |
| | D23 | 343 | Elect. app., batts & accumul. | 14.11 | 85.89 | 0.3 | -0.18 | 0.06 |
| | D23 | 362 | Rolling stock | 0.27 | 99.73 | 1.1 | -1.09 | 0.25 |
| | D23 | 424 | Distilleries & alcohol | 26.59 | 73.41 | 0.4 | -0.16 | 0.07 |
| | D23 | 438 | Carpets, floor coverings | 24.61 | 75.39 | 0.9 | -0.39 | 0.15 |
| | D23 | 467 | Wooden furniture | 4.46 | 95.54 | 0.8 | -0.67 | 0.17 |
| Total | | | | | | 34.00 | -22.41 | 16.31 |

*Legend:* X/Y: exports as a percentage of gross output, 1985.

H/Y: (100-X/Y) home market sales as a percentage of output, 1985.

L/LM: sectoral share of manufacturing employment, 1985.

dX/LM: gain in exports as a percentage of total manufacturing employment.

-dH/LM: loss in home market sales as a percentage of total manufacturing employment.

d(X/Y)*: employment-weighted percentage point change in export-output ratio, adjusted for demand conditions.

*Data sources: European Economy,* special edition 1990, part C, Greece.

Eurostat, *Structure and Activity of Industry,* Annual Enquiry – Main Results 1986/87.

Export data: Eurostat SCE 2912 – on microfiche, 1985.

**Table B.2    Ireland: Classification of the sectors to be affected by the SEM (employment weighted)**

|  |  | NACE | Sector | X/Y | H/Y | L/LM | dX/LM | d(X/Y)* |
|---|---|---|---|---|---|---|---|---|
| S1 | S11 | 330 | Office & data-processing machinery (M) | 98 | 2 | 3.8 |  | 0.00 |
|  |  | 344 | Telecommunications equipment (M) | 87 | 13 | 2.6 |  | 0.09 |
|  |  | 341 | Insulated wires and cables (M) | 70 | 30 | 2.1 |  | 0.46 |
|  | S12 | 421 | Cocoa, chocolate (I) | 62 | 38 | 1.2 |  | 0.34 |
|  | S13 | 372 | Medical & surgical equip. (M) | 99 | 1 | 2.3 |  | 0.00 |
| S2 | S21 | 251 | Basic industrial chemicals (I) | 43 | 57 | 1.2 |  | 0.19 |
|  |  | 257 | Pharmaceuticals (M) | 97 | 3 | 2.8 |  | 0.00 |
|  |  | 345 | Radios, TVs, etc. (M) | 38 | 62 | 1.1 |  | 0.19 |
|  |  | 346 | Domestic electrical appliances (M) | 78 | 22 | 1.3 |  | 0.08 |
|  |  | 351 | Motor vehicles (I) | 33 | 67 | 0.4 |  | 0.07 |
|  |  | 428 | Soft drinks (M) | 13 | 87 | 1.3 |  | 0.31 |
|  | S22 | 325 | Plant for mines, steel (M) | 69 | 31 | 0.6 |  | 0.05 |
|  |  | 364 | Aerospace equipment (I) | 40 | 60 | 1.1 |  | 0.17 |
|  |  | 413 | Dairy products (I) | 29 | 71 | 3.8 |  | 0.67 |
|  |  | 427 | Brewing, malting (I) | 13 | 87 | 1.6 |  | 0.35 |
|  | S23 | 247 | Glass & glassware (I) | 55 | 45 | 1.9 |  | 0.19 |
|  |  | 322 | Machine tools (M) | 69 | 31 | 0.6 |  | 0.04 |
|  |  | 323 | Textile machinery (M) | 69 | 31 | 0.05 |  | 0.00 |
|  |  | 324 | Food, chemical machinery (M) | 69 | 31 | 0.2 |  | 0.01 |
|  |  | 326 | Transmission equipment (M) | 69 | 31 | 0.1 |  | 0.01 |
|  |  | 327 | Other machinery (M) | 69 | 31 | 0.04 |  | 0.00 |
|  |  | 432 | Cotton industry (M) | 84 | 16 | 0.4 |  | 0.01 |
|  |  | 481 | Rubber products (M) | 85 | 15 | 1 |  | 0.03 |
|  |  | 491 | Jewellery (I) | 50 | 50 | 0.9 |  | 0.10 |
|  |  | 494 | Toys & sports goods (I) | 85 | 15 | 0.3 |  | 0.01 |
| Total |  |  |  |  |  | 32.69 | 10.90 |  |
|  |  |  |  |  |  |  | -dH/LM |  |
| D1 | D12 | 342 | Electrical machinery (M) | 90 | 10 | 1.1 | -0.00 | 0.00 |
|  |  | 361 | Shipbuilding (I) | 93 | 7 | 0.3 | -0.00 | 0.00 |
|  |  | 417 | Spaghetti, macaroni (I) | 50 | 50 | 0.02 | -0.01 | 0.01 |
| D2 | D21 | 256 | Other chemical products (M) | 77 | 23 | 0.7 | -0.05 | 0.04 |
|  |  | 321 | Agricultural machinery (M) | 69 | 31 | 0.6 | -0.06 | 0.05 |
|  |  | 493 | Photographic labs (I) | 29 | 71 | 0.1 | -0.04 | 0.02 |
|  | D22 | 431 | Wool industry (I) | 70 | 30 | 1.9 | -0.18 | 0.14 |
|  |  | 453 | Clothing (I) | 54 | 46 | 6.5 | -1.14 | 0.75 |
|  |  | 455 | Household textiles (I) | 74 | 26 | 0.5 | -0.04 | 0.03 |
|  | D23 | 248 | Ceramic goods (I) | 91 | 9 | 0.4 | -0.00 | 0.00 |
|  |  | 347 | Electric lamps (M) | 90 | 10 | 0.1 | -0.00 | 0.00 |
|  |  | 438 | Carpets, floor coverings (M) | 65 | 35 | 0.4 | -0.05 | 0.03 |
|  |  | 451 | Footwear (I) | 42 | 58 | 0.6 | -0.15 | 0.08 |
| Total |  |  |  |  |  | 13.22 | -1.72 | 4.54 |

*Legend*:  X/Y: exports as a percentage of gross output, 1986.

H/Y: (100-X/Y) home market sales as a percentage of gross output, 1986.

L/LM: sectoral share of manufacturing employment, 1987.

dX/LM: gain in exports as a percentage of total manufacturing employment.

-dH/LM: loss in home market sales as a percentage of total manufacturing employment.

d(X/Y)*: employment-weighted percentage point change in export-output ratio, adjusted for demand conditions.

*Data source*: *European Economy*, special edition 1990, part C, Ireland, pp. 247–261.

**Table B.3.　Portugal: Classification of the sectors to be affected by the SEM (employment weighted)**

| | | NACE | Sector | X/Y | H/Y | L/LM | dX/LM | d(X/Y)* |
|---|---|---|---|---|---|---|---|---|
| S1 | S11 | 341 | Insulated wires and cables | 54.9 | 45.1 | 0.6 | | 0.23 |
| | | 428 | Soft drinks | 2.6 | 97.4 | 0.5 | | 0.48 |
| | S12 | 361 | Shipbuilding | 81.4 | 18.6 | 2.7 | | 0.23 |
| | | 425 | Wine, champagne | 49.9 | 50.1 | 0.2 | | 0.08 |
| | | 427 | Brewing, malting | 2.3 | 97.7 | 0.5 | | 0.44 |
| | S13 | 248 | Ceramic goods | 58.9 | 41.1 | 2.3 | | 0.64 |
| S2 | S21 | 352 | Car bodies, trailers, caravans | 20.5 | 79.5 | 0.8 | | 0.17 |
| | | 436 | Knitwear industry | 66.9 | 33.1 | 4.7 | | 0.43 |
| | S22 | 316 | Tools, fin. metal goods | 28.1 | 71.9 | 4.9 | | 0.88 |
| | | 453 | Clothing | 74.1 | 25.9 | 7.6 | | 0.49 |
| | | 455 | Household textiles | 95.6 | 4.4 | 0.5 | | 0.00 |
| | S23 | 247 | Glass & glassware | 35.5 | 64.5 | 1.3 | | 0.19 |
| | | 324 | Food, chemical machinery | 37.3 | 62.7 | 0.2 | | 0.03 |
| | | 415 | Proc. & cons. fish & seafood | 27.2 | 72.8 | 1.4 | | 0.23 |
| | | 431/2 | Wool/cotton textiles | 15.6 | 84.4 | 15.2 | | 2.89 |
| | | 438 | Carpets, floor coverings | 27.0 | 73.0 | 0.7 | | 0.11 |
| | | 439 | Misc. textiles industries | 53.6 | 46.4 | 1.5 | | 0.16 |
| | | 451 | Footwear | 93.3 | 6.7 | 3.9 | | 0.00 |
| Total | | | | | | 49.45 | 16.48 | |
| | | | | | | | -dH/LM | |
| D1 | D11 | 257 | Pharmaceuticals | 28.3 | 71.7 | 1.3 | -0.89 | 0.88 |
| | | 330 | Office and data-processing machinery | 103.9 | -3.9 | 0.2 | 0.03 | 0.00 |
| | | 342 | Electrical machinery | 21.2 | 78.8 | 0.9 | -0.69 | 0.68 |
| | D12 | 260 | Man-made fibres | 3.8 | 96.2 | 0.3 | -0.29 | 0.26 |
| | | 315 | Boilermaking | 23.0 | 77.0 | 0.7 | -0.52 | 0.47 |
| | | 362 | Rolling stock | 25.3 | 74.7 | 0.2 | -0.14 | 0.13 |
| | | 372 | Medico-surgical app & ortho. app. | 41.1 | 58.9 | 0.1 | -0.05 | 0.05 |
| | | 417 | Spaghetti, macaroni | 1.9 | 98.1 | 0.1 | -0.10 | 0.09 |
| | | 421 | Cocoa, chocolate | 5.9 | 94.1 | 0.5 | -0.47 | 0.42 |
| | D13 | 363 | Cycles, motorcycles & parts | 33.6 | 66.4 | 0.4 | -0.25 | 0.20 |
| D2 | D21 | 251 | Basic industrial chemicals | 28.3 | 71.7 | 1.2 | -0.47 | 0.24 |
| | | 256 | Other chemical products | 28.4 | 71.6 | 1.0 | -0.39 | 0.20 |
| | | 321 | Agricultural machinery | 10.7 | 89.3 | 0.4 | -0.27 | 0.10 |
| | | 344/5 | Radio & TV, telec equipment | 75.8 | 24.2 | 2.1 | -0.16 | 0.14 |
| | | 347 | Electric lamps | 25.9 | 74.1 | 0.5 | -0.21 | 0.10 |
| | | 351 | Motor vehicles | 23.7 | 76.3 | 0.8 | -0.36 | 0.17 |
| | | 353 | Mot. veh. parts & acc. | 98.8 | 1.2 | 0.7 | -0.00 | 0.00 |
| | D22 | 325 | Plant for mines, steel | 79.0 | 21.0 | 0.4 | -0.02 | 0.02 |
| | | 328 | Other mach. & equipment | 25.2 | 74.8 | 1.3 | -0.55 | 0.24 |
| | | 346 | Domestic electrical appliances | 32.9 | 67.1 | 0.3 | -0.10 | 0.05 |
| | | 371 | Measuring & precision instruments | 24.9 | 75.1 | 0.1 | -0.04 | 0.02 |
| | | 419 | Bread & flour confectionery | 0.6 | 99.4 | 3.9 | -3.81 | 0.97 |
| | D23 | 322 | Machine tools | 40.1 | 59.9 | 0.4 | -0.111 | 0.05 |
| | | 323 | Textile machinery | 52.8 | 47.2 | 0.3 | -0.05 | 0.03 |
| | | 343 | Elect. app., batts & accumul. | 8.2 | 91.8 | 0.2 | -0.15 | 0.04 |
| | | 416 | Grain milling | 4.3 | 95.7 | 0.6 | -0.51 | 0.13 |
| | | 481 | Rubber products | 20.8 | 79.2 | 0.9 | -0.44 | 0.16 |
| Total | | | | | | 19.80 | -11.01 | 13.53 |

*Legend:*　X/Y: exports as a percentage of gross output, average 1985-87.
　　　　　H/Y: (100-X/Y) non-tradables as a percentage of output, average 1985-87.
　　　　　L/LM: sectoral share of manufacturing employment, 1985.
　　　　　dX/LM: gain in exports as a percentage of total manufacturing employment.
　　　　　-dH/LM: loss in home market sales as a percentage of total manufacturing employment.
　　　　　d(X/Y)*: employment-weighted percentage point change in export-output ratio, adjusted for demand conditions.
*Data sources: European Economy*, special edition 1990, part C, Portugal.
　　　　　Eurostat, *Structure and Activity of Industry*, Annual Enquiry – Main Results 1984/85.

## Table B.4.  Spain: Classification of the sectors to be affected by the SEM (employment weighted)

| | | NACE | Sector | X/Y | H/Y | L/LM | -dH/LM | d(X/Y)* |
|---|---|---|---|---|---|---|---|---|
| S1 | S11 | 341 | Insulated wires and cables | 18.33 | 81.67 | 0.36 | | 0.17 |
| | S12 | 425 | Wine, champagne | 9.71 | 90.29 | 1.09 | | 0.55 |
| | S13 | 494 | Toys, sports goods | 32.83 | 67.17 | 0.37 | | 0.09 |
| S2 | S21 | 351 | Motor vehicles | 35.85 | 64.15 | 4.93 | | 0.52 |
| | S22 | 346 | Domestic electrical appliances | 15.41 | 84.59 | 0.91 | | 0.12 |
| | S22 | 431 | Wool/cotton textiles | 18.01 | 81.99 | 0.29 | | 0.04 |
| | S22 | 453 | Clothing | 7.07 | 92.93 | 3.95 | | 0.55 |
| | S22 | 455 | Household textiles | 22.76 | 77.24 | 0.65 | | 0.08 |
| | S22 | 491 | Jewellery | 92.20 | 7.80 | 0.34 | | 0.00 |
| | S23 | 248 | Ceramic goods | 25.14 | 74.86 | 1.49 | | 0.15 |
| | S23 | 432 | Cotton industry | 10.48 | 89.52 | 1.13 | | 0.14 |
| | S23 | 451 | Footwear | 60.73 | 39.27 | 1.88 | | 0.00 |
| | S23 | 481 | Rubber products | 29.08 | 70.92 | 1.56 | | 0.15 |
| Total | | | | | | 18.95 | 3.34 | |
| | | | | | | | **-dH/LM** | |
| D1 | D11 | 257 | Pharmaceuticals | 10.83 | 89.17 | 1.64 | -1.34 | 0.89 |
| | D11 | 330 | Office and data-processing machinery | 69.53 | 30.47 | 0.13 | 0.00 | 0.00 |
| | D11 | 342 | Electrical machinery | 9.57 | 90.43 | 2.02 | -1.70 | 1.12 |
| | D11 | 344 | Radio & TV, telec equipment | 16.62 | 83.38 | 1.27 | -0.92 | 0.61 |
| | D11 | 428 | Soft drinks | 0.34 | 99.66 | 0.93 | -0.92 | 0.61 |
| | D12 | 315 | Boilermaking | 4.44 | 95.56 | 0.66 | -0.61 | 0.37 |
| | D12 | 361 | Shipbuilding | 41.93 | 58.07 | 1.87 | -0.56 | 0.34 |
| | D12 | 362 | Rolling stock | 1.48 | 98.52 | 0.66 | -0.64 | 0.39 |
| | D12 | 372 | Medico-surgical app & ortho. app. | 49.54 | 50.46 | 0.11 | -0.02 | 0.01 |
| | D12 | 417 | Spaghetti, macaroni | 0.00 | 100.00 | 0.05 | -0.05 | 0.03 |
| | D12 | 421 | Cocoa, chocolate | 8.48 | 91.52 | 0.76 | -0.65 | 0.39 |
| | D12 | 427 | Brewing, malting | 0.40 | 99.60 | 0.70 | -0.70 | 0.42 |
| D2 | D21 | 251 | Basic industrial chemicals | 28.39 | 71.61 | 1.15 | -0.32 | 0.14 |
| | D21 | 256 | Other chemical products | 5.66 | 94.34 | 1.28 | -0.91 | 0.20 |
| | D21 | 321 | Agricultural machinery | 12.88 | 87.12 | 0.66 | -0.33 | 0.09 |
| | D21 | 345 | Radio, TV | 8.28 | 91.72 | 0.82 | -0.51 | 0.12 |
| | D21 | 347 | Electric lamps | 18.53 | 81.47 | 0.48 | -0.19 | 0.06 |
| | D21 | 493 | Photo and cine labs | 6.98 | 93.02 | 0.13 | -0.09 | 0.02 |
| | D22 | 325 | Plant for mines, steel | 20.31 | 79.69 | 0.98 | -0.36 | 0.12 |
| | D22 | 364 | Aerospace equipment | 54.55 | 45.45 | 0.42 | -0.05 | 0.02 |
| | D23 | 247 | Glass & glassware | 12.16 | 87.84 | 1.03 | -0.54 | 0.12 |
| | D23 | 322 | Machine tools | 33.07 | 66.93 | 0.70 | -0.16 | 0.06 |
| | D23 | 323 | Textile machinery | 39.13 | 60.87 | 0.33 | -0.06 | 0.03 |
| | D23 | 324 | Food, chemical machinery | 38.35 | 61.65 | 0.58 | -0.11 | 0.05 |
| | D23 | 326 | Transmission equipment | 39.08 | 60.92 | 0.27 | -0.05 | 0.02 |
| | D23 | 327 | Other machines and equipment | 27.45 | 72.55 | 0.38 | -0.11 | 0.04 |
| | D23 | 438 | Carpets, floor coverings | 25.92 | 74.08 | 0.17 | -0.05 | 0.02 |
| Total | | | | | | 20.18 | -11.96 | 8.82 |

*Legend:*  X/Y: exports as a percentage of gross output, 1985.

H/Y: (100-X/Y) home market sales as a percentage of output, 1985.

L/LM: sectoral share of manufacturing employment, 1985.

dX/LM: gain in exports as a percentage of total manufacturing employment.

-dH/LM: loss in home market sales as a percentage of total manufacturing employment.

d(X/Y)*: employment-weighted percentage point change in export-output ratio, adjusted for demand growth.

*Data sources: European Economy,* special edition 1990, part C, Spain.

Eurostat, *Structure and Activity of Industry,* Annual Enquiry – Main Results 1984/85.

OECD STAN Database, Dec 1994 on diskettes.

**Table B.5.      Greece: Classification of the sectors to be affected by the SEM (output weighted)**

|   |   | NACE | Sector | X/Y | H/Y | Y/YM | dX/YM | d(X/Y)* |
|---|---|---|---|---|---|---|---|---|
| S1 | S11 | 341 | Insulated wires and cables | 18.48 | 81.52 | 1.05 |  | 0.82 |
|  | S11 | 351 | Motor vehicles | 3.78 | 96.22 | 0.94 |  | 0.89 |
|  | S12 | 453 | Clothing | 71.87 | 28.13 | 2.17 |  | 0.39 |
| S2 | S21 | 417 | Spaghetti, macaroni | 10.44 | 89.56 | 0.37 |  | 0.09 |
|  | S21 | 436 | Knitting mills | 100.00 | 0.00 | 1.98 |  | 0.00 |
|  | S21 | 471 | Pulp and paper manuf. | 10.03 | 89.97 | 1.22 |  | 0.30 |
|  | S22 | 431 | Wool industry | 13.04 | 86.96 | 0.56 |  | 0.12 |
|  | S22 | 432 | Cotton industry | 28.89 | 71.11 | 1.43 |  | 0.25 |
|  | S23 | 224 | Prod. of non-ferrous metal | 47.47 | 52.53 | 3.80 |  | 0.45 |
|  | S23 | 481 | Rubber products | 16.67 | 83.33 | 0.66 |  | 0.12 |
| Total |  |  |  |  |  | 14.19 | 4.73 |  |
|  |  |  |  |  |  |  | **-dH/YM** |  |
| D1 | D11 | 251 | Basic industrial chemicals | 9.38 | 90.62 | 4.23 | -3.79 | 3.75 |
|  | D11 | 344 | Telecommunications equipment | 41.83 | 58.17 | 0.29 | -0.15 | 0.15 |
|  | D11 | 442 | Leather industry | 56.67 | 43.33 | 0.03 | -0.01 | 0.01 |
|  | D12 | 256 | Other chemical products | 85.77 | 14.23 | 0.47 | -0.02 | 0.02 |
|  | D12 | 315 | Boilermaking | 3.92 | 96.08 | 0.10 | -0.09 | 0.08 |
|  | D12 | 342 | Electrical machinery | 25.40 | 74.60 | 0.63 | -0.45 | 0.41 |
|  | D12 | 427 | Brewing, malting | 0.47 | 99.53 | 1.11 | -1.11 | 0.99 |
|  | D12 | 451 | Footwear | 59.00 | 41.00 | 0.72 | -0.25 | 0.22 |
|  | D12 | 455 | Household textiles | 100.00 | 0.00 | 0.17 | 0.02 | 0.00 |
|  | D13 | 248 | Ceramic goods | 14.98 | 85.02 | 0.89 | -0.74 | 0.60 |
| D2 | D21 | 255 | Paints, varnishes & inks | 3.40 | 96.60 | 0.45 | -0.40 | 0.12 |
|  | D21 | 257 | Pharmaceuticals | 17.07 | 82.93 | 1.49 | -0.82 | 0.34 |
|  | D21 | 347 | Electric lamps | 21.38 | 78.62 | 0.05 | -0.02 | 0.01 |
|  | D21 | 352 | Car bodies, trailers, caravans | 50.89 | 49.11 | 0.22 | -0.04 | 0.03 |
|  | D21 | 411 | Manuf. of veg. & oils | 22.19 | 77.81 | 1.51 | -0.71 | 0.32 |
|  | D21 | 428 | Soft drinks | 1.18 | 98.82 | 1.00 | -0.96 | 0.27 |
|  | D21 | 441 | Leather tan & fin | 17.91 | 82.09 | 0.48 | -0.26 | 0.11 |
|  | D21 | 483 | Plastic products | 12.16 | 87.84 | 1.80 | -1.16 | 0.43 |
|  | D22 | 222 | Steel tubes | 37.53 | 62.47 | 0.73 | -0.21 | 0.11 |
|  | D22 | 247 | Glass & glassware | 15.11 | 84.89 | 0.28 | -0.16 | 0.06 |
|  | D22 | 316 | Tools, fin. metal goods | 11.28 | 88.72 | 3.04 | -2.01 | 0.67 |
|  | D22 | 325 | Plant for mines, steel | 37.18 | 62.82 | 0.04 | -0.01 | 0.01 |
|  | D22 | 328 | Other mach. & equipment | 28.50 | 71.50 | 0.54 | -0.21 | 0.10 |
|  | D22 | 346 | Domestic electrical appliances | 2.67 | 97.33 | 1.08 | -0.97 | 0.26 |
|  | D22 | 412 | Slaughtering prep. meat | 32.84 | 67.16 | 0.88 | -0.30 | 0.15 |
|  | D22 | 413 | Manuf. of dairy products | 5.77 | 94.23 | 1.93 | -1.55 | 0.45 |
|  | D22 | 419 | Bread & flour confectionery | 9.87 | 90.13 | 0.51 | -0.36 | 0.12 |
|  | D22 | 472 | Processed paper | 15.84 | 84.16 | 1.23 | -0.70 | 0.26 |
|  | D22 | 494 | Manuf. of sports goods and toys | 8.15 | 91.85 | 0.25 | -0.18 | 0.06 |
|  | D23 | 314 | Structural metal products | 8.95 | 91.05 | 0.70 | -0.50 | 0.14 |
|  | D23 | 343 | Elect. app., batts & accumul. | 14.11 | 85.89 | 0.18 | -0.11 | 0.03 |
|  | D23 | 362 | Rolling stock | 0.27 | 99.73 | 0.25 | -0.25 | 0.06 |
|  | D23 | 424 | Distilleries & alcohol | 26.59 | 73.41 | 0.47 | -0.19 | 0.08 |
|  | D23 | 438 | Carpets, floor coverings | 24.61 | 75.39 | 0.57 | -0.25 | 0.10 |
|  | D23 | 467 | Wooden furniture | 4.46 | 95.54 | 0.30 | -0.25 | 0.06 |
| Total |  |  |  |  |  | 28.61 | -19.18 | 14.05 |

*Legend:*   X/Y: exports as a percentage of gross output, 1985.

H/Y: (100-X/Y) home market sales as a percentage of output, 1985.

Y/YM: sectoral share of manufacturing output, 1985

dX/YM: gain in exports as a percentage of total manufacturing output.

-dH/YM: loss in home market sales as a percentage of total manufacturing output.

d(X/Y)*: output-weighted percentage point change in export-output ratio, adjusted for demand conditions.

*Data sources: European Economy,* special edition 1990, part C, Greece.

Eurostat, *Structure and Activity of Industry,* Annual Enquiry – Main Results 1986/87.

Export data: Eurostat SCE 2912 – on microfiche, 1985.

## Table B.6.    Ireland: Classification of the sectors to be affected by the SEM (output weighted)

| | | NACE | Sector | X/Y | H/Y | Y/YM | dX/YM | d(X/Y)* |
|---|---|---|---|---|---|---|---|---|
| S1 | S11 | 330 | Office & data-processing mach. (M) | 98 | 2 | 13.19 | | 0.00 |
| | | 344 | Telecommunications equip. (M) | 87 | 13 | 2.72 | | 0.09 |
| | | 341 | Insulated wires and cables (M) | 70 | 30 | 0.82 | | 0.18 |
| | S12 | 421 | Cocoa, chocolate (I) | 62 | 38 | 2.49 | | 0.70 |
| | S13 | 372 | Medical & surgical equip. (M) | 99 | 1 | 1.68 | | 0.00 |
| S2 | S21 | 251 | Basic industrial chemicals (I) | 43 | 57 | 2.28 | | 0.36 |
| | | 257 | Pharmaceuticals (M) | 97 | 3 | 5.96 | | 0.00 |
| | | 345 | Radios, TVs, etc. (M) | 38 | 62 | 2.12 | | 0.36 |
| | | 346 | Domestic electrical appliances (M) | 78 | 22 | 1.03 | | 0.06 |
| | | 351 | Motor vehicles (I) | 33 | 67 | 0.19 | | 0.03 |
| | | 428 | Soft drinks (M) | 13 | 87 | 1.64 | | 0.39 |
| | S22 | 325 | Plant for mines, steel (M) | 69 | 31 | 0.39 | | 0.03 |
| | | 364 | Aerospace equipment (I) | 40 | 60 | 0.50 | | 0.08 |
| | | 413 | Dairy products (I) | 29 | 71 | 12.01 | | 2.13 |
| | | 427 | Brewing, malting (I) | 13 | 87 | 5.05 | | 1.10 |
| | S23 | 247 | Glass & glassware (I) | 55 | 45 | 0.89 | | 0.09 |
| | | 322 | Machine tools (M) | 69 | 31 | 0.39 | | 0.03 |
| | | 323 | Textile machinery (M) | 69 | 31 | 0.03 | | 0.00 |
| | | 324 | Food, chemical machinery (M) | 69 | 31 | 0.13 | | 0.01 |
| | | 326 | Transmission equipment (M) | 69 | 31 | 0.07 | | 0.00 |
| | | 327 | Other machinery (M) | 69 | 31 | 0.03 | | 0.00 |
| | | 432 | Cotton industry (M) | 84 | 16 | 0.78 | | 0.03 |
| | | 481 | Rubber products (M) | 85 | 15 | 0.71 | | 0.02 |
| | | 491 | Jewellery (I) | 50 | 50 | 0.16 | | 0.02 |
| | | 494 | Toys & sports goods (I) | 85 | 15 | 0.27 | | 0.01 |
| Total | | | | | | 55.53 | 18.51 | |
| | | | | | | | **-dH/YM** | |
| D1 | D12 | 342 | Electrical machinery (M) | 90 | 10 | 0.61 | -0.00 | 0.00 |
| | | 361 | Shipbuilding (I) | 93 | 7 | 0.14 | -0.00 | 0.00 |
| | | 417 | Spaghetti, macaroni (I) | 50 | 50 | 0.04 | -0.02 | 0.01 |
| D2 | D21 | 256 | Other chemical products (M) | 77 | 23 | 0.78 | -0.05 | 0.05 |
| | | 321 | Agricultural machinery (M) | 69 | 31 | 0.39 | -0.04 | 0.03 |
| | | 493 | Photographic labs (I) | 29 | 71 | 0.12 | -0.05 | 0.02 |
| | D22 | 431 | Wool industry (I) | 70 | 30 | 0.44 | -0.04 | 0.03 |
| | | 453 | Clothing (I) | 54 | 46 | 1.43 | -0.25 | 0.16 |
| | | 455 | Household textiles (I) | 74 | 26 | 0.19 | -0.02 | 0.01 |
| | D23 | 248 | Ceramic goods (I) | 91 | 9 | 0.18 | -0.00 | 0.00 |
| | | 347 | Electric lamps (M) | 90 | 10 | 0.07 | -0.00 | 0.00 |
| | | 438 | Carpets, floor coverings (M) | 65 | 35 | 0.30 | -0.04 | 0.02 |
| | | 451 | Footwear (I) | 42 | 58 | 0.15 | -0.04 | 0.02 |
| Total | | | | | | 4.83 | -0.54 | 6.10 |

*Legend:* X/Y: exports as a percentage of gross output, 1986.

H/Y: (100-X/Y) home market sales as a percentage of gross output, 1986.

Y/YM: sectoral share of manufacturing output, 1987.

dX/YM: gain in exports as a percentage of total manufacturing output.

-dH/YM: loss in home market sales as a percentage of total manufacturing output.

d(X/Y)*: output-weighted percentage point change in export-output ratio, adjusted for demand conditions.

*Data sources: European Economy,* special edition 1990, part C, Ireland, pp. 247-261.

Irish CSO Census of Industrial Production, 1987.

**Table B.7.    Portugal: Classification of the sectors to be affected by the SEM (output weighted)**

| | | NACE | Sector | X/Y | H/Y | Y/YM | dX/YM | d(X/Y)* |
|---|---|---|---|---|---|---|---|---|
| S1 | S11 | 341 | Insulated wires and cables | 54.9 | 45.1 | 0.89 | | 0.34 |
| | | 428 | Soft drinks | 2.6 | 97.4 | 0.58 | | 0.55 |
| | S12 | 361 | Shipbuilding | 81.4 | 18.6 | 0.97 | | 0.08 |
| | | 425 | Wine, champagne | 49.9 | 50.1 | 0.13 | | 0.05 |
| | | 427 | Brewing, malting | 2.3 | 97.7 | 0.94 | | 0.82 |
| | S13 | 248 | Ceramic goods | 58.9 | 41.1 | 1.10 | | 0.31 |
| S2 | S21 | 352 | Car bodies, trailers, caravans | 20.5 | 79.5 | 0.38 | | 0.08 |
| | | 436 | Knitwear industry | 66.9 | 33.1 | 3.32 | | 0.30 |
| | S22 | 316 | Tools, fin. metal goods | 28.1 | 71.9 | 2.69 | | 0.48 |
| | | 453 | Clothing | 74.1 | 25.9 | 3.99 | | 0.26 |
| | | 455 | Household textiles | 95.6 | 4.4 | 0.25 | | 0.00 |
| | S23 | 247 | Glass & glassware | 35.5 | 64.5 | 1.00 | | 0.14 |
| | | 324 | Food, chemical machinery | 37.3 | 62.7 | 0.08 | | 0.01 |
| | | 415 | Proc. & cons. fish & seafood | 27.2 | 72.8 | 1.14 | | 0.19 |
| | | 431/2 | Wool/cotton textiles | 15.6 | 84.4 | 8.71 | | 1.65 |
| | | 438 | Carpets, floor coverings | 27.0 | 73.0 | 0.54 | | 0.09 |
| | | 439 | Misc. textiles industries | 53.6 | 46.4 | 0.74 | | 0.08 |
| | | 451 | Footwear | 93.3 | 6.7 | 2.26 | | 0.00 |
| Total | | | | | | 29.69 | 9.90 | |
| | | | | | | | -dH/YM | |
| D1 | D11 | 257 | Pharmaceuticals | 28.3 | 71.7 | 1.55 | -1.06 | 1.05 |
| | | 330 | Office and data-processing machinery | 103.9 | -3.9 | 0.16 | 0.02 | 0.00 |
| | | 342 | Electrical machinery | 21.2 | 78.8 | 0.65 | -0.49 | 0.49 |
| | D12 | 260 | Man-made fibres | 3.8 | 96.2 | 0.74 | -0.71 | 0.64 |
| | | 315 | Boilermaking | 23.0 | 77.0 | 0.45 | -0.33 | 0.30 |
| | | 362 | Rolling stock | 25.3 | 74.7 | 0.27 | -0.20 | 0.18 |
| | | 372 | Medico-surgical app & ortho. app. | 41.1 | 58.9 | 0.08 | -0.04 | 0.04 |
| | | 417 | Spaghetti, macaroni | 1.9 | 98.1 | 0.28 | -0.27 | 0.25 |
| | | 421 | Cocoa, chocolate | 5.9 | 94.1 | 0.39 | -0.36 | 0.33 |
| | D13 | 363 | Cycles, motorcycles & parts | 33.6 | 66.4 | 0.26 | -0.16 | 0.13 |
| D2 | D21 | 251 | Basic industrial chemicals | 28.3 | 71.7 | 5.33 | -2.07 | 1.05 |
| | | 256 | Other chemical products | 28.4 | 71.6 | 2.62 | -1.01 | 0.52 |
| | | 321 | Agricultural machinery | 10.7 | 89.3 | 0.23 | -0.15 | 0.06 |
| | | 344/5 | Radio & TV, telec equipment | 75.8 | 24.2 | 2.26 | -0.17 | 0.15 |
| | | 347 | Electric lamps | 25.9 | 74.1 | 0.32 | -0.13 | 0.06 |
| | | 351 | Motor vehicles | 23.7 | 76.3 | 2.44 | -1.09 | 0.51 |
| | | 353 | Mot. veh. parts & acc. | 98.8 | 1.2 | 1.10 | -0.00 | 0.00 |
| | D22 | 325 | Plant for mines, steel | 79.0 | 21.0 | 0.20 | -0.01 | 0.01 |
| | | 328 | Other mach. & equipment | 25.2 | 74.8 | 1.04 | -0.44 | 0.19 |
| | | 346 | Domestic electrical appliances | 32.9 | 67.1 | 0.41 | -0.14 | 0.07 |
| | | 371 | Measuring & precision instruments | 24.9 | 75.1 | 0.09 | -0.04 | 0.02 |
| | | 419 | Bread & flour confectionery | 0.6 | 99.4 | 1.56 | -1.52 | 0.39 |
| | D23 | 322 | Machine tools | 40.1 | 59.9 | 0.17 | -0.05 | 0.02 |
| | | 323 | Textile machinery | 52.8 | 47.2 | 0.19 | -0.04 | 0.02 |
| | | 343 | Elect. app., batts & accumul. | 8.2 | 91.8 | 0.28 | -0.21 | 0.06 |
| | | 416 | Grain milling | 4.3 | 95.7 | 2.39 | -2.02 | 0.51 |
| | | 481 | Rubber products | 20.8 | 79.2 | 0.75 | -0.37 | 0.13 |
| Total | | | | | | 26.20 | -13.07 | 12.62 |

*Legend:*    X/Y: exports as a percentage of gross output, average 1985-87.
H/Y: (100-X/Y) non-tradables as a percentage of output, average 1985-87.
Y/YM: sectoral share of manufacturing output, 1987.
dX/YM: gain in exports as a percentage of total manufacturing output.
-dH/YM: loss in home market sales as a percentage of total manufacturing output.
d(X/Y)*: output-weighted percentage point change in export-output ratio, adjusted for demand conditions.
*Data sources: European Economy,* special edition 1990, part C, Portugal.
Eurostat, *Structure and Activity of Industry,* Annual Enquiry – Main Results 1984/85 and 1986/87.

## Table B.8. Spain: Classification of the sectors to be affected by the SEM (output weighted)

| | | NACE | Sector | X/Y | H/Y | Y/YM | dX/YM | d(X/Y)* |
|---|---|---|---|---|---|---|---|---|
| S1 | S11 | 341 | Insulated wires and cables | 18.33 | 81.67 | 0.46 | | 0.21 |
| | S12 | 425 | Wine, champagne | 9.71 | 90.29 | 1.62 | | 0.82 |
| | S13 | 494 | Toys, sports goods | 32.83 | 67.17 | 0.28 | | 0.07 |
| S2 | S21 | 351 | Motor vehicles | 35.85 | 64.15 | 10.01 | | 1.06 |
| | S22 | 346 | Domestic electrical appliances | 15.41 | 84.59 | 0.96 | | 0.12 |
| | S22 | 431 | Wool/cotton textiles | 18.01 | 81.99 | 0.20 | | 0.02 |
| | S22 | 453 | Clothing | 7.07 | 92.93 | 1.92 | | 0.27 |
| | S22 | 455 | Household textiles | 22.76 | 77.24 | 0.39 | | 0.05 |
| | S22 | 491 | Jewellery | 92.20 | 7.80 | 0.15 | | 0.00 |
| | S23 | 248 | Ceramic goods | 25.14 | 74.86 | 0.92 | | 0.09 |
| | S23 | 432 | Cotton industry | 10.48 | 89.52 | 0.88 | | 0.11 |
| | S23 | 451 | Footwear | 60.73 | 39.27 | 0.91 | | 0.00 |
| | S23 | 481 | Rubber products | 29.08 | 70.92 | 1.34 | | 0.13 |
| Total | | | | | | 20.05 | 3.53 | |
| | | | | | | | -dH/YM | |
| D1 | D11 | 257 | Pharmaceuticals | 10.83 | 89.17 | 1.91 | -1.57 | 1.03 |
| | D11 | 330 | Office and data-processing machinery | 69.53 | 30.47 | 0.51 | 0.00 | 0.00 |
| | D11 | 342 | Electrical machinery | 9.57 | 90.43 | 1.45 | -1.22 | 0.80 |
| | D11 | 344 | Radio & TV, telec equipment | 16.62 | 83.38 | 1.12 | -0.81 | 0.54 |
| | D11 | 428 | Soft drinks | 0.34 | 99.66 | 1.09 | -1.09 | 0.72 |
| | D12 | 315 | Boilermaking | 4.44 | 95.56 | 0.40 | -0.37 | 0.22 |
| | D12 | 361 | Shipbuilding | 41.93 | 58.07 | 0.73 | -0.22 | 0.13 |
| | D12 | 362 | Rolling stock | 1.48 | 98.52 | 0.31 | -0.30 | 0.18 |
| | D12 | 372 | Medico-surgical app. & ortho. app. | 49.54 | 50.46 | 0.05 | -0.01 | 0.01 |
| | D12 | 417 | Spaghetti, macaroni | 0.00 | 100.00 | 0.06 | -0.06 | 0.04 |
| | D12 | 421 | Cocoa, chocolate | 8.48 | 91.52 | 0.69 | -0.59 | 0.36 |
| | D12 | 427 | Brewing, malting | 0.40 | 99.60 | 0.86 | -0.85 | 0.51 |
| D2 | D21 | 251 | Basic industrial chemicals | 28.39 | 71.61 | 3.77 | -1.04 | 0.45 |
| | D21 | 256 | Other chemical products | 5.66 | 94.34 | 1.73 | -1.24 | 0.27 |
| | D21 | 321 | Agricultural machinery | 12.88 | 87.12 | 0.39 | -0.20 | 0.06 |
| | D21 | 345 | Radio, TV | 8.28 | 91.72 | 0.68 | -0.42 | 0.10 |
| | D21 | 347 | Electric lamps | 18.53 | 81.47 | 0.27 | -0.11 | 0.04 |
| | D21 | 493 | Photo and cine labs | 6.98 | 93.02 | 0.10 | -0.06 | 0.01 |
| | D22 | 325 | Plant for mines, steel | 20.31 | 79.69 | 0.87 | -0.32 | 0.10 |
| | D22 | 364 | Aerospace equipment | 54.55 | 45.45 | 0.28 | -0.03 | 0.02 |
| | D23 | 247 | Glass & glassware | 12.16 | 87.84 | 0.87 | -0.45 | 0.10 |
| | D23 | 322 | Machine tools | 33.07 | 66.93 | 0.56 | -0.13 | 0.05 |
| | D23 | 323 | Textile machinery | 39.13 | 60.87 | 0.31 | -0.06 | 0.03 |
| | D23 | 324 | Food, chemical machinery | 38.35 | 61.65 | 0.35 | -0.07 | 0.03 |
| | D23 | 326 | Transmission equipment | 39.08 | 60.92 | 0.15 | -0.03 | 0.01 |
| | D23 | 327 | Other machines and equipment | 27.45 | 72.55 | 0.22 | -0.06 | 0.02 |
| | D23 | 438 | Carpets, floor coverings | 25.92 | 74.08 | 0.16 | -0.05 | 0.02 |
| Total | | | | | | 19.89 | -11.35 | 8.78 |

*Legend*: X/Y: exports as a percentage of gross output, 1985.

H/Y: (100-X/Y) home market sales as a percentage of output, 1985.

Y/YM: sectoral share of manufacturing output, 1987.

dX/YM: gain in exports as a percentage of total manufacturing output.

-dH/YM: loss in home market sales as a percentage of total manufacturing output.

d(X/Y)*: output-weighted percentage point change in export-output ratio, adjusted for demand growth.

*Data sources: European Economy*, special edition 1990, part C, Spain.

Eurostat, *Structure and Activity of Industry*, Annual Enquiry – Main Results 1984/85 and 1986/87.

OECD STAN Database, Dec 1994 on diskettes.

## Table B.9.    Ireland: Classification of the indigenous sectors to be affected by the SEM (output weighted)

| | | NACE | Sector | X/Y | H/Y | Y/YM | dX/YM | d(X/Y)*. |
|---|---|---|---|---|---|---|---|---|
| S1 | S12 | 421 | Cocoa, chocolate (I) | 62 | 38 | 2.49 | | 0.70 |
| S2 | S21 | 251 | Basic industrial chemicals (I) | 43 | 57 | 2.28 | | 0.36 |
| | | 351 | Motor vehicles (I) | 33 | 67 | 0.19 | | 0.03 |
| | S22 | 364 | Aerospace equipment (I) | 40 | 60 | 0.50 | | 0.08 |
| | | 413 | Dairy products (I) | 29 | 71 | 12.01 | | 2.13 |
| | | 427 | Brewing, malting (I) | 13 | 87 | 5.05 | | 1.10 |
| | S23 | 247 | Glass & glassware (I) | 55 | 45 | 0.89 | | 0.09 |
| | | 491 | Jewellery (I) | 50 | 50 | 0.16 | | 0.02 |
| | | 494 | Toys & sports goods (I) | 85 | 15 | 0.27 | | 0.01 |
| Total | | | | | | 23.84 | 7.95 | |
| | | | | | | | -dH/YM | |
| D1 | D12 | 361 | Shipbuilding (I) | 93 | 7 | 0.14 | -0.00 | 0.00 |
| | | 417 | Spaghetti, macaroni (I) | 50 | 50 | 0.04 | -0.02 | 0.01 |
| D2 | D21 | 493 | Photographic labs (I) | 29 | 71 | 0.12 | -0.05 | 0.02 |
| | D22 | 431 | Wool industry (I) | 70 | 30 | 0.44 | -0.04 | 0.03 |
| | | 453 | Clothing (I) | 54 | 46 | 1.43 | -0.25 | 0.16 |
| | | 455 | Household textiles (I) | 74 | 26 | 0.19 | -0.02 | 0.01 |
| | D23 | 248 | Ceramic goods (I) | 91 | 9 | 0.18 | -0.00 | 0.00 |
| | | 451 | Footwear (I) | 42 | 58 | 0.15 | -0.04 | 0.02 |
| Total | | | | | | 4.83 | -0.41 | 4.78 |

*Legend*:   X/Y: exports as a percentage of gross output, 1986.

H/Y: (100-X/Y) home market sales as a percentage of gross output, 1986.

Y/YM: sectoral share of manufacturing output, 1987.

dX/YM: gain in exports as a percentage of total manufacturing output.

-dH/YM: loss in home market sales as a percentage of total manufacturing output.

d(X/Y)*: output-weighted percentage point change in export-output ratio, adjusted for demand conditions.

*Data sources: European Economy*, special edition 1990, part C, Ireland, pp. 247–261.

Irish CSO Census of Industrial Production, 1987.

APPENDIX C

# Assessment of the impact of the SEM on the services sector

Market services play a considerable role in the European Union; they accounted for nearly 50% of GDP and 42% of employment in 1990. From 1980 to 1990 employment in services rose by 23.4% while it fell by 13% in manufacturing. Therefore in employment terms services are also the main providers of new jobs. At the same time, labour productivity in market services (1.5%) has been considerably weaker than in manufacturing (2.8%) over the 20 years from 1970 to 1990. This is due to the high degree of regulation which has hindered competition and slowed down productivity growth. Another factor is that the substitutability of capital for labour has traditionally been more limited in services. With deregulation of services as part of the 1992 single market programme along with technological improvements, increased levels of labour productivity are likely to occur.

Since services were more sheltered from competition due to high government regulation, this in turn implied higher inflation in the services sectors than that experienced in manufacturing sectors.

**Table C.1.    Weight of services in Member States' economies (%)**

|  | GDP | | Employment | |
|---|---|---|---|---|
|  | 1990 | Increase 1980–90 | 1990 | Increase 1980–90 |
| Greece | 39.3 | 1.4 | : | : |
| Ireland | 36.9 | 3.0 | : | : |
| Portugal | 43.5 | 3.5 | 28.8 | 5.0 |
| Spain | 44.8 | -0.2 | 38.6 | 1.1 |
| EUR-12 | 48.2 | 5.8 | 42.0* | 5.6* |

* For employment, EUR-10 instead of EUR-12.

*Source:* Buigues and Sapir (1993a), Table 1, p. 6.

For the peripheral countries, services accounted for a lower share of GDP and employment than the Community average, as can be seen in Table C.1 above. Sapir (1993) believes that the higher level of government regulation has hindered the scope for increased competition within the peripheral economies.

Assessing the impact of the single market on services proves a harder task than for the manufacturing sector. Data constraints – usually the lack of consistency across countries (or the total lack of data for Greece, for example) – makes empirical work next to impossible. Trade in services is much more difficult to record than merchandise trade due to the intangibility aspect, and the lack of detailed international nomenclature for trade in services means that individual country data is not perfectly comparable.

This problem is frequently mentioned in the literature on services. The *European Economy* (1993) special issue on market services and European integration refers to the aforementioned problem of data constraints and notes that this is especially true of the peripheral countries.

While assessing the impact of the single market on services we review two main publications, the *European Economy* Issue (1993) and Emerson *et al.* (1988.) We discuss the implications of their findings for our own research and draw some general conclusions.

## C.1. *European Economy* (1993): Market services and European integration

The main characteristics, noted by Buigues and Sapir (1993b), of the services sector were the low degree of internationalization, a high degree of government intervention and regulation, low levels of technological change and a relatively low growth in labour productivity. They found that for the peripheral countries these characteristics are more pronounced, especially in sectors such as distribution (low trade level) and hotels (high government regulation). They predicted that these economies are likely to undergo important structural changes with increased competition, due to the introduction of new technologies, resulting in greater productivity (especially labour productivity), but that the negative impact this would have on employment would be offset by the growth in services due to income growth.

Buigues and Sapir stated that the main challenge with respect to services for policy-makers at the Community level was likely to be employment; with increased competition and technological change, they felt, leading to sectoral shifts and changes in skill requirements. This point was also emphasized in another paper in the *European Economy* (1993): Lebrun *et al.* stressed that restructuring in the southern Member States, given the high proportion of total employment in distribution (40% of services employment in 1990) would be a key factor in analysing the impact of 1992 on employment in Europe.

Buigues and Sapir noted that inflation in services has generally been higher than inflation in manufacturing, as firms in services pass on their poorer levels of productivity through higher prices as compared to manufacturing. They found that the southern peripheral countries also experienced lower productivity and higher inflation than the northern countries, due to higher levels of regulation in the periphery which hindered competition.

As regards internationalization of services, Buigues and Sapir noted that trade in services was on average four times smaller than trade in goods. Trade in services accounted for 20% and 19% of total exports and imports of goods and services respectively in 1990. For the southern peripheral economies, the weight of exports of services was much higher (Greece 53%, Spain 36%, 1989) and that of imports lower; according to Buigues and Sapir this was a reflection of the strong specialization in tourism.

Services are generally considered as non-traded activities since production and consumption occur at the same time. Buigues and Sapir found that an important consequence of this feature was the fact that foreign direct investment had played a crucial role in international services transactions. FDI flows to services accounted for over half of total FDI flows in the EC during the early 1980s. Sapir (1993) pointed out that the FDI flows had been on the increase since 1984 and suggested that the surge in foreign direct investment was not just particular to the EC nor was it related to 1992. In our analysis of FDI flows into manufacturing industries in the peripheral economies, we found that there was a significant increase in FDI flows to Spain and Portugal when they joined the European Community in 1986; we attribute this increase to their accession to the EC which attracted increased foreign investment (see tables in Chapter 5).

Ilzkovitz (1993) singled out three services sectors as playing a significant role in terms of employment and value added for the peripheral countries: distribution, tourism and transport, in particular road transport. These three sectors have a high unskilled labour content, and price competition is strong. They accounted for 62% to 76% of employment in services and 47% to 57% of value added in services in 1990 within the peripheral countries.

Ilzkovitz considered indicators such as intra-EC export market shares, coverage ratios (ratio of intra-EC exports to intra-EC imports) and export specialization indices (average for 1987–92) to assess the trade performance in services. He reminded us that services differ from manufacturing and therefore, although the tools of analysis are the same, they are not as reliable as indicators of the strengths and weaknesses of trade in services due to the difference in internationalization and FDI between services and manufacturing. He stressed the statistical problems, already mentioned, with respect to services trade data.

Of the three service sectors, he found that productivity and trade performance were strong in tourism alone. In distribution, Spain and Portugal perform poorly, with Spanish firms being targeted by foreign competitors. He suggests that this poor performance is due to the lack of modernization, the small concentration and the predominance of small firms in comparison with northern Europe. He predicted that the impact of 1992 would lead to a dominance of foreign ownership in Spain and Portugal.

The lower wages costs in the southern economies benefit road transportation. Ilzkovitz predicted that one of two scenarios would occur due to the SEM: either modernization would occur as it had in the northern economies, or else they would remain specialized in the more traditional segment of road transportation where price rather than quality competition dominated. In general, he predicted that a dualism would emerge where the southern states would specialize in traditional labour-intensive services with strong price competition and the northern Member States in high-tech and capital-intensive services where quality was important.

The *European Economy* (1993) special edition analysed the impact of 1992 at a sectoral level. Below, we concentrate on those service sectors that are significant in the southern peripheral countries and Ireland. These include road haulage, distribution and hotel chains. The analysis is sector specific and not country specific; therefore, the conclusions drawn by the authors do not, in general, refer to specific countries. We focus on the information we see as being relevant to the peripheral economies.

## C.2. Road haulage

Road haulage accounted for between 85% and 96% of all inland transport for the southern periphery countries and Ireland in 1987; this is higher than in Germany, for example, where it accounted for 63%. Sleuwaegen (1993) predicted that the impact of 1992 would reduce freight rates and reduce regulation which in turn would lead to greater efficiency. The author warned that with harmonization, rules would have to be laid down in order that increased competition would not encourage a reduction in quality and relaxation of road safety and environmental regulations. He predicted a move towards concentration, with a number of small firms being squeezed out of the market. Sleuwaegen did not draw any specific conclusions for the southern peripheral countries or Ireland.

## C.3.  Distribution

This sector is the largest services sector both in terms of output and employment. It accounted for nearly 40% of employment in services in the European Community in 1990. This sector includes both retailing and wholesaling activities. Fitz Gerald *et al.* (1993) noted how hard it is to separate out this service from the goods that were being sold, as well as the difficulty in deriving measures of efficiency of the sector. The distinction between wholesaling and retailing has also become blurred, which makes individual analysis of these subsectors difficult. They noted that consumer tastes are reflected in the size of distribution: for example, in Ireland clothing was more frequently sold in large shops, while the opposite occurred in the southern states and France, where the smaller shops still accounted for the bulk of trade. They made these distinctions in order to show that there is no optimal structure for distribution and also that the degree of internationalization is limited due to cultural differences in tastes. They found that the share of retail sales in consumer expenditure was inversely correlated with the standard of living, hence in the peripheral economies (lowest standard of living) retail sales accounted for over 50% of consumer expenditure in 1987.

They concluded that there was likely to be a greater concentration in the distribution sector, particularly in the southern countries where traditional forms of retailing were still predominant. They also predicted that price differences would persist between Member States, due to differences in the competitive position of manufacturers and local distributors.

## C.4.  Hotel chains

Viceriat (1993) stated that accommodation and tourist services accounted for the largest share of GDP in the southern European countries (7.7% of GDP for Greece, 6.6% for Spain and 3.2% for Portugal, 1986). In employment terms a similar pattern emerged. With regards to hotel chains, the author found that they were more highly developed in the UK and France, while in Spain the importance of independent hotels was noticeable. There were no specific conclusions drawn by the author for the peripheral economies. In general, he predicted that the trend in concentration was likely to continue and that hotel chains were likely to take advantage of economies of scale, with mergers and take-overs likely to increase.

In general, the *European Economy* (1993) special issue on the services sectors does not carry a disaggregated level of analysis at country level for our needs. This may be due to data constraints: for example, the lack of data for Greece was often cited. The overall conclusion that we draw from this analysis is that the southern peripheral economies and Ireland are likely to be dominated by foreign affiliates as integration continues, especially in services sectors such as hotel chains. In most of the above-mentioned studies, economies of scale are expected to lead to the squeezing out of a number of small transport haulage firms to be replaced, for example, by large international companies which increased productivity levels. Buigues and Sapir predict that the loss in employment due to such factors would be outweighed by the overall growth in services due to income expansion.

## C.5.  Emerson *et al.* (1988)

In his study of the single market, Emerson outlined case studies for services sectors: financial services, business services, surface and air transport and telecommunications services. These sectors accounted for over half of total services in the economy in terms of value added and 15% of the EC total value added in 1985. These sectors, according to Emerson, were those which experienced the most international business. Spain was the only peripheral economy included in Emerson's analysis, notably for financial services.

In general, Emerson suggested that the regulatory function of government not only acts as a prudential and safety objective but that it often tended to limit entry. He suggested that the objective of European integration was to provide adequate safety standards in tandem with increased market openness and competition and he forecasted that the potential gains would be quite large.

## C.6. Financial services

For financial services Spain is close to the Community average in terms of value added as a percentage of GDP (6.4% for both) and employment as a percentage of total employment (2.8% compared to 2.9%) (data for 1985). Emerson stated that the completion of financial market integration was dependent on the relaxation of remaining exchange controls, which were more apparent in the southern peripheral economies. Possible reductions in the cost of financial services due to the removal of regulatory barriers and the abolition of exchange controls varied widely across countries; he forecasted that Spain would benefit greatly from reductions in prices. His analysis was based on estimates of a range of financial products, before and after European integration, taken from a study by Price Waterhouse (European Commission, 1988). For Spain the estimated potential fall in the price of financial products as a result of the single market was 21%; this was by far the highest fall (the EUR-8 average fall is 10%). The reason given was that Spain had the highest price level to begin with and was heavily regulated, therefore liberalization would have a major impact on financial services prices in Spain.

## C.7. Bradley *et al.* (1992)

As mentioned in our earlier literature review of the impact of the single market (Chapter 4), we noted that Bradley *et al.* (1992) had quantified the liberalization of financial services in Ireland and compared it to the average value calculated by Cecchini. The authors predicted that capital market integration would force interest rates to equalize as capital became free to locate wherever the rate of return was highest. They forecasted that this would lead to a 1.1% rise in GNP by the year 1998 and a 1% fall in consumer prices. These medium-term results were lower than those predicted by Cecchini both in terms of prices and growth. This suggested that Ireland would not gain as much from the liberalization of financial services as the core European economies.

## C.8. Conclusion

The above two results on the impact of financial services liberalization for Spain and Ireland are the only quantitative results that we have come across in our review of the literature. Quantification of the impact of the single market on prices or on productivity in services in the peripheral economies of the EU is not available. This means that we are forced to rely largely on qualitative analyses, such as those of Buigues and Sapir (1993a), for our assessment of the overall impact of the SEM on the services sector.

# Bibliography

Alogoskoufis, G. 'Traded goods, competitiveness and aggregate fluctuations in the United Kingdom', *Economic Journal*, No. 100, Cambridge, Blackwell, 1990a, pp. 141–163.

Alogoskoufis, G. 'Competitiveness, wage adjustment and macroeconomic policy in the dependent economy: the case of Greece', *Greek Economic Review*, Vol. 12, 1990b, pp. 15–57.

Aquino, A. 'Intra-industry trade and inter-industry specialization as concurrent sources of international trade in manufactures', *Weltwirtschaftliches Archiv*, Vol. 114, 1978.

Argimon, I. and Gonzalez-Paramo, J. M., Martin, M. J. and Roldan, J. M., *Productividad e infrastructuras en la economia española*, Working Paper No. 9313, Madrid, Banco de España, 1993.

Aschauer, D.A. 'Is public expenditure productive?', *Journal of Monetary Economics*, Vol. 3, Amsterdam, Elsevier Science, 1989, pp. 177–200.

Bajo-Rubio, O. and Sosvilla-Rivero, S. 'Does public capital affect private sector performance? An analysis of the Spanish case, 1964–88', *Economic Modelling*, Vol. 10, 1993, pp. 179–185.

Bajo-Rubio, O. and Sosvilla-Rivero, S. 'An econometric analysis of foreign direct investment in Spain, 1964-89', *Southern Economic Journal*, Vol. 61, 1994, pp. 104–120.

Baldwin, R. 'The growth effects of 1992', *Economic Policy*, October 1989, pp. 248–281.

Baldwin, R. and Venables, A. *Methodologies for an Aggregate Ex Post Evaluation of the Completion of the Internal Market: Feasibility Study and Literature Survey*, Draft Report prepared for the European Commission, DG II, 16 July 1989.

Barro, R. 'Government spending in a simple model of endogenous growth', *Journal of Political Economy*, Vol. 98, No. 5, University of Chicago Press, 1990, pp. 103–126.

Barro, R. and Sala-i-Martin, X. 'Public Finance in Models of Economic Growth', National Bureau of Economic Research Working Paper No. 3362, 1990.

Barro, R. and Sala-i-Martin, X. *Economic Growth*, New York, McGraw Hill, 1995.

Barry, F. 'Payroll taxes, capital grants and Irish unemployment', *Economic and Social Review*, Vol. 21, No. 1, Dublin, Economic and Social Studies, 1989, pp. 107–121.

Barry, F. 'The Irish recovery 1987-90: an economic miracle?', *Irish Banking Review*, Winter 1991, pp. 23–40.

Barry, F. 'Exchange Rate Policy when the Labour Market Exhibits Hysteresis', *Manchester School of Economic and Social Studies*, 1997.

Barry, F. 'Peripherality in economic geography and modern growth theory: Evidence from Ireland's adjustment to free trade', *World Economy*, Vol. 19, No. 3, May 1996, pp. 345–365.

Barry, F. and Bradley, J. 'On the causes of Ireland's unemployment', *Economic and Social Review*, Vol. 22, No. 4, Dublin, Economic and Social Studies, 1991, pp. 253–286.

Barry, F., Bradley, J., Kennedy, K. and O'Donnell, N. 'Labour Market Performance in the EU Periphery: Lessons and Implications', *Papers and Proceedings of the European Economic Forum* (ed. J. Mortensen), The Hague, Central Planning Bureau, 1994.

Barry, F., Bradley, J. and Duggan, D. 'Economic structure and structural change in the EU periphery', in B. Fynes and S. Ennis (eds.) *Competing from the Periphery*, Dublin, Oaktree Press, 1996.

Barry, F., Bradley, J. and Hannan, A. *An Evaluation of the Impact of the SEM on the EU Periphery with the Aid of Macroeconometric Models*, Economic and Social Research Institute Seminar, Dublin, November 1995.

Barry, F. and Devereux, M. 'The expansionary fiscal contraction hypothesis: a neo-Keynesian analysis', *Oxford Economic Papers*, 47, 1995, pp. 249–246.

Barry, F. and Hannan, A. 'On comparative and absolute advantage: FDI and the sectoral and spatial effects of market integration', UCD Working Paper No. 96/19, University College Dublin, 1996.

Ben-David, D. 'Equalizing Exchange: Trade Liberalization and Income Convergence', *Quarterly Journal of Economics*, 108(3), 1993, pp. 653–679.

Beutel, J. *The Economic Impacts of the Community Support Frameworks for the Objective 1 Regions 1989–93*, report prepared for the European Commission, DG XVI, Luxembourg, Office for Official Publications of the European Communities, 1993.

Beyers, W., Tofflemire, J., Stranahan, H. and Johnson, E. *The Service Economy: Understanding Growth of Producer Services in the Central Puget Sound Region*, Seattle, Central Puget Sound Economic Development District, 1986.

Biehl, D. *The contribution of infrastructure to regional development*, No. 2, Luxembourg, Office for Official Publications of the European Communities, 1986.

Bliss C. and de Macedo J. (eds.). *Unity with Diversity in the European Economy*, Cambridge, Cambridge University Press, 1990.

Bourguignon, F., Branson, W. and de Melo, J. 'Adjustment and income distribution: a micro-macro model for counter factual analysis', *Journal of Development Economics*, Vol. 38, 1993, pp.17–39.

Bourguignon, F., Lolos, S., Suwa-Eisermann, A. and Zonzilos, N.G. 'Evaluating the Community Support Framework with an Extended Computable General Equilibrium Model: the Case of Greece (1988–95)', paper presented at the Annual Conference of the European Economics Association, Trinity College Dublin, 1992.

Bradley, J. and Fitz Gerald, J. 'Industrial output and factor input determination in an econometric model of a small open economy', *European Economic Review*, 32, 1988, pp. 1227–1241.

Bradley, J. and Fitz Gerald, J. 'Production structures in a small open economy with mobile and indigenous investment', *European Economic Review*, 34, 1990, pp. 364–374.

Bradley, J. and Fitz Gerald, J. 'The ESRI Medium Term Economic Model', in J. Bradley, J. Fitz Gerald and D. Mc Coy *Medium Term Review 1991-1996*, Dublin, The Economic and Social Research Institute, 1991.

Bradley, J., Fitz Gerald, J. and Kearney, I. (eds.) *The Role of the Structural Funds: Analysis of the Consequences for Ireland in the Context of 1992*, Policy Research Series Paper No. 13, Dublin, The Economic and Social Research Institute, 1992.

Bradley, J., Fitz Gerald, J. and Kearney, I. 'Modelling supply in an open economy using a restricted cost function', *Economic Modelling*, January 1993, pp. 11–21.

Bradley, J., Fitz Gerald, J. and Mc Coy, D. *Medium Term Review 1991-1996*, Dublin, The Economic and Social Research Institute, 1991.

Bradley, J., Herce J. and Modesto, L. 'Modelling in the EU periphery: the HERMIN Project', *Economic Modelling*, special edition, 1995b.

Bradley, J. and McCartan, J. *Annotated listings of HERMIN models in SIMPC format: Greece, Ireland, Portugal and Spain*, mimeo, Dublin, The Economic and Social Research Institute, May 1996.

Bradley, J., O'Donnell, N., Sheridan, N. and Whelan, K. *Regional Aid and Convergence: Evaluating the impact of the Structural Funds on the European periphery*, Avebury, Aldershot, 1995a.

Bradley, J. and Whelan, K. 'The Irish experience of monetary linkages with the United Kingdom and developments since joining the EMS', in R. Barrell (ed.) *Economic Convergence and Monetary Union in Europe*, London, Sage Publications in association with the NIESR, 1992.

Bradley, J. and Whelan, K. 'The Irish expansionary fiscal contraction: a tale from one small European economy', *Economic Modelling*, April 1997, pp. 175–202.

Bradley, J., Whelan, K. and Wright, J. *Stabilization and Growth in the EC Periphery: A Study of the Irish Economy*, Avebury, Aldershot, 1993.

Bryant, R. and Zhang, L. 'Alternative Specifications of Intertemporal Fiscal Policy in Macroeconomic Models', mimeo, Washington, Brookings Institution, 1994.

Buffie, E.F. 'Labour market distortions, the structure of protection and direct foreign investment', *Journal of Development Economics*, 27, 1987, pp. 149–163.

Buigues, P., Ilkovitz, F. and Lebrun, J-F. 'The Impact of the Internal Market by Industrial Sector: The Challenge for the Member States', special edition of *European Economy/Social Europe*, Luxembourg, Office for the Official Publications of the European Communities, 1990.

Buigues, P., Ilkovitz, F., Lebrun, J-F. and Sapir, A. (eds.). *Market services and European integration: The challenges for the 1990s, European Economy*, Reports and Studies, No.3, Luxembourg, Office for Official Publications of the European Communities, 1993.

Buigues, P. and Sapir, A. 'Market Services in the Community economy', in *Market services and European integration: The challenge for the 1990s, European Economy*, special issue, No. 3, Part A, Luxembourg, Office for Official Publications of the European Communities, 1993a, pp. 3–22.

Buigues, P. and Sapir, A. 'Market services and European integration: issues and challenges', in *Market services and European integration: The challenge for the 1990s, European Economy*, special issue, No. 3, Part A, Luxembourg, Office for Official Publications of the European Communities, 1993b, pp. ix–xx.

Cabral, S. 'Comparative Export Behaviour of Foreign and Domestic Firms in Portugal', *Banco de Portugal Economic Bulletin*, Lisbon, March 1995.

Callan, T. 'Returns to Educational Investment: New Evidence for Ireland', in *The Community Support Framework 1989-93: Evaluations and Recommendations for CSF 1994-99*, Dublin, ESRI, 1993.

Calmfors, L. and Viotti, S. 'Wage indexation, the Scandinavian model and macroeconomic stability in the open economy', *Oxford Economic Papers*, 34, 1982, pp. 546–566.

Calvo-Gonzalez, J. and Gonzalez-Romero, A. 'El Mercado Unico: Perspectivas para España', Working Paper 9202, Departamento de Analisis Economico, UNED, 1992.

Capros, P. and Karadeloglou, P. 'Macroeconomic Impacts of Structural Funds on the Greek Economy', Report to the Economic and Industrial Research Institute, Athens, 1989.

Capros, P., Karadeloglou, P. and Mentzas, G. 'The GEM-NTUA Annual Econometric Model of the Greek Economy', Working Paper, Energy Policy Unit, National Technical University of Athens, 1988.

Capros, P., Karadeloglou, P. and Mentzas, G. 'Macroeconomic Effects of 1992 on the Greek Economy', paper presented at the 2nd Conference of the Hellenic Economic Association, Athens, 12–13 December 1990.

Catinat, M. and Italianer, A. 'Completing the Internal Market, Primary Microeconomic Effects and their Implementation in Macroeconometric Models', Report Prepared for the European Commission, DG II, 20 April 1988.

Cecchini, P. *The European Challenge 1992, The Benefits of a Single Market*, London, Wildwood House, 1988.

Christodoulakis, N. *Public infrastructures and private productivity*, Discussion Paper 93-07, Department of International and European Economic Studies, Athens University of Economics and Business, 1993.

Christodoulakis, N. and Kalyvitis, S. 'A Four-Sector Macroeconometric Model for Greece', mimeo, Athens University of Economics and Business, November 1993.

Collado, J. *et al. Efectos del Mercado Unico sobre los sectores productivos españoles*, Madrid, Instituto de Estudios Economicos, 1992.

Collado, J. 'Estructura occupacional y convergencia europea de los sectores productivos', *Papeles de Economia Española*, 63, 1995, pp. 223–233.

Cuddington, J. and Viñals, J. 'Budget deficits and the current account: an intertemporal disequilibrium approach', *Journal of International Economics*, Vol. 21, Amsterdam, Elsevier Science, 1986a, pp. 1–24

Cuddington, J. and Viñals, J. 'Budget Deficits and the Current Account in the Presence of Classical Unemployment', *Economic Journal*, No. 96, Cambridge, Blackwell, 1986b, pp. 101–119.

Cuddy, M. and Keane, M. 'Ireland: A Peripheral Region', in A. Foley and M. Mulreany (eds.) *The Single European Market and the Irish Economy*, Dublin, IPA, 1990.

de la Oliva, P. and Orgaz, L. 'Algunos efectos del Mercado Unico sobre la economia industrial', *Boletin Economico de ICE*, 2182, 1989, pp. 1901–1906.

de Macedo, J.B. 'External liberalization with ambiguous public response: the experience of Portugal', in C. Bliss and J.B. de Macedo (eds.), *Unity with Diversity in the European Economy*, Cambridge, Cambridge University Press, 1990.

de Melo, J. and Robinson, S. 'Productivity and externalities: models of export-led growth', *Journal of International Trade and Development*, Vol. 1, No. 1, London, Routledge, 1992, pp. 41–69.

Diaz Alejandro, C. 'Latin America in the 1930s', in R. Thorp (ed.) *Latin America in the 1930s: The Role of the Periphery in World Crisis*, London, Macmillan, 1984.

Don, H. *SIMPC 3.3 Manual*, The Hague, Don Econometrics, 1993.

Dornbusch, R. 'Expectations and exchange rate dynamics', *Journal of Political Economy*, 84, University of Chicago Press, 1976, pp. 1161–1176.

Dornbusch, R. *Open Economy Macroeconomics*, New York, Basic Books, 1980.

Draper, M. and Herce, J. A. 'Infraestructuras y crecimiento, un panorama', *Revista de Economia Aplicada*, Vol. 6, 1994, pp. 129–168.

Drèze, J.H. and Bean, C. 'Europe's Unemployment Problem: Introduction and Synthesis', in J.H. Drèze and C. Bean (eds.) *Europe's Unemployment Problem*, Cambridge, Mass., MIT Press, 1992.

Durkan, J. and Reynolds-Feighan, A. 'Transport' in *The Role of the Structural Funds: Analysis of the Consequences for Ireland in the Context of 1992*, Policy Research Series Paper No. 13, Dublin, The Economic and Social Research Institute, 1992.

Duggan, D. 'The Core and Peripheral Regions of the European Union: Distinctive Characteristics and Core-Periphery Comparisons', M.A. thesis, Dept. of Economics, University College Dublin, 1995.

Emerson, M. *et al., The Economics of 1992: The EC Commission's Assessment of the Economic Effects of Completing the Internal Market*, Oxford, Oxford University Press, 1988.

European Commission. *The cost of non-Europe in financial services*, Vol. 9, *The Cost of Non-Europe*, Luxembourg, Office for Official Publications of the European Communities, 1988.

European Commission. 'One Market, One Money: An Evaluation of the Potential Benefits and Costs of Forming an Economic and Monetary Union', *European Economy*, No. 44, 1990a.

European Commission. 'The impact of the internal market by industrial sector', *European Economy/Social Europe*, special issue, 1990b.

European Commission. *Community Support Framework, 1994-99: Greece*, Luxembourg, Office for Official Publications of the European Communities, 1994a.

European Commission. *Community Support Framework, 1994-99: Ireland*, Luxembourg, Office for Official Publications of the European Communities, 1994b.

European Commission. *Community Support Framework, 1994-99: Portugal*, Luxembourg, Office for Official Publications of the European Communities, 1994c.

European Commission. *Community Support Framework, 1994-99: Spain*, Luxembourg, Office for Official Publications of the European Communities, 1994d.

European Commission. *Community Support Framework, 1989-93: Portugal*, Luxembourg, Office for Official Publications of the European Communities, 1989.

European Commission. *Community Support Framework, 1989-93: Greece*, Luxembourg, Office for Official Publications of the European Communities, 1990a.

European Commission. *Community Support Framework, 1989-93: Ireland*, Luxembourg, Office for Official Publications of the European Communities, 1990b.

European Commission. *Community Support Framework, 1989-93: Spain*, Luxembourg, Office for Official Publications of the European Communities, 1990c.

European Commission. *Foreign Direct Investment*, Single Market Review, Vol. IV.1, Luxembourg, Office for Official Publications of the European Communities, London, Kogan Page Publishers, 1997.

Eurostat. *National Accounts ESA*, Luxembourg, Office for Official Publications of the European Communities, 1993.

Farinas, J. 'La economia española en la Europa del Acta Unica', in J. Garcia-Delgado (ed.) *España. Economia*, Madrid, Espasa Calpe, 1993.

FEDEA. *Evaluación del Marco de Apoyo Comunitario 1989-1993*, mimeo, Madrid, 1994.

Ferris, T. 'Transport', in A. Foley and M. Mulreany (eds.) *The Single European Market and the Irish Economy*, Dublin, IPA, 1990.

Fitz Gerald, J. and Knipper, I. 'Distribution' in *Market services and European integration: The challenge for the 1990s, European Economy*, special issue, No. 3, Part C, Luxembourg, Office for Official Publications of the European Communities, 1993, pp. 340–362.

Foley, A. 'Indigenous Manufacturing', in A. Foley and M. Mulreany (eds.) *The Single European Market and the Irish Economy*, Dublin, IPA, 1990.

Foley, A. and Mulreany, M. (eds.) *The Single European Market and the Irish Economy*, Dublin, IPA, 1990.

Gaspar, V. and Pereira, A. 'The Impact of Financial Integration and Unilateral Public Transfers on Investment and Economic Growth', Working Paper, Department of Economics, University of California, San Diego, 1991.

Giavazzi, F. and Pagano, M. 'Can Severe Fiscal Contractions be Expansionary? A Tale of Two Small Economies', in O. Blanchard and S. Fischer (eds.) *National Bureau of Economic Research Macroeconomics Annual 1990*, 1990, pp. 75–110.

Goncalves, P. 'Portugal', in *European Economy/Social Europe*, special issue, Part C, 1990, pp. 301–323.

Gonzalez-Romero, A. 'El Mercado Interior en la CEE: Aspectos bàsicos y efectos sobre la economía española', *Economía Industrial*, No. 269, 1989, pp. 147–160.

Grinols, E. 'Unemployment and foreign capital: the relative opportunity costs of domestic labour and welfare', *Economica*, No. 58, Cambridge, Blackwell, 1991, pp. 107–121.

Gual, J., Torrens, L.I. and Vives, X. 'El impacto de la integración económica europea en los sectores industriales españoles. Anàlisis de sus determinantes', in J. Viñals (ed.) *La economía española ante el Mercado Unico europeo. Las claves del proceso de integración*, Madrid, Alianza Editorial, 1992, pp. 229–312.

Hansen, N. 'Do Producer Services Induce Regional Economic Development?', *Journal of Regional Science*, Vol. 30, No. 4, 1990, pp. 465–476.

Heffernan, S. and Sinclair, P. *Modern International Economics*, Oxford, Basil Blackwell, 1990.

Helpman, E. 'Macroeconomic policy in a model of international trade with a wage restriction', *International Economic Review*, 17, 1976, University of Pennsylvania, pp. 262–277.

Helpman, E. 'Non-traded goods and macroeconomic policy under a fixed exchange rate', *Quarterly Journal of Economics*, XCI, 1977, pp. 469–480.

Honohan, P. 'Ireland and the Small Open Economy', Central Bank of Ireland Technical Paper, 11/RT/81, Dublin, 1981.

Honohan, P. 'The Role of the Adviser and the Evolution of the Public Service', in M. Hederman (ed.) *The Clash of Ideas: Essays in Honour of Patrick Lynch*, Dublin, Gill and Macmillan, 1988.

Honohan, P. 'The link between Irish and UK unemployment', *ESRI Quarterly Economic Commentary*, Spring 1992, pp. 33–44.

Ilzkovitz F. 'Sectoral/country dimension', in *Market services and European integration: The challenge for the 1990s, European Economy*, special issue, No. 3, Part A, Luxembourg, Office for Official Publications of the European Communities, 1993, pp. 41–62.

Jacobson, D. and Andreosso, B. 'Ireland as a Location for Multinational Investment', in A. Foley and M. Mulreany (eds.) *The Single European Market and the Irish Economy*, Dublin, IPA, 1990.

Katseli, L. 'Economic integration in the enlarged European Community: structural adjustment of the Greek economy', in C. Bliss and J. de Macedo (eds.) *Unity with Diversity in the European Economy*, Cambridge, Cambridge University Press, 1990.

Keeble, D., Offord, J. and Walker, S. *Peripheral Regions in a Community of 12 Member States*, Luxembourg, Office for Official Publications of the European Communities, 1988.

Keegan, O. and Hennessy, G. 'Building and Construction', in A. Foley and M. Mulreany (eds.) *The Single European Market and the Irish Economy*, Dublin, IPA, 1990.

Kennedy, K. and Foley, A. 'Industrial Development', in B. Dowling and J. Durkan (eds.) *Irish Economic Policy: A Review of Major Issues*, Dublin, ESRI, 1978.

Kouri, P. 'Profitability and Growth in a Small Open Economy', in A. Lindbeck (ed.) *Inflation and Unemployment in Open Economies*, Amsterdam, North Holland, 1979.

Krugman, P. 'Economic Integration in Europe: Some Conceptual Issues', in T. Padoa-Schioppa (ed.) *Efficiency, Stability and Equity*, Oxford, Oxford University Press, 1987.

Krugman, P. *Geography and Trade*, Cambridge, Massachusetts, MIT Press, 1991.

Krugman, P. and Venables, A. 'Integration and the Competitiveness of Peripheral Industry', in C. Bliss and J.B. de Macedo (eds.) *Unity With Diversity in the European Economy*, Cambridge, Cambridge University Press, 1990.

Larre, B. and Torres, R. 'Is Convergence a Spontaneous Process? The Experience of Spain, Portugal and Greece', *OECD Economic Studies*, 16, Paris, 1991, pp. 169–198.

Layard, R., Nickell, S. and Jackman, R. *Unemployment: macroeconomic performance and the labour market*, Oxford, Oxford University Press, 1991.

Lebrun, J., Petit, P. and Winter, C. 'Employment dimension', in *Market services and European integration: The challenge for the 1990s, European Economy*, special issue, No. 3, Part A, Luxembourg, Office for Official Publications of the European Communities, 1993, pp. 63–80.

Leddin, A. and Walsh, B. *The Macroeconomy of Ireland* (3rd ed.), Dublin, Gill and Macmillan, 1995.

Lindbeck, A. 'Imported and structural inflation and aggregate demand: the Scandinavian model reconstructed', in A. Lindbeck (ed.) *Inflation and employment in open economies*, Amsterdam, North Holland, 1979.

Lolos, S.E.G. and Zonzilos, N.G. 'The Impact of European Structural Funds Growth: The Case of Greece', Working Paper, Economic Research Department, Bank of Greece, 1992.

Lucas, R. 'On the mechanics of economic development', *Journal of Monetary Economics*, Vol. 22, Amsterdam, Elsevier Science, 1988, pp. 3–42.

Mardas, D. and Varsakelis, N. 'Greece', in *European Economy/Social Europe*, special edition, Part C, 1990, pp. 175–202.

Martin, C. 'Spain', in J.B. de Macedo 'External liberation with ambiguous public response: the experience of Portugal', in C. Bliss and J. de Macedo (eds.) *Unity with Diversity in the European Economy*, Cambridge, Cambridge University Press, 1990.

Martin, P. and Rogers, C. 'Trade Effects of Regional Aid', Discussion Paper No. 910, London, Centre for Economic Policy Research, 1994.

Masson, P., Symansky, S. and Meredith, G. *MULTIMOD Mark II: A Revised and Extended Model*, Occasional Paper No. 71, Washington, International Monetary Fund, July 1990.

Modesto, L. and das Neves, J.C. 'Hysteresis and sluggishness in Portuguese unemployment, 1977-88', *International Review of Applied Economics*, Vol. 7, No. 2, 1993, pp. 197–207.

Molinas, C., *et al.* 'MOISEES: Un modelo de investigación y simulación de la economia española', Instituto de Estudios Fiscales, Secretaria de Estado de Hacienda, Ministerio de Economia y Hacienda, Madrid, 1990.

Munnell, A.H. 'Infrastructure investment and economic growth', *Journal of Economic Perspectives*, 6, 1992, pp. 189–198.

Munnell, A.H. 'An assessment of trends in and economic impacts of infrastructure investment', in *Infrastructure policies for the 1990s*, Paris, OECD, 1993.

Neary, J.P. 'Non-traded goods and the balance of trade in a neo-Keynesian temporary equilibrium', *Quarterly Journal of Economics*, 1980, pp. 403–429.

Neary, J.P. 'Neo-Keynesian Macroeconomics in an Open Economy', in R. Van der Ploeg (ed.) *Advanced Lectures in Quantitative Economics*, New York, Academic Press, 1990.

NESC. *Ireland in the European Community: Performance, Prospects and Strategy*, Report No. 88, Dublin, National Economic and Social Council, 1989.

NESC. *The economic and social implications of emigration*, Report No. 90, Dublin, National Economic and Social Council, 1991.

Neven, D. 'EEC integration towards 1992: some distributional aspects', *Economic Policy*, No. 10, 1990.

Newell, A. and Symons, J. 'The causes of Ireland's unemployment', *The Economic and Social Review*, Vol. 21, Dublin, Economic and Social Studies, 1990, pp. 409–429.

Norton, D. *Economics for an Open Economy: Ireland*, Dublin, Oak Tree Press, 1994.

OECD. *International Direct Investment Statistics Yearbook*, Paris, OECD, 1993.

O'Grada, C. and O'Rourke, K. 'Irish Economic Growth, 1945-1988', Discussion Paper No. 975, London, Centre for Economic Policy Research, 1994.

O'Hagan, J. (ed.). *The Economy of Ireland: Policy and Performance of a Small European Country*, Dublin, Gill and Macmillan, 1995.

O'Malley, E. 'Ireland', in *European Economy*, special edition, Part C, Luxembourg, Office for Official Publications of the European Communities, 1990, pp. 247–261.

O'Malley, E. 'Industrial structure and economies of scale in the context of 1992', in *The Role of the Structural Funds: Analysis of the Consequences for Ireland in the Context of 1992*, Policy Research Series Paper No.13, Dublin, The Economic and Social Research Institute, 1992.

Ortega, E. 'La Inversión Extranjera Directa en España', *Banco de España Estudios Economicos*, No. 51, Madrid, 1992.

O'Sullivan, L. 'Macroeconomic Effects of 1992', in J. Bradley, and J. Fitz Gerald (eds.), *Medium Term Review 1989-1994*, Dublin, The Economic and Social Research Institute, 1989.

Pereira, A. 'Structural Policies in the European Community: An International Comparison', Report prepared for the European Commission, DG XII, Brussels, 1992.

Polo, C. and Sancho, F. 'An analysis of Spain's integration in the EEC', *Journal of Policy Modelling*, 15, 1993, pp. 157–178.

Prados de la Escosura, L., Daban Sanchez T. and Sanz Oliva, J. 'De Te Fabula Narratur? Growth, Structural Change and Convergence in Europe, 19-20th Centuries', mimeo, Universidad Carlos III, Madrid, 1993.

Pratten, C. 'A survey of economies of scale' in Vol. 2 of *Studies on the economics of integration: Research on the 'costs of non-Europe'*, European Commission, Luxembourg, Office for Official Publications of the European Communities, 1988.

Psacharopoulos, G. 'Returns to investment in education: a global update', *World Development*, Vol. 22, No. 9, 1994, pp. 1325–1343.

Purvis, D. 'Exchange rates: real and monetary factors', *Economic and Social Review*, Vol. 13, No. 4, Dublin, Economic and Social Studies, 1982, pp. 303–314.

Romer, P.M. 'Endogenous technical change', *Journal of Political Economy*, Vol. 98, No. 5, University of Chicago Press, 1990, pp. S70–S102.

Sapir, A. 'Sectoral dimension', in *Market services and European integration: The challenge for the 1990s, European Economy*, special issue, No. 3, Part A, Luxembourg, Office for Official Publications of the European Communities, 1993, pp. 23–39.

Sarris, A. *Rigidities and Macroeconomic Adjustment under Market Opening: Greece and 1992*, Discussion Paper No. 364, London, Centre for Economic Policy Research, 1990.

Simoes, V.C. 'European Integration and the Pattern of FDI Inflow into Portugal', in J. Cantwell (ed.) *Multinational Investment in Modern Europe: Strategic Interaction in the Integrated Community*, Aldershot, Edward Edgar, 1992.

Sleuwaegen, L. 'Road Haulage', in *Market services and European integration: The challenge for the 1990s, European Economy*, special issue, No. 3, Part C, Luxembourg, Office for Official Publications of the European Communities, 1993, pp. 211–250.

Smith, A. and Venables, A. 'Completing the internal market in the European Community', *European Economic Review*, 32, 1988, pp. 1501–1525.

Smith, A. and Venables, A. 'The costs of non-Europe: an assessment based on a formal model of imperfect competition and economies of scale', in *Studies on the economics of integration: Research on the 'costs of non-Europe'*, Vol. 2, Chapter 5, European Commission, Luxembourg, Office for Official Publications of the European Communities, 1988.

Toulemonde, J. 'Is it Possible to Evaluate the Effectiveness of EC Structural Funds? A Study Based on the Irish Case', Seminar Paper, Dublin, Economic and Social Research Institute, 9 December 1993.

Viceriat, P. 'Hotel chains', in *Market services and European integration: The challenge for the 1990s, European Economy*, special issue, No. 3, Part C, Luxembourg, Office for Official Publications of the European Communities, 1993, pp. 366–379.

Viñals, J. *et al.*, 'Spain and the "EEC cum 1992" shock', in C. Bliss and J.B. de Macedo (eds.) *Unity with Diversity in the European Economy*, Cambridge, Cambridge University Press, 1990, pp. 145–234.

Viñals, J. (ed.) *La economia española ante el Mercado Unico Europeo. Las claves del proceso de integración*, Madrid, Alianza Editorial, 1992.

Walsh, B. 'Expectations, information and human migration: specifying an econometric model of Irish migration to Britain', *Journal of Regional Science*, Vol. 14, 1974, pp. 107–120.

Walsh, B. 'Why is unemployment so high in Ireland today?', *Perspectives on Economic Policy*, Centre for Economic Research, University College Dublin, 1987.

Walsh, B. 'The Contribution of Human Capital Formation to Post-War Economic Growth in Ireland', Discussion Paper No. 819, London, Centre for Economic Policy Research, 1993.

Weale, M. 'A Critical Evaluation of Rate of Return Analysis', *The Economic Journal*, 103, 1993, pp. 729–737.

Williamson, J.G. 'Regional inequality and the process of national development: a description of the patterns', *Economic Development and Cultural Change*, Vol. 13, No. 4(2), 1965, pp. 3–84.

Wier, T. *Service Sector Development in a Hierarchy of Central Places: A Regional Analysis of 7 Southern States*, unpublished Ph.D. thesis, University of Tennessee, 1992.